The Way Companion to the Sunday Missal

The Way Companion to the Sunday Missal

Peter Edmonds SJ

This edition first published 2014
by
Way Books, Campion Hall
Oxford, OX1 1QS
www.theway.org.uk

Cover design: Elizabeth Lock, with thanks to Brendan Callaghan SJ and Joseph A. Munitiz SJ

Cover image: St John and the Angel, Chinese, 18th century, Campion Hall, Oxford. Photograph: Dan Mai SJ

ISBN 978 0 904717 43 3

Contents

YEAR B
THE YEAR OF MARK

The Sundays of Advent and the Christmas Season

FOREWORD

EVERY COMMITTED PREACHER, when preparing a Sunday homily, yearns for guides that are exegetically up to date and at the same time clearly written. Such 'helps to homilies' are very difficult to find. Sometimes these guides are too long, because they include material that is far too abstruse for the average reader. Or they are written in a complicated grammatical style that wearies the reader.

Peter Edmonds's book is an answer to a preacher's prayer. The author has had years of teaching scripture to people who need to see the relevance of Christ's message in their daily lives. The book is scholarly but simply written at the same time. From a mass of biblical research material the author has the ability to select insights that are especially important to people today. The author almost apologises for the brevity of his commentaries (one page for each Sunday's readings), but I believe this brevity is one of the great qualities of the book.

This book was written while the author was working in Africa. No doubt he had an African audience primarily in mind, but his scholarship and style of presentation make the book highly relevant to any culture and congregation.

Gerald A. Arbuckle SM
Sydney, Australia

HOW DO I USE THIS BOOK? After I have prayed over the biblical text and examined it for myself, often with the help of other translations of the relevant passage, I read Edmonds's book and another commentary. I often find in *The Way Companion to the Sunday Missal* interesting insights and explanations that I have not come across elsewhere. This is certainly the result of a scholarship accumulated over years of teaching and pastoral experience.

With regards to the scope of the book, Edmonds has lived up to the reader's expectations. He has wonderfully succeeded in combining brevity with scholarship. It is precisely this feature that earns the book its merit, as concision is not always a well-imparted gift to many scholars. I warmly recommend this book to all those interested in scripture and biblical pastoral, particularly to those who do not have access to specialised commentaries.

Mpay Kemboly SJ
Kinshasa, Congo

PREFACE

THESE PAGES ARE DESIGNED as a brief guide to help towards the understanding of the texts from scripture that are read out in every Catholic church in the world on Sundays. The principles used in the choice of readings are explained in the *Introduction to the Lectionary*.

These notes are not homilies, and they are not to be read out to a congregation. They belong rather to the time of preparation for the Sunday celebration of the Eucharist. We may keep in mind the experience of the two disciples on the Emmaus road who recognised Jesus 'at the breaking of bread' after they had been prepared for it by hearing Jesus explain the scriptures to them. They realised that their hearts had been burning within them while Jesus spoke (Luke 24:13–35). Likewise on the road from Jerusalem to Gaza, Philip helped the Ethiopian understand the passage from Isaiah that he had been reading (Acts 8:30–31).

One page is devoted to each Sunday. Despite the brevity of the comments, it is hoped that they will repay meditative reading and that the reader will take advantage of the references to other scripture passages that are offered. A complete text of the Bible, preferably one that supplies other cross-references and notes on the text, should be kept open close by. We can learn more about a text by employing two or more translations.

A sound principle for scriptural interpretation is that the book from which a passage is taken, is often the best commentary on that passage. Then to compare and contrast the passage with other relevant biblical passages is often an enjoyable and illuminating exercise.

If these notes are used as 'helps to homilies', then their aim is to assist the preacher to discover what the texts meant when they were originally written. The homilist is to apply them to the needs of a congregation today. As one bishop wrote to his priests, 'The preacher is more likely to grasp what a passage means today if he has understood what it meant yesterday'.

A careful reading of a passage will frequently lead us to isolate matters that interest us, but it can also produce problems that puzzle us. After all, it is around two thousand years since even the most recent biblical texts were written. But for two hundred years, careful disciplined study of scripture has been going on. We should take advantage of this by looking out for relevant commentaries and dictionaries. And we do not overlook the advantage to be gained by quiet prayer over the texts.

This work has its origin in booklets produced by the Pastoral Centre of the Catholic Bishops Conference of Zimbabwe. These were subsequently brought together in a single volume by Pauline Publications Africa in Nairobi. This is a corrected and modified version of that text.

Peter Edmonds
St Ignatius
Stamford Hill, London

YEAR A
THE YEAR OF MATTHEW

MATTHEW'S GOSPEL is a revision of Mark for a Jewish Christian audience. His 1,068 verses are divided into 28 chapters. He expands Mark by beginning with stories about the birth of Jesus and he concludes with resurrection narratives. His main contribution is the five discourses, or sermons, which enable us to call it the teaching Gospel, of which the best known is the Sermon on the Mount (chapters 5–7). Over the centuries, this has proved the most popular of the Gospels for the Church in its doctrine and its liturgy. Its Jesus is a figure of majesty, worshipped and addressed as 'Lord'. The Magi are but the first of many to worship him (Matthew 2: 11). The disciples, although they are of 'little faith' (Matthew 8: 26), continuously call upon him as their 'Lord' (Matthew 8:25). He is 'Emmanuel', God with us. This is the title the angel gave him at the start (Matthew 1:23; Isaiah 7:14), and the last words of Jesus in the Gospel confirm it, because he would be with his disciples until the end of the ages (Matthew 28: 20). These final verses have the Risen Lord commissioning his disciples to make disciples, to baptize and to teach all that he has commanded them. The church in every age is to continue speaking out boldly the teaching that astonished the crowds who heard him in his own time (Matthew 7:28).*

* Peter Edmonds, *Rediscover Jesus: A Pilgrim's Guide to the Land, the Personalities and the Language of Luke* (Stowmarket: Kevin Mayhew, 2007), 25.

Year A
The Year of Matthew

THE SUNDAYS OF ADVENT*

*The **First Readings**, taken from the Old Testament, are described as 'prophecies about the messiah and the messianic age, especially from Isaiah'. They have therefore an importance of their own apart from the gospel readings.*

*The **Second Readings** 'from an apostle serve as exhortations and proclamations in keeping with the various themes of Advent'. In this Year A, we have three readings from Paul's letter to the Romans and one from the letter of James.*

*The **Responsorial Psalms** are designed to help with the understanding of the First Reading, to deepen some significant theme, to clarify its message.*

*In the **Gospel Readings** we reflect on the three comings of Christ: at the end of time, in his public ministry, in his birth. The evangelist selected is the one whom we will hear for the remainder of the year.*

THE CHRISTMAS SEASON

The readings for Christmas and Epiphany are taken 'from the Roman tradition'. On other days, we learn, by means of the readings, about Jesus' childhood, the virtues of family life, the mystery of the incarnation, the Virgin Mother of God and the mystery of the baptism of Jesus.

* Quotations from 'General Introduction', *The Roman Missal: Lectionary*, 3 volumes (London: Collins, 1981), nn.93–95.

Advent I A

Isaiah 2:1–5
Psalm 121:1–2, 4–5
Romans 13:11–14
Matthew 24:37–44

The Coming of the Lord

Many passages in scripture encourage hope for the future. **Isaiah** wants his hearers to cease brooding on the ruins of their city after the Assyrian invasions and to reflect on God's promise to make Zion—Jerusalem—a place of pilgrimage for all peoples who want to live out God's law in peace and justice. We find the same prophecy in Micah (4: 1–5). The journey of the magi was one way in which it found fulfilment (Matthew 2: 1–12).

The **Psalm** is a song which pilgrims, obeying instructions in their Law to go up to Jerusalem (Deuteronomy 16: 16), would sing on their safe arrival. Jesus made several such journeys (Luke 2: 51; 9: 51). His was the true throne of David (Luke 1: 69) and he was the agent of God's peace (John 14: 27).

Paul concludes his exhortation on Christian conduct in **Romans**. Thanks to Christ, Christians live in peace with God (5: 1); God's love has been poured into their hears (5: 5); and their behaviour is to reflect their status in new life (6: 4). Paul uses the imagery of light and darkness familiar in the New Testament (John 3: 19–21) and argues from the common belief of the time that the second coming of Christ was imminent (1 Thessalonians 1: 10). Christians were to prepare for this coming negatively, by not conforming themselves to the sinful ways of their neighbours (1 Peter 4: 3), and positively, by putting on the armour of Christ (Ephesians 6: 13–17). Paul's words may well echo sermons addressed to the newly baptized in the first years of Christianity.

Often when Jesus speaks to his disciples in **Matthew**, he is also speaking to those who first heard this Gospel. They knew that Jesus' prophecies about the destruction of Jerusalem and the Temple had already come about (23: 38). There remained his future coming as Son of Man, their Lord, to whom all authority on heaven and earth had been given (28: 18). This is described as his *parousia*, the word used of a king taking possession of his city.

After his first prediction of his passion, Jesus spoke of his future coming as Son of Man in judgment (16: 27). He now reveals more details. It will happen suddenly. The surprise of the godless generation of Noah at the flood will be repeated (Genesis 6: 6–9). Among its effects will be separation. Men working in the fields and women at the mill will find themselves parted. The division of the weeds and the wheat of which Jesus spoke in his parables will then take place (13: 30). The bad fish will be thrown out of the net that they share with the good (13: 48). The thief who comes at night gives no warning; neither will the Son of Man. Paul made a similar prediction (1 Thessalonians 5: 2). The only remedy is watchfulness, the subject of the next section of the Gospel.

Warnings of judgment are common in Matthew. His readers may have included lax second-generation Christians who had lost Christianity's first fervour, such as the people of Ephesus who were urged in Revelation to recover their original love and enthusiasm (Revelation 2: 1–7). Matthew wanted from his readers a busy, active Christianity rather than passive endurance (7: 21). They were to greet their Lord at his *parousia* with the enthusiasm that the city of Jerusalem showed when he entered as the Son of David (21: 9). We must not forget that threats of judgment in Matthew are outnumbered by words of encouragement (6: 25; 11: 28).

Advent 2 A

Isaiah 11:1–10
Psalm 71:1–2, 7–8, 12–13
Romans 15:4–9
Matthew 3:1–12

The Preaching of the Baptist

Jesse was the father of King David. At a time of fickle leadership, **Isaiah** looks forward to the coming of a Davidic king who will possess all the qualities that good government demands, including concern for the poor. His rule will establish peace even in the animal kingdom. Jesus was descended from Jesse (Matthew 1:5). During his temptations he was among the wild beasts (Mark 1:13). He brought the good news to the poor (Matthew 11:5). His death made creation look for liberation from bondage (Romans 8:21).

The **Psalm** reflects the hopes of Isaiah and other writers about the Davidic royal family (2 Samuel 7) and offers a blueprint for every Christian ruler. It articulates common human hopes for prosperity, peace and justice for all.

The final chapters of **Romans** address the particular problems of a community consisting of Christians of both Jewish and Gentile origin. First, Paul offers a reflection on scripture, which for him means the Old Testament, including the passage we have read about Jesse. Though written long ago, such scripture encourages us and gives us hope in the present (2 Timothy 3:16). He prays for unity in a community with such diverse backgrounds. In particular, he pleads for a spirit of hospitality. After all, his readers have all been welcomed by God because of Christ. In accepting both Jews and Gentiles into the Christian family, God fulfilled his promises to the patriarchs (4:11). And, for Paul, 'God never takes back his gifts or revokes his choice' (11:29).

Each Gospel tells us about the ministry of John the Baptist in its own way. **Matthew** alone tells us that he preached the imminence of the Kingdom. In this, he anticipated the beginning of the ministry of Jesus (4:17) and the mission of Jesus' disciples (10:7). The Baptist's activity is described in Old Testament terms. He is the one prophesied by Isaiah at the beginning of the Book of Consolation (40:3). His clothing and his diet put him in the tradition of Elijah (2 Kings 1:8). He proclaims his call to repentance at the same Jordan river through which Israel passed on its way to the promised land (Joshua 4:1). Thanks to him, all the people of Judaea return to this Jordan and confess their sins. They commit themselves again to the ideals of their covenant with God (Exodus 19:3–6).

In Matthew the warnings of the Baptist are addressed to the Pharisees and Sadducees; they prepare us for the woes that Jesus pronounced on the Pharisees (Matthew 23). Like Jesus in the Sermon on the Mount, John refers to the fruit that a good tree must produce (7:18). By speaking of God raising up children to Abraham from the stones, he anticipates Jesus' words about the Gentiles eating at the feast in the Kingdom with Abraham (8:11).

His picture of Jesus is very fierce. He describes Jesus as a preacher of judgment in terms reminiscent of Malachi, the last of the prophets, who foresaw God purifying his people as silver is purified (Malachi 3:1–3). The reader is hardly prepared for the quiet appearance of Jesus himself for baptism (3:13) and his gentle call of the four disciples by the lake of Galilee (4:18–22). John did not know that Jesus would imitate the conduct of the Servant of Isaiah, who would not 'brawl or shout' (Matthew 12:19). He would fail to gather the wheat into the granary but, in the words of his parable, would allow the crop to reach maturity with the weeds still in the fields (13:24–30).

Advent 3 A

Isaiah 35:1–6, 10
Psalm 145:6–10
James 5:7–10
Matthew 11:2–11

The Baptist in Prison

Joy always characterises the first reading on this Sunday. **Isaiah** rejoices because he views the earth producing crops, flowers blooming in the desert, the blind and the lame seeing and walking again. No longer does the people have its eyes shut and its ears stopped (6:10). Everything achieves the purpose of its creation. This physical renewal of the world prepares for the spiritual renewal that Christ brings.

The **Psalm**, the first of the praise psalms which conclude the Psalter, praises God in language that echoes Isaiah. His care for those whom the world neglects prepares us for Jesus' message to the Baptist.

We find in **James** three references to the coming, the *parousia*, of the Lord (Matthew 24:27). Twice he urges patient and hopeful waiting for this coming. Farmers must be patient until the rain comes to make their crops grow. So too the Christian cannot be at ease until Christ comes (Hebrews 13:14). Because the Christian is one who has to carry the cross daily (Luke 9:23), the coming of the Lord will mean release and relief from this burden. Finally, he uses the prospect of the Lord's coming as a warning against grumblers in the community, since the Lord will come as judge (Mark 13:29). 'Do not judge, and you will not be judged', Jesus had taught (Matthew 7:1). His teaching is firmly based on traditional Jewish ideas. For examples of steadfastness in face of hardship he makes a typical appeal, not to the teaching of Christ (Matthew 11:28) but to the Old Testament prophets (Jeremiah 20:9).

The mission of John the Baptist concludes with his imprisonment and death. His trials are mental as well as physical. He has lost his former confidence that Jesus is the one who was to come. The one whose mission he has prepared has failed to 'clear his threshing-floor' through a ministry of judgment (3:12). Jesus has not preached the Kingdom in the way that John pioneered. Jesus reassures him by describing his mission in terms that John would recognise from the prophets. In the Sermon on the Mount (chapters 5–7), he had preached good news to the poor (Isaiah 61:1). Through his many miracles (8–9) he had brought the messianic programme of Isaiah to reality (29:18; 35:5). A blessing awaits John if he acknowledges the validity of the means by which Jesus proclaims the Kingdom. But even the Baptist could misunderstand Jesus. In this story **Matthew** may well be appealing to synagogue members in Antioch who refused to accept Christ.

John has witnessed to Jesus (3:11–12); now Jesus witnesses to the Baptist. The crowds did not flock to him because he told them what they wanted to hear; he was not a reed shaken by the wind of popular enthusiasm. They did not go to him as royalty or some influential politician, powerful in this world's affairs; he did not live in any palace. They recognised him as a prophet, a Malachi who would 'purify the sons of Levi' (Malachi 3:3). He had indeed prepared the way of the Lord (Isaiah 40:3). His loyalty to his prophetic mission would shortly bring him to a miserable death (14:10).

Despite his greatness in the old dispensation, John is the least in the Kingdom of Heaven. The greatest are the 'little ones' who realise their dependence on God (18:6). John lived before the establishment of the Kingdom through the death and resurrection of Jesus (26:29).

Advent 4 A

Isaiah 7:10–14
Psalm 23:1–6
Romans 1:1–7
Matthew 1:18–24

The Annunciation to Joseph

The prophecy of **Isaiah** to Ahaz, a king of the house of David, concerns the young woman who was to become the mother of Hezekiah, son of Ahaz. The Greek Bible called her a virgin and Matthew quotes this version. The name that the child is given, Emmanuel, is significant for Matthew since in his Gospel Jesus promises to be present wherever two or three are gathered in his name (Matthew 18:20) and to be with his Church until the end of time (Matthew 28:20).

The **Psalm** was originally used in processions of the Ark of the Covenant. Only participants who lived a sound moral life were welcome. Such just men prepare us for Joseph in the Gospel.

The opening sentence of **Romans**, possibly quoting an early Christian creed, calls Jesus both Son of David and Son of God. The first title recalls Isaiah's prophecy to Ahaz and prepares us for the angel's words to Joseph, addressing him as a Son of David who would accept Mary's child as his own. The second title might suggest that Jesus was only appointed Son of God after the resurrection, but Matthew makes it clear that he was so right from the beginning (Matthew 2:15). Paul understands all this so well through his conversion experience (Galatians 1:16) that he readily accepts being called a 'servant of Christ Jesus'. His mission is to bring the whole world to believe and obey, and to belong to, the Christ who is its Lord. All nations are to recognise his identity and live their lives accordingly.

Matthew tells the story of the birth of Jesus from the point of view of Joseph. In his genealogy, Matthew has already told us that Joseph was not the real father of Jesus (1:16). We now learn from the words of the angel that Mary was with child 'through the Holy Spirit', the agency by which God had created the world at the beginning (Genesis 1:2). In the conception of Jesus a new creation has taken place, which prefigures the new creation that all who are 'in Christ' become (2 Corinthians 5:17). The angel addresses Joseph as 'Son of David'. In this role, he accepts Mary and her child, and thus gives Jesus all the legal rights and privileges of a son of David. The reader would be reminded of God's promise to David through Nathan that his throne should be established forever (2 Samuel 7:16).

Matthew's infancy story makes many allusions to the persons and events of the Old Testament. The quotation of the prophecy to Ahaz is explicit. Less obvious is the link between Joseph the foster-father of Jesus and Joseph the patriarch. Both had dreams and both went down to Egypt. God was with the patriarch Joseph (Genesis 39:21). According to Stephen's speech in Acts, this patriarch was a type of Christ in his sufferings and rejection by his own people (Acts 7:9).

Joseph is said to be a just man. In the Sermon on the Mount, Jesus demanded of his disciples a deeper righteousness than that of the scribes and the Pharisees (5:20). As a pious Jew, Joseph would know the Law of Deuteronomy about the sanctity of marriage (Deuteronomy 22:20–21). He could have applied the Law rigorously. A woman who had committed adultery was to be stoned (John 8:5). Joseph does not presume Mary's guilt, but sends her away quietly. He knows that she may be quite innocent. He puts into practice the obedience of faith of which Paul wrote (Romans 1:5).

Christmas (Midnight)

Isaiah 9:1–7
Psalm 95:1–3, 11–13
Titus 2:11–14
Luke 2:1–14

Birth of the Saviour

Isaiah provides us with a fine overture to introduce the Christmas Gospel. Our passage begins with expressions of joy and rejoicing, such as break out when people celebrate a good harvest or a victory in battle. The real reason seems to have been the birth of a child, probably Hezekiah, one of the more worthy of Israel's kings. Traditional titles express the hopes they have of this new king: he will be a protector of his people and bring them peace. He will exercise all the qualities expected of the house of David (2 Samuel 7: 11). Christians transfer these hopes to the Christ born at Christmas time.

The **Psalm** is a hymn that was used in temple worship to celebrate the presence of God in the liturgy. It calls on all creation to join in the praise, because God himself, not a human king, is going to rule the earth.

The letter to **Titus** gives us a summary of what Christians came to believe about Jesus Christ. They see him as the personification of God's grace. He is this grace come into the world; it is no longer a matter of future expectation, as for Isaiah. Because of Christ's self-sacrifice on the cross, a new people has come into being, freed from the sin and wickedness of the past. In the future this Christ will come again into the world as its God and saviour. Rarely indeed is Jesus called God in the New Testament, as here; it means that he is seen as possessing not just the virtues of Israel's rulers, as listed by Isaiah, but the qualities of God himself. He is also called saviour; as such, he meets the expectations of the Gentiles, who in those days looked for salvation from all kinds of philosophies.

In our Christmas reading from **Luke** we hear three voices. The first is that of the narrator. He introduces us to the characters involved in the story. The first two are Romans: the emperor, Caesar Augustus, and his local delegate, Quirinius. They have issued the decree that causes Joseph and Mary to travel from Nazareth to Bethlehem. Thanks to them, the child Jesus will be born where the prophet Micah said the birthplace of the messiah would be, Bethlehem (Micah 5:2). Then we hear about Joseph and Mary. Luke has already told us that Joseph was betrothed to Mary, that Mary had had a visit from an angel and that she will bear a son who will be called Jesus, the Son of God, born of the Holy Spirit. Mary had called herself handmaid of the Lord, and poured out her gratitude and praise in the canticle we call the Magnificat. We also meet shepherds, poor people forced to spend the night in the open, looking after their sheep.

The second voice we hear is that of an angel, probably Gabriel, who has already announced two births in this Gospel: the birth of John the Baptist and that of Jesus. Once again he gives a description of the child to be born. He calls him 'a saviour' who is 'Christ the Lord'. Each of these terms is significant. The nations of the time were hoping for a *saviour*, to deliver them from the confusion and chaos of a disordered age. The *Christ* was the anointed one, whom the prophet Nathan had promised to King David centuries before (2 Samuel: 12–16); *Lord* was the title claimed by Roman emperors of the time. They demanded that their subjects cry out 'Caesar is Lord' as proof of their loyalty. Now this newborn child is Lord.

The third voice is the voice of the heavenly choir. According to Isaiah, they sang in heaven, acclaiming the glory of God (Isaiah 6: 3). Now their hymn is heard here below, announcing not only glory to God, but also peace on earth. True peace is not that claimed by the emperor in Rome, but is brought by the child born in a manger in the city of David.

Holy Family A

Sirach 3:2–6, 12–14
Psalm 127:1–5
Colossians 3:12–21
Matthew 2:13–15, 19–23

The Flight into Egypt

The teaching of the book of **Sirach** on the family, dating from 200 years before Christ, would have been familiar to Joseph, Mary and Jesus, whom we know as the Holy Family. Ben Sira, its author, writes in the tradition of the Decalogue handed on by Moses, which commands us to honour father and mother (Exodus 20:12)—a commandment quoted by Jesus himself (Matthew 15:4). The theology is a simple one. He promises blessings in return, which include the forgiveness of sins, children of one's own and a long life. But he is realistic, too, in warning of the difficulties that old age may bring. Kindness in dealing with these also cancels sin.

The **Psalm** is a blessing pronounced on pilgrims visiting the Holy City (Deuteronomy 16:16). Here too the poet expects fear of the Lord to be rewarded by abundance of family and possessions.

In **Colossians**, the author reflects on the consequences for Christian life of what God has done for us in Christ. For the vices abounding in the pagan society of the time, its audience is to substitute the virtues that reflect the values of Christ, especially love (1 Corinthians 13). As to worship and liturgy, the whole of life and daily activity are to be accomplished in the name of the Lord Jesus (Romans 12:1). In family life, inspiration is to come from Jewish sources such as Sirach or, as in our reading, from 'household codes', in which pagan writers of the time listed the various duties of the different members of a household. All of these are to be part of our life 'in the Lord' and of our service to God.

One of the few incidents in the gospel tradition in which the Holy Family as a whole takes part is the flight into Egypt reported by **Matthew**. The story falls into three sections, each marked by a dream of Joseph. Matthew roots Jesus firmly in the history of his people, identifying him either as the representative or as the successor of a great personage in its history.

A quotation from Hosea, 'I called my son out of Egypt' (11:1), links the journey of the child to Egypt and back with that of the people of Israel who, centuries before, went down to Egypt (Genesis 46:8) and returned (Exodus 12). This child represents not only a new creation on God's part (Matthew 1:20), but also a new redemption. Through him, God's people has a new beginning.

The words of the angel to Joseph in his second dream about 'those who wanted to kill the child' are a quotation from Exodus, about how Pharaoh wanted to kill the child Moses (Exodus 4:19). Matthew hints several times in his Gospel that the career of Moses, who gave the people the Law on Mount Sinai (Exodus 19), is recapitulated in that of Jesus and his disciples. These disciples will hear Jesus speaking with the authority of God in the Sermon on the Mount (5:1) and, on another mountain in Galilee, will receive their mission to make disciples of all the nations (28:19).

Because of a warning in a third dream, Joseph takes his family to Nazareth. The precise meaning of the words 'spoken through the prophet' about the Nazarene is not clear, but they may call to mind the great Nazirite of the book of Judges, Samson, who delivered God's people from the Philistines (Judges 13:7). Matthew knew that Jesus was to deliver his people from their sins (1:21). In all this, Joseph hears the words of God and acts on them (7:24).

Sunday 2 of Christmas

Sirach 24:1–2, 8–12
Psalm 147:12–15, 19–20
Ephesians 1:3–6, 15–18
John 1:1–18

The Word Made Flesh

Was God alone when he created the world? Later Jewish speculation, as recorded in **Sirach**, following the teaching of Proverbs (8:23), suggests that he was not. He was in the company of Wisdom. Today, we hear her boasting in the heavenly court about how God created her at the beginning of creation and how she now has a home in the earthly Zion where God himself lives. The Christian recognises how her pitching of her tent in Jerusalem was an anticipation of God's own dwelling on earth through the incarnation of his Son.

We know from Genesis that God spoke when he created the world (1:3). The **Psalmist** knows that this was not God's final word. As he looks at the crops ready for harvest, this psalmist sees the fruit of further words of God. When he reflects on the Law, God's greatest gift to his people (Psalm 119), he identifies this Law with God's Word.

What was in the mind of God when he created the world? According to the opening of **Ephesians**, it was not only his Son but all those who would believe in his Son. Like Wisdom, all were included in God's plans from the beginning of time. The author blesses God for this truth, and then prays a double prayer—first that his hearers might all grow in the understanding of the wonders of their calling and make progress in wisdom to knowledge of God. He prays that they all may have eyes to see how to live a life in hope. They are to share in the inheritance of the glory that belongs to God. Such a prayer makes a fine climax to the Christmas season.

John was the last of the evangelists to write. Mark began his story of Jesus with John the Baptist (1:2). By his genealogy, Matthew began the story of Jesus with Abraham (1:2), and Luke began it with Adam (3:38). John goes back to where the Bible began: 'In the beginning' (Genesis 1:1). Even then, the Word was. It had no beginning. Then, as now, the Word was with God and was God.

The lively city of Ephesus could well have been the birthplace of John's Gospel. Luke in Acts tells us the sort of people who could be found there (Acts 19). They included Jews who frequented the synagogue (Acts 19:8). In the Word, these Jews would recognise the figure of Wisdom, who was present when God created the world (Proverbs 8:23) and said, 'Let us make man ...' (Genesis 1:26). By the power of the Word, God created the world (Psalm 33:6). The same Word brought God's revelation to the prophets (Amos 3:7). This Word becomes flesh in Jesus and pitches his tent in our world (Exodus 25:8). Moses brought the word of the Law (Exodus 24), but this gift is far surpassed by the Word that personifies the grace and truth defining God (Exodus 34:6). Moses, like the other heroes of Israel's past, loses his significance in comparison to Christ (8:58).

In Ephesus, philosophers such as Tyrannus (Acts 19:9), familiar with the best thought of the time, would attract many students. The opening of this Gospel would remind them of the doctrine of the Word taught by Heracleitus, Ephesus' own philosopher of centuries before. Stoic teachers, too, spoke of the Word as the principle that kept creation in order. The evangelist wanted to lead them to believe in the truth that was Christ. The disciples of the Baptist in Ephesus (Acts 19:3) had to learn that John was not the light. His only function in this Gospel is to witness to the light that was Christ. In this, he prefigures every believer, who continues the mission of Christ, to witness to the truth (18:37; 20:21).

Mary, the Mother of God

Numbers 6:22–27
Psalm 66:2–3, 5, 6, 8
Galatians 4:4–7
Luke 2:16–21

At the Crib

One of the functions of priests in Israel was to bless the people. At the beginning of Luke, the people praying outside the Temple were waiting for the blessing of Zechariah (Luke 1:10). **Numbers** gives us an example of such a text. This falls into three parts. The first refers to the traditional blessing of all that makes life possible and full (Deuteronomy 28:1–14). The second speaks of God's shining face, which means that God will deliver people from trouble. The third part bestows peace. This includes harmony between God and humanity, among human beings themselves, between the human family and nature, and within the individual. Paul intends such a peace at the beginning of his letters (1 Corinthians 1:3); it has been won for us by Christ (Romans 5:1).

The **Psalm** echoes the blessing of Numbers. It was probably originally a prayer for a good harvest. It reflects the Psalmist's confidence in a God who cares for the world and its peoples.

God's greatest blessing was the gift of his Son. In **Galatians,** Paul tells us how this came about. Humanity was enslaved. The Jew was imprisoned by the Law, since the Law could give information about sin, but could not give power to overcome its effects (3:23). The Gentile was enslaved to what he calls 'the elemental principles of this world' (4:3). God's remedy was to send his Son. He was born of a woman. Nowhere else does Paul mention the mother of Jesus; but thanks to the fact of her motherhood, we all have the possibility of being children of God, able to call upon God as our *Abba*, our Father, like Jesus himself (Mark 14:36; Romans 8:15).

There are three groups in the Gospel scene from **Luke**. The first is that of the shepherds; they have obeyed the message of the angels and found everything as they were told. Unlike the magi in Matthew, they do not worship the child Jesus (Matthew 2:11). They simply relate their story and then return to their obscurity, glorifying and praising God At the end of the Gospel, the disciples will likewise praise God (24:53). We never hear of these shepherds again, but by praising and glorifying God they are taking the first steps in Christian prayer (11:2).

The second group is 'everyone who heard it'. Their reaction is one of astonishment, like those present at the birth of John the Baptist (1:63). While those bystanders had pondered in their hearts and led others to ask, 'What will this child turn out to be?' (1:66), here no such sequel is described. They do not join the shepherds in their praise. Like the characters in the parable of the sower, they receive the word with joy but have no root (8:13).

The third group consists only of Mary. Previously she has declared, 'let what you have said be done to me' (1:38). Elizabeth called her blessed among women (1:42). Mary does not forget what has happened to her but, like others in Luke, she reflects. She resembles the other Mary who sat at Jesus' feet listening to him (10:39) and the crowds who stood by the cross watching (23:48). As in the parable of the sower, she takes the word to herself 'with a noble and generous heart' (8:15). She is included among those whom Jesus will later praise because they 'hear the word of God and keep it' (11:28).

The final scene of our reading is the circumcision of Jesus, according to Jewish custom (Genesis 17:12). He was born under the Law (Galatians 4:4). This was the time when a child's name was formally given. There is no argument about the name of this child, as there was with John the Baptist (1:63). He is *Jesus*, a form of *Joshua*, a saviour. The name came from God himself through the words of the angel Gabriel (1:31).

Epiphany

Isaiah 60:1–6
Psalm 71:1–2, 7–8, 10–13
Ephesians 3:2–3, 5–6
Matthew 2:1–12

The Coming of the Magi

A ruined city and a devastated land are what **Isaiah** sees, but the words that God speaks to him concern a new city and a prosperous land. Once again light will overcome darkness, as it had when God first created the world (Genesis 1:3). Jerusalem is to be rebuilt. Processions will again come to her. Her scattered sons and daughters will return. Foreign nations, too, will march, this time not for conquest but to rebuild the city. With the gold and incense they bring, fitting worship will again be offered to God in a temple.

The successors of King David were a disappointment, and God's promises seemed to be failing (2 Samuel 7). But the **Psalmist** does not lose hope. He foresees a new Davidic king who will bring true justice to God's people and receive fitting respect and tribute from foreign nations and their rulers.

Paul was the great apostle to the Gentiles in the early Church (Galatians 1:16). As a Jew, 'enthusiastic ... for the traditions of my ancestors' (Galatians 1:14), he would have been looking out for the new city and temple foreseen by Isaiah, and for the appearance of the new king celebrated in the Psalm. His conversion experience (Acts 9) taught him that these expectations have been fulfilled in Christ, and that the Gentiles have no need to worship a foreign king in a foreign city. They themselves possess the same promises and inheritance as those who had before regarded themselves exclusively as God's people. The wall between Jew and Gentile has been broken down through the work of Christ. This is a major theme of **Ephesians** (2:14).

Matthew would have surprised, even shocked, his Jewish-Christian readers by telling the story of the magi immediately after his account of the birth of Jesus. Foreigners, identified by later piety as Melchior, Balthasar and Gaspar, rather than his own people, were first to worship the newborn child. Later tradition, influenced by Isaiah 60 and Psalm 71, identified them as kings. The Gospel calls them *magi*, a title paying tribute to their learning. This most Jewish of the Gospels will also end with a reminder of the universality of Christianity when Jesus, the Risen Lord, commands his apostles to 'make disciples of all the nations' (28:19).

The magi come to King Herod, looking for the 'King of the Jews'. Theirs is a dangerous mission. Herod had killed even his own sons when he suspected them of ambition towards his office as king of the Jews. By the end of this Gospel, the reader knows that Jesus is indeed king of the Jews, but his kingship is displayed on a cross (27:37): a peaceful kingship symbolized by his entering the city on a donkey rather than a warhorse (21:5; Zechariah 9:9); a kingship mocked by the powerful of the world on Calvary (27:42); and a kingship that will finally be exercised at the last judgment (25:34).

God used the natural means of a star to bring the learned magi to Jerusalem, but, to continue their journey, they need the revelation of scripture (Micah 5:2; Romans 1:20). Ironically, those who tell them about the scriptures do not use their own knowledge. As 'chief priests with the scribes and elders', they will later mock the King of the Jews as he dies on the cross (27:41). The story of the magi is a prediction of the future passion; in it, the saying of Jesus about those who came from the east and the west to enjoy the banquet in the Kingdom with Abraham, Isaac and Jacob was finding fulfilment, while the sons of the Kingdom were rejecting it (8:11–12). Was the star that brought the magi to Jerusalem the same star that the prophet Balaam had seen centuries before (Numbers 24:17)?

Baptism of the Lord A (Sunday I A)

Isaiah 42:1–4, 6–7
Psalm 28:1–4, 9–10
Acts 10:34–38
Matthew 3:13–17

Fulfilling Righteousness

There are four 'songs of the Servant' in Deutero-**Isaiah** (42: 1–4; 49: 1–6; 50: 4–9; 52: 13 – 53: 12). The identity of this Servant has caused great debate. Perhaps he is the prophet himself, or Jeremiah (Jeremiah 38: 6), or one of the many prophets who suffered in the service of God (Matthew 23: 30). The term may be collective, describing the faithful remnant in Israel that conformed itself completely to God's salvific plan. Whoever he was, the Servant's fidelity to God ensures that he becomes a light to the nations and a means of salvation for the blind and the imprisoned (Isaiah 6: 10). In the New Testament this figure is identified with Christ (Mark 10: 45; Acts 8: 34).

The **Psalm** may be an adaptation by Israel of a foreign hymn dedicated to the god of thunder. The voice of the Lord upon the waters prepares us for the voice from heaven in the Gospel.

The Cornelius incident in **Acts** enables Peter to grasp that God's salvific plan extends to all peoples. For the first time, Peter understands the words of Deuteronomy about God's impartiality (Deuteronomy 10:17). Like the Servant of whom Isaiah wrote, Jesus originated in Israel, but his mission, as Lord of all, was for all. Peter begins the story of Jesus with his baptism, when he was anointed with the Holy Spirit and power. Paul was to recognise that these same forces were behind his own mission (1 Thessalonians 1: 5). Like the Servant, he became the source of salvation for others.

Matthew reports only one meeting between Jesus and John the Baptist. On his own initiative, Jesus makes his way to the Jordan for baptism. John's reaction shows how superior to himself he knows Jesus to be. It is as if he has read the birth story of Jesus in Matthew, which makes it clear that Jesus brought the Old Testament prophecies to their climax through his birth as God's son.

The conversation between Jesus and John is unique to Matthew. This contains the first words spoken by Jesus in this Gospel. He explains that he must be baptized, not because he is a sinner (Mark 1: 4), but in order to 'do all that righteousness demands'. Both of these terms are important. Jesus has already fulfilled many prophecies in his birth story. His teaching will fulfil the Law and the prophets (5: 17). His actions will continue to fulfil 'the words spoken through the prophets' (2: 23). For this reason did he heal (8: 17), withdraw from his enemies (12: 15–18) and die on the cross (26: 54–56). We can understand righteousness in two ways. He will reveal by his 'Good News of the kingdom' (4: 23) the righteousness that belongs to God. He will train his disciples to live out the righteousness that is God's will for his people. This righteousness is to exceed that of the scribes and the Pharisees (5: 20). It is a righteousness for which his disciples are to hunger and thirst (5: 6).

Matthew concludes with the story of the baptism of Jesus. In it, heaven and earth meet. God's Spirit comes down in the shape of dove, a bird to remind us of God's Covenant after the flood story (Genesis 8: 8–12). God speaks. He does not address Jesus directly, as in Mark (1: 11), but speaks in the third person, for the sake of the bystanders. His words quote a psalm which was probably sung at the coronation of a king (Psalm 2: 7). They also recall the first Servant Song (Isaiah 42: 1). As God's Son, Jesus is to be King and Servant at once.

Year A
The Year of Matthew

THE SUNDAYS OF LENT*

*The **First Readings** take us through the 'history of salvation':*

Sunday 1	*The sin of Adam and Eve*	*Genesis 2:7–9; 3:1–7*
Sunday 2	*The promise to Abraham*	*Genesis 12:1–4*
Sunday 3	*Moses provides water from the rock*	*Exodus 17:3–7*
Sunday 4	*Samuel anoints David*	*1 Samuel 16:1, 6–7, 10–13*
Sunday 5	*Ezekiel and the dry bones*	*Ezekiel 37:12–14*
Passion Sunday	*The Suffering Servant of Isaiah*	*Isaiah 50:4–7*

***Second Readings:** 'The readings from the letters of the apostles have been selected to fit the gospel and the Old Testament readings, and, to the extent possible, to provide a connection between them.'*

Sunday 1	*Adam and Christ*	*Romans 5:12–19*
Sunday 2	*The appearing of our Saviour*	*2 Timothy 1:8b–10*
Sunday 3	*God loves us*	*Romans 5:1–2, 5–8*
Sunday 4	*Light in the Lord*	*Ephesians 5:8–14*
Sunday 5	*He who raised Jesus*	*Romans 8:8–11*
Passion Sunday	*Jesus humbled and exalted*	*Philippians 2:6–11*

*The **Responsorial Psalms** are designed to help with the understanding of the First Reading, to deepen some significant theme, to clarify its message.*

*The **Gospel Readings** of **Sundays 1 and 2** are always about the temptations and transfiguration of Jesus, this year according to Matthew. **Sundays 3 to 5** are texts from John: the Samaritan woman (John 4), the man born blind (John 9) and the raising of Lazarus (John 11), 'gospels of major importance in regard to Christian initiation'. On Passion Sunday (**Sunday 6**), the passion story according to Matthew is read.*

* Quotations from 'General Introduction', *Roman Missal*, nn. 97, 100.

EASTER AND THE SUNDAYS AFTER EASTER

*The **First Readings** are always from the Acts of the Apostles, about 'the life, witness and growth of the primitive Church'. Every year, we hear on Easter Sunday about the preaching of Peter to Cornelius, on Ascension Day the story of the ascension and on Pentecost Day the descent of the Holy Spirit. We learn about the life of the early Christians in Jerusalem. In this year A, we hear other samples of Peter's preaching, about the appointment of the Seven and the mission of Philip in Samaria.*

*The **Second Readings** form a semi-continuous reading of the First Letter of Peter, which gives depth to the narratives about Peter recorded in the Acts of the Apostles. This letter fits 'especially well with the spirit of joyous faith and sure hope proper to this season'.*

*The **Responsorial Psalms** are designed to help with the understanding of the First Reading, to deepen some significant theme, to clarify its message.*

*The **Gospel Readings** are always the same on **Sundays 1 and 2**: they are taken from John and tell of the three people at the tomb on Easter Day and the story of Thomas on the second Sunday. **Sunday 3** introduces Luke's account of the appearance of the Risen Lord to the disciples on the road to Emmaus. **Sunday 4** always provides a passage from John 10, the shepherd chapter. **Sundays 5, 6 and 7** provide extracts from the Last Supper discourse in John—on Jesus as the Way, on the paraclete and the beginning of the final prayer of Jesus to the Father.*

[Ascension Day and Body and Blood of Christ are often celebrated on the Sunday following rather than the traditional Thursday; hence they are included here.]

Lent I A

Genesis 2:7–9; 3:1–7
Psalm 50:3–6, 12–14, 17
Romans 5:12–19
Matthew 4:1–11

Temptations in the Desert

Lent is a time when we are reminded of key moments in the history of salvation, and we begin with **Genesis**. Its author wrote not to give us a scientific account of creation but to teach us how a good God created a good world and how man and woman, made in his own image, were the crown of all his work. This world was spoilt not through God's intention but through the ambition of the man and woman whom he had created. Desiring equality with God, they disobeyed his commandment and sinned. As a result, they found themselves weak, vulnerable and helpless. They knew themselves as God knew them.

Psalm 50 is traditionally associated with the sin of David with Bathsheba (2 Samuel 11:2–25). Because it expresses so accurately the feelings and emotions that go with sorrow for sin, it is included among the seven penitential psalms.

Paul in **Romans** reflects on Christ in the light of Genesis. He contrasts him with Adam. By his sin of disobedience, Adam brought death into the world and alienation from God. In contrast, Christ, by his obedience—demonstrated in today's temptation story and, above all, by his death on the cross (Philippians 2:8)—brought us a verdict of acquittal in God's law court. We cannot compare the single sin of Adam with the many sins forgiven by God as a free gift brought about through Christ. The tyranny of sin and death introduced by Adam is no more. For Paul, this tyranny has been overthrown by the salvific work of Christ. When we meet Satan in temptation, we have the power to resist; we will not be tested beyond our strength (1 Corinthians 10:13).

In his infancy story, Jesus relived the history of Israel in Egypt, 'I have called my son out of Egypt' (Matthew 2:15). In the temptation story, the traditional gospel reading on this first Lenten Sunday, **Matthew** has him repeat Israel's desert experience. Whereas Israel murmured against God and Moses (Psalm 95:8), Jesus remains faithful, despite all the temptations that Satan puts before him.

After a fast of forty days and nights, the same period that Moses spent on the mountain with God (Exodus 24:18), Satan (Job 1:6) comes to Jesus to test the quality of divine sonship proclaimed at his baptism (3:17). The suggestions Satan makes seem reasonable enough. Surely the Son of God does not to have suffer the pains of hunger? Later the rulers of Israel will likewise tell him to come down from the cross (27:42). He reminds Satan quoting Deuteronomy, that he does not live by bread alone (Deuteronomy 8:3) but by doing the will of the Father (7:21).

To find Satan in the wilderness is hardly a surprise, but to find him in the 'Holy City', speaking a Psalm (Psalm 91:12), is another matter. He is disguising himself as an angel of light (2 Corinthians 11:14). Jesus again repels the tempter and the temptation, to throw himself off the Temple, by quoting Deuteronomy (6:16). Those faithful to God do not force him to rescue them from their folly.

Before his death Moses viewed the whole of the Promised Land from Mount Nebo (Deuteronomy 34:1). Satan now shows Jesus all the kingdoms of the world and tells him that they can be his. By the end of the Gospel, they are his (28:18), but not because he worships Satan. He accepts the Father's will in drinking the cup of Calvary (26:39). The devil is dismissed; God's representatives, the angels, minister to Jesus. We realise that God has never been absent. He did not allow his Son to be tempted beyond his strength (1 Corinthians 10:13). He could recognise that even what appeared to be good suggestions had their origin in Satan and his demonic purposes.

Lent 2 A

Genesis 12:1–4
Psalm 32:4–5, 18–20, 22
2 Timothy 1:8b–10
Matthew 17:1–9

Transfiguration on a Mountain

With the story of Abraham, **Genesis** turns aside from the history of sin and begins the story of God's merciful response. Abraham has settled in Haran (11:31). Now, without warning, the voice of God tells him to abandon land, family and nation. He does not hesitate, believing the promises that God makes of a new land, family and nation. These promises cancel the curses laid on the sinful Adam and Eve (3:15–17). In place of a hostile earth, God promises fertile land; instead of pain in childbearing, abundant progeny; instead of endless toil, prosperity. And these blessings will, through Abraham, extend to all the nations of the earth.

Our **Psalm** is a meditation on the power of the 'Word of God'. By it, God created the universe and maintains it. If this Word spoke to Abraham, it would accomplish what it promised (Isaiah 55:11). God is faithful.

Our passage from **2 Timothy** can be applied both to Abraham's call and to the transfiguration. Abraham did not earn his call or the promises: it came by God's 'own purpose and ... grace', as Paul never tires of stressing (Romans 4; Galatians 3). The summons to Timothy to overcome his timidity and to take his share of hardships associates him with the disciples at the transfiguration; its purpose was to enable them to accept the passion of Christ and their share in it. The appeal to the 'Appearing of the glory of our great God and saviour Christ Jesus' is to the incarnation (Titus 2:11–13), but in our liturgy it is applied to the 'appearing' of the glory of the Lord in his Transfiguration. It prepares us, too, for the 'appearing' of the Risen Jesus to his disciples at the end of the Gospel (Matthew 28:16–20).

In **Matthew**, as in Mark and Luke, the transfiguration takes place after Jesus' first passion prediction and Peter's refusal to accept Jesus' warning about a suffering messiah (16:22). The three disciples who are privileged to witness Christ in his glory will later be present at his agony and prayer in Gethsemane (26:37). The first purpose of the transfiguration is to encourage the disciples to persevere with Jesus by a glimpse of the glorified Christ. The brightness of his face does not belong to this world, but is like that of the just in the world to come (13:43). The presence of Moses, the law-giver, and Elijah, the prophet, confirms Jesus' mission to fulfil both the Law and the Prophets (5:17). Peter, who had protested at the first passion prediction (16:21), proves his lack of understanding again by proposing to build three tents. Tents were dwellings of the world to come: Peter wants the vision to last and to withdraw Jesus from this earth.

A voice from a cloud, symbol of the glory of God (1 Kings 8:10), causes Peter and his companions to fall down in fear. They hear again the words spoken at the baptism of Jesus (3:17), which identified him as Son of God and the Servant spoken of by Isaiah (Psalm 2:7; Isaiah 42:1). The additional words, 'Listen to him', give Jesus the authority of the prophet, like Moses who was to come (Deuteronomy 18:15). Peter is not to build tents but to listen to Jesus, especially when he speaks a message Peter does not like (6:22).

The final section is unique to Matthew. Jesus touches the disciples and reassures them, speaking of his future resurrection. Their experience is like that of an apocalyptic seer. The prophet Daniel had received a message from God, and been touched and strengthened by an angel (Daniel 10:10–12). This same touch from Jesus cured a leper (8:2) and raised the dead to life (9:25). Thanks to this personal contact, the disciples lose their fear and understand Jesus' words about the Baptist and Elijah as they come down the mountain (17:13).

Lent 3 A

Exodus 17:3–7
Psalm 94:1–2, 6–9
Romans 5:1–2, 5–8
John 4:5–42

The Woman of Samaria

Famine drove Abraham's descendants to Egypt, where they endured slavery and oppression. **Exodus** relates how God raised up Moses to deliver them from their distress. One of the crises that Moses meets in his wearisome task of leading a people always on the verge of rebellion is their complaint of thirst. They blame Moses for having led them out of Egypt. God responds to the mediation of Moses by giving the people water from a rock. Paul will identify this rock with Christ (1 Corinthians 10:4). Jesus will speak of living water in our gospel reading.

The **Psalmist** uses this hardening of the people's hearts in the desert to warn his own generation against similar infidelity, a warning repeated in the letter to the Hebrews (Hebrews 3–4). The God of the Psalmist is creator, saviour and shepherd.

Paul, in **Romans**, offers us a little treatise on faith, hope and love. Faith in Christ restores peace between God and humanity, who were formerly enemies because of sin, the tyrant which held all in its power (3:9). Humanity can now look forward in hope to the fullness of the salvation that, in principle, it already possesses (Galatians 5:5) because of the reconciliation that comes from God's initiative in Christ. God's love guarantees this through the Holy Spirit that he pours into our hearts. Given all this, there is no place in Christian life for complaints against God such as the Israelites made in the desert and for divisions such as those that separated Jew and Samaritan, about which we will hear in our gospel reading. The chapters that follow will develop these themes in the detail they deserve.

John's Gospel includes a series of meetings between Jesus and individuals. One of these was Nicodemus, a learned ruler of the Jews who, failing to grasp the revelation Jesus offered, retired into the darkness from which he came (3:2). If Nicodemus could not understand Jesus, what chance would a woman from Samaria have to do better? Samaritans were traditional enemies of the Jews and women in the culture of that time were quite without status. A weary and thirsty Jesus meets the woman at a well, and plays the part of the model missionary.

Jesus leads this woman, step by step, to a level of understanding as deep as any in the Gospel. Asked for water by this alien traveller, she is hostile and sarcastic, but by calling him 'a greater man than our father Jacob', she unconsciously speaks the truth. Jesus' persistence brings her to ask him for water. Water in this Gospel symbolizes either the revelation Jesus offered (1:18) or the Spirit he brought (7:39); the reader would think of baptism (3:5). The story continues with Jesus asking for the woman's husband. Then Jesus tells her how true worship must be 'in spirit and truth'. This is not an attack on external worship but a demand that it be inspired by the Holy Spirit (Romans 8:26) and be conformed to the truth that is, ultimately, Jesus himself (14:6). The woman recognises him as a prophet and Jesus is able to identify himself with the messiah, something that he otherwise never does in his ministry.

An exemplary disciple, the woman goes off to inform others of what she has learnt (1:41). These too are Samaritans, who go on to make their own unique confession of Jesus, calling him 'saviour of the world'. The contribution of the disciples is to urge Jesus to eat. In reply, he used proverbs to turn their thoughts to the spiritual harvest that will later come to pass in the mission of Philip to Samaria (Acts 8:5). The reader is to take to heart this portrait of Jesus as patient teacher and the woman as exemplary learner.

Lent 4 A

1 Samuel 16:1, 6–7, 10–13
Psalm 22
Ephesians 5:8–14
John 9:1–41

The Man Born Blind

Once the people of Israel was settled in the land promised to Abraham, they were at first ruled by judges. **Samuel** was the last of these. He combined the roles of priest and prophet. However the people demanded a king like the other nations who surrounded them. Their first king was Saul, but in God's eyes he was unfit and God rejected him. God now orders Samuel to anoint David instead. Samuel is surprised at God's choice. David is a younger brother whose life has been spent herding sheep. The choice would not have surprised Samuel's mother, Hannah. She had sung in her canticle, 'The bow of the mighty is broken but the feeble have girded themselves with strength' (1 Samuel 2:4). Her words will be echoed by those of Mary in her Magnificat (Luke 1:52).

The selection of David the shepherd boy as king makes the 'Good Shepherd' **Psalm** an appropriate choice. God's care for his people as good shepherd mirrors his description of himself as the ideal shepherd who would make up for the deficiencies of human ones (Ezekiel 34).

The letter to the **Ephesians**, in its address to recent converts (4: 17), describes the moral behaviour that is to be expected in their new way of life. It uses the language of light and darkness, including a hymn familiar to them from their liturgy, to contrast the Christian life with that which they knew before their conversion and baptism. It prepares us for the Gospel, which depicts Christ as the Light of the World who gives sight to the blind (John 8: 12) and reminds us of Jesus' words in the Sermon on the Mount which describe his disciples as the 'light of the world' (Matthew 5: 14).

If Jesus' encounter with the Samaritan woman was typical of his relationships with the alienated of society, his healing of the man born blind typifies his care for the sick. Such healings were understood as signs of the messianic times (Isaiah 29: 18). Yet **John** did not want his readers to think of Jesus merely as a physical healer. The real healing he brought was for spiritual health. Before he begins the story, he makes it clear that physical defect does not imply personal guilt (Luke 13: 2–3).

From physical blindness, the cured man advances in stages to full spiritual vision. Like that of the Samaritan woman, his understanding of Jesus deepens. At first, he describes Jesus simply as 'the man called Jesus', then he recognises him as a prophet and, finally, told that Jesus is the Son of Man, he worships Jesus as Lord. Meanwhile, the 'Jews', representing the authorities who are the enemies of Jesus, fail to realise how they themselves are slipping from physical sight into spiritual blindness. They refuse to accept that the blind beggar was ever blind or, indeed, that he is the same man at all. The story concludes with a warning from Jesus that their spiritual blindness is a far worse condition than the physical blindness of the healed man.

Of special interest is the role of the man's parents. They refused to accept the consequences of their knowledge. They represent those who will not witness to their faith openly because of what it might cost. Their passivity contrasts with Jesus' activity as the 'Good Shepherd' (10: 14). As such, he cures the blind man, seeks him out in trouble, encourages him and helps him to recognise Jesus' true identity as Son of Man. In Christian tradition, baptized Christians have recognised their own experience in this man who washes in 'Siloam', the one 'sent'. Jesus was the one sent by the Father (20: 21), and their own responsibility and need are to grow in their faith in the person of Jesus, the true light.

Lent 5 A

Ezekiel 37:12–14
Psalm 129
Romans 8:8–11
John 11:1–45

The Raising of Lazarus

In 587 BC, Jerusalem was invaded and its Temple destroyed. The people went into exile in Babylon. **Ezekiel** was a prophet active at the time of this exile. The nation of Israel seemed as good as dead. God sent Ezekiel a vision of a valley full of dry bones and as he watched, these bones were restored to life through the Spirit of God (37:10). In our passage, the vision is explained. The bones symbolize the Israel that has died. God promises that her people will live and possess its land again, because his Spirit will make its home in them (Psalm 104:30).

In the **Psalm**, the penitent makes no excuses for past infidelity. He knows that God is a God who forgives, who in his loving kindness is faithful to his people. The watchman's wait will not be in vain. God will bring his people to life again.

In **Romans**, Paul contrasts the state of those who live by and for themselves without Christ—'who are interested only in unspiritual things'—with those in whom 'the Spirit of God has made his home'. This Spirit is given various names: 'Spirit of God', 'Spirit of Christ', 'the Spirit of him who raised Jesus from the dead'. It cancels the spiritual death brought by sin (5:12). Unlike Ezekiel's Spirit, it is not something external to God's creation, but dwells within it. Christian life is characterized by the indwelling of this Spirit, as opposed to the indwelling of sin (7:17). Physical death remains the lot of the Christian as a result of sin, but the possession of the Spirit assures us that this is not the end of the story. Life is a gift for ever (Wisdom 1:14). Nothing can separate us from the love of Christ (Romans 8:35). God's love has been poured into our hearts through the Holy Spirit (Romans 5:5).

When Jesus told his enemies that he was the Good Shepherd, he insisted that he had power to lay down his life and to raise it up again (John 10:15, 17, 18). In **John**, he gives a 'sign' of this truth by raising Lazarus from the dead. Other Gospels relate how Jesus raised the dead, but never with such detail. And neither Jairus' daughter nor the son of the widow of Nain had been in a tomb for three days (Mark 5:42; Luke 7:15).

As with the Samaritan woman and the man born blind, the account is dramatic, with tension at the beginning when we wonder whether Jesus will go to his friend or not, and tension at the end as we wait for Lazarus to come out of the tomb. Within the story, we are surprised at the quality of Martha's confession of Jesus as 'the Christ, the Son of God, the one who was to come into this world', which is as profound as that of Peter in Matthew (Matthew 16:16). It is the confession that the reader of the Gospel is to make (20:31). We are struck by the weeping of Jesus. Is this a proof of his true humanity? Or does he weep because of his friends' unchristian reaction to the death? Are they so without hope? Have they forgotten his teaching in Capernaum that 'everybody who believes has eternal life' (6:47) and his words in Jerusalem, 'the hour is coming when the dead will leave their graves at the sound of his voice' (5:28). Paul met similar problems in Thessalonica with those who lacked Christian hope about the fate of the dead (1 Thessalonians 4:13).

Finally Lazarus emerges from the tomb, but his resurrection is not like that of Jesus. He is still wearing his burial clothes, whereas Jesus would leave his in the tomb (20:6). In contrast to Lazarus, Jesus rose to a completely new life and would never die again. The believer hopes for a share in the resurrection of Jesus, leading to a life whose quality we have yet to discover. 'What we are to be in the future has not yet been revealed' (1 John 3:2). On previous Sundays, we have met Jesus as the giver of living water (John 4:10) and the light of the world (John 9:5); today we encounter him as the 'Resurrection and the Life'.

Passion Sunday A

Isaiah 50:4–7
Psalm 21:8–9; 23–24
Philippians 2:6–11
Matthew 26:14–27:66

The Passion of Jesus

Before and during the exile, many in Israel were unfaithful. We read in the third of **Isaiah**'s 'Servant Songs' about one who remains steadfast. Whether an individual or a group, this Servant listens to and passes on God's word and does not rebel or give up because of the affliction and shame it brings. Knowledge of God's presence and support keeps him faithful.

Our **Psalm** is a 'song of the innocent sufferer'. It supplements the Servant Song and prepares for the passion story. Jesus spoke its first words as his last (Matthew 27:46). Its descriptions of mocking bystanders and divided garments describe his sufferings. Its ending, in which God is praised and the sufferer vindicated, anticipates his resurrection.

The hymn from **Philippians** describes the career of Christ. Some find in it a description of Christ in his pre-existent and divine life. He did not hold on to this but emptied himself so as to die on a cross. Others compare Christ with Adam. Like Adam, he was in the image of God (Genesis 1:26), but he did not look for equality with God as Adam did (Genesis 3:5), but accepted the human condition in all its weakness. His fidelity to God led him to a slave's death on a cross. God's response was the opposite of his response to Adam, whom he condemned to return to the dust from which he came (Genesis 3:19); he exalted Jesus to divine status. The description that Isaiah applied to God is now used to depict the risen Christ (Isaiah 45:23): he is now the 'Lord'. Paul wanted his friends in Philippi to lay aside their selfishness and arrogance, so that the grace of God could find its full scope in them. The pattern of the career of Christ was a pattern to be lived in their lives too.

The story of the sufferings and death of Jesus is the most extended narrative in the Gospels, and **Matthew**'s is the longest of the four. His revisions of Mark's story indicate how he wants these events to be understood. Mark did not play down the horror of the story; he portrayed Jesus as silent, despised and deserted until the moment of death when, by the tearing of the Temple veil and the centurion's confession, God vindicated his cause as a prelude to his resurrection (Mark 15:38–39).

Matthew's account helps the reader, and the teachers in his community, better to understand the meaning of the events. Jesus announces the start of the drama, 'My time is near'. At the supper he explains the sacrificial nature of his death, which is for the 'forgiveness of sins'. He prays to his Father in Gethsemane, knowing that he could be given twelve legions of angels; his refusal to resist reflects his own teaching in the Sermon on the Mount (5:39). As he dies, his enemies mock him as 'Son of God' (Wisdom 2:13), but the reader knows from the temptation story (4:6) that he will not misuse this intimacy with his Father. This was his identity from the beginning (2:15) and his disciples recognised it during the ministry (14:33; 16:16). The title on the cross, 'Jesus, the King of the Jews', is no error, since it was as a child king that the wise men gave him gifts (2:2) and he had entered Jerusalem as a humble king on a donkey (21:5–9).

Meanwhile the scriptural prophecies are fulfilled. Old Israel formally rejected Jesus before Pilate, treating him as an impostor, so that it, like every other nation, became in need of the forgiveness brought by his blood. Meanwhile, we remember Paul's words that 'God never takes back his gifts or revokes his choice' (Romans 11:29). The nations are symbolized by Pilate's wife, who pleads to her husband for Jesus. Finally, the earthquake and resurrection of the just show that the turning point of the ages, expected in the future, has already come with this death.

Easter Sunday

Acts 10:34, 37–43
Psalm 117:1–2 , 16–17, 22–23
Colossians 3:1–4
John 20:1–9

The Empty Tomb

During the Easter season, our first reading is always from the **Acts**. Today, we hear the speech of Peter to Cornelius, the first Gentile to be accepted as a Christian. This speech is significant for its statement that God wants the salvation of all (1 Timothy 2:4) and for giving us the fullest outline of the life of Jesus outside the Gospels. By contrast with his other speeches in Acts, Peter begins with the mission of John the Baptist and ends with the commission of the apostles. They are to bear witness to what the Risen Lord proclaimed and to his future return as judge (Luke 24:46–47; Acts 1:11).

The **Psalm** is one of the *hallel* Psalms, sung at the Last Supper by Jesus and his disciples (Mark 14:26). The phrase about the rejected stone, originating in Isaiah (28:16), is one of the prophetic texts testifying to Jesus that Peter includes in his speech (Acts 10:43). It is also quoted in Luke's Gospel, in Jesus' parable of the vineyard workers (Luke 20:17).

In **Colossians**, we find a profound understanding of the dignity of Christ as one who is 'the image of the unseen God, and the firstborn of all creation' (1:15). Through baptism, Christians share this dignity (2:12; Romans 6:3). Christ, now seated at the right hand of God, will come again in glory. Paul makes a personal appeal to the people of Colossi. They are to live the sort of life fitting for those who have been raised with Christ. Their gaze is to be set on heaven where Christ is; their destiny is to share in the glory of Christ when he comes again. This ancient summons is repeated to us every Easter Sunday. We, too, are to recognise the nobility that belongs to us as Christians and to live it out in practice.

Jesus himself never appears in our passage from **John**. The time is early and it is still dark, which means for John that Christ, who is the 'light of the world' (8:12), is absent. Three disciples react to this absence. Mary Magdalene is the first; we read only the first half of her story, but we notice how primitive her faith is. Her devotion has brought her to the tomb, but the missing body can only mean that someone has taken it away. Jesus himself will have to search her out to bring her to full belief (20:15).

The second disciple is Peter. At the end of the discourse on the Bread of Life, he made an impressive personal commitment to Jesus as 'the Holy One of God' (6:69), but later, after Jesus' arrest, he denied three times that he even knew Jesus (18:15–18, 25–27). So wounded is he spiritually by these denials that, even though he sees that the tomb is empty and the grave clothes are lying there, he cannot arrive at the truth. The resurrection of Jesus is of a different order from that of Lazarus, whose hands and feet were bound with bandages and whose face was wrapped in a cloth when he was raised (11:44).

The third disciple is not named. He is simply called 'the one Jesus loved'. He lay close to Jesus at the Last Supper (13:23) and was present at the foot of the cross (19:26). He enjoyed such an intimacy with Jesus because he already had the right relationship with him, that of mutual love. For this reason, he can run faster than Peter and draw the correct conclusion from the grave clothes that have been left behind by Jesus in the tomb. As a model believer, he became not only the authority for his community for the material contained in this Gospel, but an example to them. They were to believe as he had believed (20:31). Usually, he is identified with the disciple John, but he represents all faithful disciples of Jesus in every age of the Church. Their loving intimacy with Jesus ensures that, though they do not see Jesus physically, they believe without seeing (20:29).

Easter 2

Acts 2:42–47
Psalm 117:2–4, 13–15, 22–24
1 Peter 1:3–9
John 20:19–31

My Lord and My God

In his initial summary description of the first Christian community in Jerusalem, Luke in **Acts** stresses four points. New converts are to understand what they believe by attending to the teaching of the apostles (Luke 8:12). Through fellowship, they express the truth that Christianity implies a sharing of life and resources (Luke 12:33). The practice of prayer proves that they take the example of Jesus in Luke's Gospel seriously (Luke 18:1). Through the breaking of bread, they continue in their Eucharists the meals that they shared with Jesus in his life with them (Luke 22:14; 24:30).

The pilgrim **Psalm** of last Sunday is continued. All are invited to join in the praise of God. God has given victory to the one who was failing, to Christ who was buried in the tomb.

1 Peter is a letter for 'those living among foreigners in the Dispersion' (1:1), for groups whose lives in this world are alienated and marginalised. The 'blessing' with which it begins (2 Corinthians 1:3–14) introduces the themes of the letter. They may be homeless in this world, but, as fellow-heirs of Christ, they have homes in heaven (Romans 8:17). Just as Christ was raised from the dead, they too possess new life through baptism (Romans 6:3). Hardship may be their lot now, but this is just for a time. This testing is helping them prove the quality of their faith (James 1:2). Their fundamental attitude is to be the Easter attitude of joy (John 20:20). Even though they did not see Jesus in the flesh, they still love him (John 15:9). Tradition hears the voice of the disciple Peter behind these words. He has overcome his failure and infidelity during the passion of Jesus (John 18:15–18, 25–27).

At his final meal with his disciples in **John**, Jesus had promised not to leave them as orphans (14:18). His appearances to them after his resurrection are part of his fulfilment of this pledge. When he shows himself to them as they hide behind locked doors in Jerusalem, he makes real the joy (16:20) and the peace (14:27) of which he spoke at the Last Supper. His words then were preparing them for this future.

They are to continue the mission that Jesus has been given by the Father (8:42). Just as he has never been alone, since the Father is always with him (16:32), neither will they be. He solemnly breathes the Spirit over them (Genesis 1:2). John the Baptist had seen this Spirit coming down on Jesus and remaining on him at the beginning, at his baptism (1:31–32). Jesus has spoken of the Spirit during his ministry (7:39). He described it in detail as the paraclete at the Supper (14:15–17, 26; 15:26–27; 16:7–11, 12–15). It was symbolized in the water flowing from Jesus' side at his death (19:34). When the disciples in turn pass it on to others, then sins will be forgiven.

Jesus performed many signs in his lifetime (20:30), with the purpose of producing belief (2:23). In the new age of the Spirit, faith is no longer to depend on this sort of sign. Thomas seeks for the reassurance of touch and feeling as the price for his belief in the Risen Lord. Jesus refuses to give such reassurance. There are two beatitudes in John's Gospel: one is concerned with mutual service at the foot-washing (13:17), and the other with belief that does not depend on sight.

It is easy to identify with Thomas. He is the pessimist among the disciples, who regarded an invitation to go to Jerusalem with Jesus as an invitation to death (11:16). When Jesus called himself the 'Way', Thomas said bluntly, 'How can we know the way?' (14:5). As good shepherd, Jesus sought Thomas out. He knew him as one of his own (10:15) and enabled him to make a confession of Jesus surpassing all others in the Gospel, 'My Lord and my God!'.

Easter 3 A

Acts 2:14, 22–33
Psalm 15:1–2, 5, 7–11
1 Peter 1:17–21
Luke 24:13–35

The Emmaus Road

There are many speeches in the **Acts** of the Apostles. Five of them are attributed to Peter. This week and next, we hear from his pentecost speech. Its centre is the proclamation of the death and resurrection of Jesus. Typically, he backs up his argument with a quotation from scripture. He uses verses from a psalm to show that King David of old foresaw the resurrection (Psalm 16:8–11). Quotations like this one help us to understand how Jesus explained to his disciples passages from scripture that were about himself (Luke 24:27).

The **Psalm** is a traditional song of the Levites, a tribe that possessed no land (Joshua 18:7) and had God alone as 'my heritage, my cup'. The phrase 'my body, too, will rest securely' makes it appropriate for Easter.

We can speculate that **1 Peter** reflects the encouragement offered to the newly baptized. They learn about God. God is a judge, fair and thorough in his judgments, but he is also a father, concerned for the welfare of those for whom he is responsible. He is the one who raised Jesus from the dead. They learn about Christ. Although he existed before the world began, he has poured out his life-blood in sacrifice. He has been put to death like the lamb that the Israelites slaughtered each year to commemorate their escape from Egyptian oppression centuries ago (Mark 14:14). His death is described as a ransom, a word used by Jesus himself to his disciples as he anticipated it (Mark 10:45). The result of all this is that they are to have faith and hope in God, even though they are exiles and living away from their homes, scattered over various parts of the Roman empire (1:1).

For **Luke**, as for the other evangelists, Easter is first proclaimed to the faithful women disciples who have followed Jesus from Galilee (24:5–6). The other disciples do not believe them (24:11), so Jesus himself sets out in search of his doubting followers, like a shepherd going after the lost sheep (15:4). He meets two of them travelling away from Jerusalem towards Emmaus.

Cleopas and his companion are talking about the very Jesus who walks beside them unrecognised. They are not short of information. Recalling Peter's sermons in Acts, they describe Jesus as 'a great prophet by the things he said and did'. They know all about his death and speak about the hope they had that he would deliver Israel. They have even heard the Easter message of the women. The facts they know, but they need a spark to make them flame out in belief. They are people whose 'own hope had been that he would be the one to set Israel free'.

Their unknown companion brings their faith to life again in three stages. First, he reproaches them for their failure to heed the warnings he had given them that the Christ had to suffer and enter into his glory (9:22, 44; 18:31–32) and for their lack of understanding of the scriptures, which they thought they knew. They are like the foolish man in the Psalms who said there was no God (Psalm 14:1). Secondly, he explains the scriptures to them with such effect that they say their hearts 'burn within us'. We read how the prophets wrote about Christ in the various speeches in Acts. Thirdly, he breaks bread with them, a phrase applied in Acts to the Eucharist (20:7). This is the spark that rekindles their belief. They rush back to Jerusalem to share the good news with the other disciples, to find them already repeating the Easter proclamation, 'it is true. The Lord has risen.'

The narrative of the journey is a model liturgy. First the scriptures are read and explained, and then the bread is broken. This should lead to a recognition of the Risen Lord and an enthusiasm for bearing witness to him to the ends of the earth (Acts 1:8).

Easter 4 A

Acts 2:14, 36–41
Psalm 22:1–6
1 Peter 2:20–25
John 10:1–10

Jesus, the Gate and the Shepherd

Peter concludes his speech at pentecost in **Acts** by proclaiming the crucified Jesus as 'Lord and Christ'. The people respond, 'What must we do?', the same question the crowds had asked John the Baptist (Luke 3:10). John had replied in terms of elementary social justice. Peter demands far more: repentance, a complete change of attitude to be manifested in baptism. Peter makes three thousand converts that day. He is a fisher of men, as Jesus promised at his call by the lake (Luke 5:10). He is also exercising his role as a witness to the Risen Lord (Luke 24:47).

The **Psalm** of the Good Shepherd gives confidence to those who obey Peter by repenting as he demands. The shepherd they follow is characterized by goodness and kindness. He guides along the right path; he is the Jesus portrayed in the Gospel.

Among those who heard **1 Peter** read out were poor slaves who would often have to endure unjust punishment from their pagan overseers. Peter encourages them by describing the experience of Christ in his passion. He endured it all in patience and he did so for the sake of his followers. Now they have the power to live in holiness, as people set aside for the service of God. The author uses the language of the fourth Servant Song of Isaiah (Isaiah 52:13–53:12). The early Church identified the Servant with Christ. We find confirmation of this in the story of Philip and the Ethiopian (Acts 8:32). Last week, Christ was compared to a lamb. Here, he is called 'shepherd'. This prepares us for the Gospel, and for the description of church elders as shepherds later in this letter (5:1–2).

Each year on this Sunday, a passage from **John**'s Good Shepherd chapter is read. The context is one of controversy. After having healed the man born blind, Jesus finds himself in conflict with his critics. His response is to compare himself first to the gate of a sheepfold and then to a shepherd. This is the nearest he comes in John to speaking in parables. Later, at the Last Supper, he will call himself the vine to which the disciples must be attached and in which they must abide (15:4).

Today, Jesus speaks about the gate of a sheepfold. The genuine shepherd of the sheep passes through this gate. The sheep are happy to follow such a shepherd. They will not follow one who enters by some other route. These sayings of Jesus, like his parables in the synoptic Gospels, are not understood (Mark 4:10) and he has to explain. He identifies himself with the gate, the proper entrance to the sheepfold. Thieves find other ways in. Such are the Pharisees, who have disgraced themselves in their treatment of the blind man, and such are the present rulers, who have brought God's people to the crisis of being 'sheep without a shepherd' (Mark 6:34).

Jesus is the way to good pasture (14:6), as we have learnt already from this Gospel. He gave drink to the Samaritan woman (4:1–42) and bread to the starving crowds of Galilee (6:1–72). Food and drink symbolize the life he wishes to give in abundance. Sheep do not pay attention to bad shepherds, just as the man born blind spoke up against the Pharisees (9:25). Such shepherds have Satan as their father, a 'murderer from the start' (8:44). This imagery is from the Old Testament: the rulers of Israel were called shepherds; David was summoned from pasturing his father's flocks (1 Samuel 16:11). God complained about the shepherds of the people (Jeremiah 23; Ezekiel 34), promising to become their shepherd himself. The Psalmist praised him as the good shepherd of his people (Psalm 23; Psalm 80). At the end of the Gospel, Peter in his turn will be appointed to feed the sheep of Christ (21:15–17).

Easter 5 A

Acts 6:1–7
Psalm 32:1–2, 4–5, 18–19
1 Peter 2:4–9
John 14:1–12

Jesus, the Way, the Truth and the Life

A turning point in **Acts** is provided by the activity and death of Stephen, the first martyr. So far, apart from the incident with Ananias and Sapphira (5:1–11), the Christians have enjoyed internal peace. A dispute between the Hebrews and the Hellenists about widows interrupts this. In reaction, the twelve apostles, who now include Matthias (1:13, 26), agree to appoint seven others, 'men of good reputation', to 'give out food'. They do more than this. Stephen is to make a long speech about the Temple and we will soon meet Philip on his missionary journeys (8:4–5). All have Greek names, which hints at the evangelization of the Greek world outside Jerusalem. Their ministry of service (*diakonein*) anticipates the service of deacons (*diakonoi*) in the Church.

The **Psalm** celebrates in song the virtues of the God of the covenant, which came to a climax in Christ (John 1:17). The reference to rescuing souls from death makes it a suitable Easter hymn.

Though the recipients of **1 Peter** might feel themselves homeless and leaderless, the writer informs them that this is not the reality. They are a spiritual house built with living stones, and Christ is their cornerstone. This imagery derives from sayings about stones in Isaiah (28:16) and the Psalms (118:22). To build up the community further, he gives them four titles that God bestowed on Israel when he chose it as his people (Exodus 19:6; Revelation 1:6). Their task and privilege is to proclaim to the world the wonders of God who has called them out of darkness into light (Colossians 1:12; Acts 26:18).

We read in the scriptures how Jacob said farewell to his sons (Genesis 49:1) and how David said farewell to Solomon (1 Kings 2:1). They had no expectation of meeting again in the future. However, when Jesus makes his farewell speech to his disciples at the Last Supper in **John**, he assures them that they will see him again. He first promises them that he is going ahead of them to prepare a place for them. He will meet them once more after their death, because they, too, will have a room in his Father's house. He will return to take them there (1 Thessalonians 4:14). But then he has to deal with interjections from two of his disciples.

The first comes from Thomas, whom we met before the raising of Lazarus (11:16). He interrupts Jesus by asking him about the way they are to take. Thanks to his interruption, we have another 'I am' saying of Jesus to treasure. We learn that not only is he the gate (10:7) and the shepherd (10:14), but also the Way, and he defines this as the truth and the life. Truth in John is often the equivalent of wisdom (17:17). Jesus would tell Pilate that he came into the world to testify to the truth (18:37), and life, as he told Martha, the sister of Lazarus, is that which death cannot destroy (11:26). Jesus was himself the 'resurrection and the life' (11:25).

Then Philip (1:43) breaks in, and we owe to his intervention a lesson on the relationship between Jesus and the Father (Matthew 11:25). The key word here is 'living'. When the disciples first met Jesus, they asked him, 'Where do you live?' (1:38). Now they are given their answer. The Son lives with the Father; the Father lives in the Son. All this is a preparation for Jesus' revelation later in this chapter, 'If anyone loves me he will keep my word, and my Father will love him, and we shall come to him and make our home with him' (14:23). The same Greek word is translated by the English 'live' and 'make our home'. The disciple does not have to wait for death in order to meet Jesus again. Jesus is speaking language with which the mystic is at home.

Easter 6 A

Acts 8:5–8, 14–17
Psalm 65:1–7, 16
1 Peter 3:15–18
John 14:15–21

The Paraclete

Jesus announced the programme of **Acts** when he commissioned his disciples, before his ascension, to be his witnesses in Jerusalem, in Samaria and to the ends of the earth (1:8). After Stephen's death (7:60), the mission to Samaria at last begins, through Philip, one of the Seven. Like Jesus, he heals and casts out demons (Luke 4:40–41). Peter and John bring the approval of Jerusalem by the laying on of hands. In the words of Jesus in the chapter of John's Gospel about Samaria, Philip has sown but Peter and John have reaped (John 4:37). Thus the Samaritans receive the Holy Spirit and had their own day of pentecost (2:4).

The **Psalm**, traditionally used as a resurrection hymn, thanks God for the new life he has granted to his people. The Exodus from Egypt and deliverance from exile in Babylon foreshadow the resurrection of Jesus.

Life for the scattered readers of **1 Peter** is not easy. Their way of life puzzles the society around them. They are subject to false accusations. Sometimes their faith brings them suffering. Their response is to be twofold. On the human level, they are not to be silent and passive. They must defend and explain their attitudes and conduct. They are to exercise courtesy. Their way of life has to be beyond reproach. But they also have to keep Christ in mind. His name occurs at the beginning and end and in the middle of our passage. They are to reverence him as their Lord. They have to base their behaviour on his example and they are to remember that, though innocent himself, he died for the guilty.

We continue the Supper Discourse of **John**. Two words claim our attention. The first is *advocate* or, in Greek, *paraclete*. Jesus is explaining a further way in which he will continue to be present with his disciples after his imminent departure. This will be through the Paraclete, who will take the place of Jesus in the life of his followers. Various texts help us build up a picture of his role. Like Jesus himself, the paraclete comes from the Father (14:26). He is the Spirit of truth who continues the revelation that Jesus brought. He will be the teacher of the disciples, telling them more about Jesus (15:26) and about his teaching (16:12). The world will no more accept the paraclete than it accepted Jesus, because he would prove it wrong 'about sin, and about who was in the right, and about judgement' (16:8). As long as the paraclete is with them, the followers of Jesus cannot be orphans. This is the novel way in which the Holy Spirit and its role is explained in this Gospel. In the first letter of John, the author portrays Jesus himself in heaven exercising the role of paraclete with the Father on behalf of anyone who sinned (1 John 2:1).

The second word that dominates our passage is *love*. This comes at both the beginning and the end. It also marked the opening of John's account of the Last Supper, 'he showed how perfect his love was' (13:1), and the end of the discourse in which Jesus prays to his Father, that 'the love with which you loved me may be in them' (17:26).

It is easy to collect texts that show that love is the key word in the second half of John's Gospel. The Father loves the Son (17:26); the Son loves the disciples (17:23). At the very centre of the discourse, Jesus tells the disciples that they are to love one another (15:12). There is no greater love than to lay down one's life for one's friends (15:13). The story of the passion is proof of how much God loves the world: he gave up his only Son (3:16). It is only in the First Letter of John that we read, 'God is love' (1 John 4:8, 16).

The Ascension A

Acts 1:1–11
Psalm 46:2–4, 6–9
Ephesians 1:17–23
Matthew 28:16–20

The Exalted Christ

The opening of **Acts** solemnly describes the start of the third stage of world history for Luke. The time of Israel and the time of the earthly Jesus are past, and the time of the Church begins. Moses was prepared for his mission by a forty-day stay on the mountain (Exodus 24:18). Elijah (1 Kings 19:8) and Jesus spent forty days in the desert (Matthew 4:2). At the end of a similar period, the disciples were promised the same Holy Spirit that had anointed Jesus as he began his mission (Luke 3:22) and they were appointed his witnesses to the ends of the earth. This mission was symbolically completed by the arrival of Paul in Rome but meanwhile the disciples are to cease gazing upward into heaven and devote themselves to the continuation of Jesus' ministry in this world.

The **Psalm** was probably first sung after some great military victory. The Ark of the Covenant was solemnly carried through Jerusalem to the Temple, where God was greeted as the Lord Most High (Genesis 14:18) and as Great King. On Ascension Day we apply it to Christ, now exalted in heaven as the Lord of all creation.

In **Ephesians**, in a prayer of personal thanksgiving, the author uses various pictures to express the power of God that has been exercised in Christ. He raised him from the dead. He made him sit at his right hand (Psalm 110:1) like a newly installed king. He subordinated all the powers in the universe to him. He appointed him head of the Church, which is his body. This author expresses in doctrine what Luke intended by his description of the physical ascent of Jesus from earth to heaven by means of a cloud.

Though **Matthew** does not mention the Ascension, its significance is contained in the solemn conclusion to his Gospel. The setting is a mountain, a place of special revelation in scripture like Sinai in the Old Testament (Exodus 19:3) and like the other mountains in Matthew (5:1; 17:1). The place is Galilee of the Gentiles, the region where Jesus began his ministry (4:15). The audience is the 'Eleven' (10:2). Like the magi at the beginning (2:11), they worship Jesus, though 'some hesitated'. They are still people of little faith (14:31), a microcosm of the Church to come, described in the parables as a mixed field of wheat and weeds (13:25).

In the Gospels generally, whenever Jesus speaks of himself he uses the title Son of Man (16:27), an expression found in Daniel (7:13). Here on the mountain, he claims directly for himself the authority given to this figure in Daniel (7:14). He is the Exalted One (Philippians 2:9). The kingdoms of the world and their glory, offered Jesus by Satan in the Temptations (4:8) in return for his worship, are now his because of his acceptance of the cross and the will of the Father (16:21; 26:39).

He formally gives the Eleven their mission. This is no longer restricted to Israel (10:6; 15:24); all nations are to become his disciples. They are to be baptized in the name of the Trinity, to experience what Jesus himself did at his baptism (3:16–21). They are to belong to the divine family of Father, Son and Spirit (2 Corinthians 13:13). For the first time in Matthew, Jesus commissions the disciples to teach. They are to make the teaching of the five great discourses of this Gospel (5–7, 10, 13, 18, 24–25) their own and pass it on. Jesus himself, as Lord of the Church, will encourage and support them. He promises his presence until the end of time. The Emmanuel prophecy of the infancy is now fulfilled (1:23). Wherever two or three are gathered in his name, there he is in their midst (18:20).

Easter 7 A

Acts 1:12–14
Psalm 26:1, 4, 7–8
1 Peter 4:13–16
John 17:1–11

The Prayer of the Hour

Between the ascension of Jesus and the coming of the Holy Spirit at pentecost, according to **Acts**, the apostles prepare to be 'clothed with the power from on high' (Luke 24:49), as they wait for 'what the Father had promised' (Acts 1:4). The place is Jerusalem, 'the dwelling of the Most High' (Psalm 46:4), where Luke had begun his gospel story with the vision of Zechariah (Luke 1:11–12). Once again we are given the names of the apostles (Luke 6:13–16). Mary, the mother of Jesus, and his 'brothers' join them. This is Mary's final appearance in Luke's work. These make up the nucleus of the Church. They are the new family of God (Mark 3:34–35). Like Jesus before his baptism with the Holy Spirit, they pray (Luke 3:21).

The **Psalm** acknowledges the presence of God in the Jerusalem Temple, a God who meets every human need. It would be a prayer treasured by the family of Jesus and the apostles as they await the Spirit.

The recipients of **1 Peter** are being 'tested by fire' (4:12). The author gives them encouragement in various ways. He has already told them that affliction cannot destroy their joy in Christ (1:6). Like Paul before him, he affirms that sharing the sufferings of Christ will mean a share in his glory (Romans 8:17). Echoing words of Jesus, he assures them of a special blessing if they are reviled for the sake of Christ (Matthew 5:10). Recalling Isaiah, he assures them that the Spirit of God will rest on them (Isaiah 11:2). Their suffering will give glory to God, just as Paul's had given glory to Christ (Philippians 1:20). They are to keep clear of crime as of the other vices of the age (4:3). This is the only place outside Acts (11:26; 26:28) where believers are called Christians.

Jesus concludes his Supper Discourse in **John** with the longest prayer in the Gospels. We read part of it each year; it provides a good supplement to the pre-pentecost prayer of his mother and his disciples (Acts 1:12–14). It is often called the 'priestly' prayer, because Jesus prays that his disciples be consecrated in the truth, but a better title is the 'prayer of the hour'. His hour has now come (John 2:4), when he is to pass from this world to the Father (13:1). In the prayer, he takes up again themes of the Discourse and of this Gospel as a whole.

He prays for glory. For those with the eyes to see, his glory has been visible throughout this Gospel (1:14; 2:11). This is why there has been no account of the transfiguration. The supreme manifestation of this glory will come through his imminent passion, death and resurrection. For John, these are not to be separated. His lifting up on the cross is part of it; then he will draw all people to himself (12:32). The theme of glory leads into that of eternal life. This is the life of God himself which he desires to share with those who believe (6:68). Unusually, it is defined here in terms of the knowledge of the Father and the Son whom he sent.

The main task of the Son is to reveal the name of the Father. This name, 'I am who I am', was long ago given to Moses at the burning bush (Exodus 3:14). It has constantly been recalled in the Gospel by the 'I am' sayings of Jesus (8:58). Jesus tells Philip that the one who has seen the Son, has already seen the Father (14:9). This revelation of Jesus is not something secret; he will shortly emphasize to the high priest, Annas, how his teaching is for all who will hear it (18:20–23). Surprisingly, Jesus refuses to pray for the world, because in John the world belongs to the evil one (14:30). The world has to be subjected to the judgment of the paraclete (16:8); then all the scattered children of God will be brought into one (11:52). Thus the glory belonging to Jesus and to the Father is offered to all (1:14).

Pentecost A

Acts 2:1–11
Psalm 103:1, 24, 29–31, 34
1 Corinthians 12:3–7, 12–13
John 20:19–23

The Coming of the Holy Spirit

Pentecost, fifty days after Passover, is the festival when the Jews thank God for the harvest and for the Law. The apostles and the relatives of Jesus are waiting for 'what the Father had promised' (Acts 1:4). Pilgrims have come from every corner of the empire. God chooses this time to fulfil Joel's prophecy of the last days (Joel 2:28–32). The wind and fire recall the giving of the Law at Sinai (Exodus 19:16). The many languages newly understood cancel out the confusion of Babel (Genesis 11:9). God's creative Spirit that 'hovered over the water' (Genesis 1:2), the Spirit that inspired the prophets (Isaiah 61:1), the Spirit promised as a source of renewal in the future (Ezekiel 36:26), is poured out over renewed Israel. In **Acts**, the Holy Spirit comes across as a powerful, external force.

The poet in the **Psalm** reflects on God's goodness in creation. Those who appreciate his fidelity and kindness also appreciate his world. His Spirit renewed the face of the earth at pentecost.

Paul mentions the Holy Spirit five times in our passage from **1 Corinthians**. For him, this Spirit is an *internal* force, dwelling within the believer (Romans 8:9; 1 Corinthians 3:16). It influences the interior faith life of prayer and religious confession (Romans 8:26). It expresses itself in the service and contribution each person makes to the life of the community in working to build it up for the common good (12:8–11). It is also the force that keeps the community together and enables it to absorb within itself a diverse range of people, overriding the ethnic and social differences that so easily threaten its unity. Later Christian thought would identify this Spirit as the third person of the Trinity.

For **John**, pentecost took place on Easter Sunday! (There are many such chronological problems with the post-resurrection narratives.) For his way of understanding the Spirit, it is useful to glance back over his Gospel and at the Old Testament. Jesus 'breathed' the Spirit on to his disciples, just as God had 'breathed' the breath of life into the first man, who thus became a living being (Genesis 2:7). John the Baptist had seen the Spirit descend on Jesus as a dove from heaven and remain on him (1:33). John recognised Jesus as one who baptized with the Holy Spirit (1:33).

On his first visit to Jerusalem, Jesus taught Nicodemus of the necessity to be born of 'water and the Spirit' in order to enter the Kingdom of God (3:5). At the feast of Tabernacles, he spoke of the living water that would flow from his breast. This he explained in terms of the Spirit that those who believed were to receive (7:39) At the Last Supper, he described this Spirit to his disciples as the paraclete that would constitute for them his own continuing presence, once he had returned to the Father. This paraclete was the Spirit of truth (14:17). He would be their teacher (14:26) and would testify on behalf of Jesus (15:26). He would prove the world wrong about sin and righteousness and judgment (16:7–14).

On this first Easter Day, Jesus associates the Spirit particularly with the forgiveness of sins. This must include not only sins committed before baptism, but post-baptismal sins too since, as we read in the first letter of John, the brethren admitted their sinfulness (1:8) and prayed for forgiveness of one another (5:16). The note about the retaining of sins reminds us of Paul exercising his authority in 1 Corinthians (5:3) and of the instructions in Matthew (18:18). Twice in this gospel passage, Jesus greets his disciples with a word of peace. He has spoken of this peace in his Supper Discourse: it is not the peace that the world gives (14:27). For Paul, peace was part of the fruit of the Holy Spirit (Galatians 5:22).

Trinity Sunday A

Exodus 34:4–6, 8–9
Daniel 3:52–56
2 Corinthians 13:11–13
John 3:16–18

Father, Son and Spirit

After the incident of the Golden Calf (Exodus 32), **Exodus** reports how God gives Moses the Law a second time. When he first revealed this Law, God spoke of his compassion and his severity in equal terms (Exodus 20:5–6). This second time, he stresses his tenderness and compassion. He is slow to anger and rich in kindness and faithfulness, a description dear to the Psalmist (Psalm 86:15). Such attributes distinguish Israel's God from the gods of other peoples, and anticipate the character of the Father of our Lord Jesus Christ whom Jesus reveals in the Gospels and who is identified with love itself in the letters of John (1 John 4:8, 16).

Instead of a Psalm, verses from the song of the three men in the furnace from **Daniel** are sung. They invite all creation to praise God, who is active in this world, in heaven above and in the depths below.

Paul concludes **2 Corinthians** with the most elaborate of his blessings. He describes the Trinity in terms that correspond to the later understanding of the Church. He gives a specific function to each of its Persons. To Jesus Christ he attributes grace. He loved us and gave himself for us as a free gift (Galatians 2:20; Romans 3:24). To the Father he attributes love. The love of God was poured into our hearts and the Father did this through the Holy Spirit (Romans 5:5). To the Spirit he attributes fellowship. This can be understood actively and passively. The Spirit binds together the body of Christ (1 Corinthians 12:4–11) and Christians, who constitute this body, are themselves brought into union with the Spirit since the Spirit dwells within the Christian (Romans 8:11).

Jesus told Nicodemus in **John**'s Gospel that a person must be born of water and the Spirit to enter the Kingdom of God (3:5). But once Nicodemus has returned to the darkness from which he came, the evangelist adds his own reflections on the dialogue that has just concluded, concentrating on the roles of the Father and the Son. He speaks of God the Father giving up his only Son out of his love for the world. The background here is the story of Abraham who, in obedience to God's command, was prepared to sacrifice his son Isaac. At the last moment, a substitute was provided and Abraham was able to sacrifice a ram in place of his son (Genesis 22:13). No substitute was provided for Jesus. In the words of Paul, God did not spare his own son, but gave him up for us all (Romans 8:32). In describing Jesus' journey to Calvary, John makes it clear that Jesus carried his own cross, just as Isaac carried the wood for the sacrifice (19:17).

As for the Son, John stresses that his role is not to condemn the world but to save it. He offered living water to the Samaritan woman, and this water was a symbol of the Spirit which would well up to eternal life (4:14). He promised that 'From his breast shall flow fountains of living water. He was speaking of the Spirit which those who believed in him were to receive ....' (7:38–39) When the soldier pierced his side on Calvary, 'at once blood and water came out' (19:34). Thus the birth of the Spirit of which Jesus spoke to Nicodemus became possible (3:5).

In the Gospels there is no formal declaration of the later doctrine of the Trinity, but we catch a glimpse of each person of the Trinity playing his part and exercising his function as God works to take away the sin of the world (1:29) and to bring it the peace that the world cannot give (14:27). God does this because the Son is in the Father (14:20). The Spirit of truth proceeds from the Father and bears witness to the Son (15:26).

Body and Blood of Christ A

Deuteronomy 8:2–3, 14–16
Psalm 147:12–15, 19–20
1 Corinthians 10:16–17
John 6:51–58

The Bread of Life

Moses in **Deuteronomy** reminds Israel that, without God's care, they would never have survived their journey through the desert. A particular instance of this care is his provision for them of bread in the form of manna. But manna does not give life; this comes from the word of God. Jesus quoted this passage when he was tested by Satan in the desert (Matthew 4:4). In his discourse about the bread of life to the crowds in Galilee, Jesus contrasted manna, which did not give life, with the bread that he was offering, which was the source of eternal life. This bread was himself who had come down from heaven (John 6:33).

The **Psalm** offers many reasons to Jerusalem to praise God. Among them is God's twofold gift of food: the material food of wheat which gives bread and the spiritual food of his Word.

Surprisingly, Paul in his letters says little about the Eucharist. But he does refer to it in **1 Corinthians**, while discussing whether Christians are permitted to eat meat that has been sacrificed to idols. We learn three things about it. First, Paul plainly understands that the Eucharist has a sacrificial efficacy for Christians similar to that which their pagan neighbours claimed for their sacrifices. Secondly, he clearly affirms that Christ is truly present with his people in the Eucharist. Thirdly, he stresses that the Eucharist is to be a sign of the communion of Christians among themselves. It is to bring about not only union between believers and Christ, but also unity between Christians themselves as the one body of Christ. Paul has much more to say about the Eucharist in his next chapter (1 Corinthians 11:23–34).

The longest instruction on the Eucharist in the Gospels is found in **John**. We find it not, as we might expect, in his account of the Last Supper, where he reports the washing of the feet rather than the Eucharist (13:1–20), but in the sequel to his account of the Feeding of the Five Thousand. On the day following that miracle, a great crowd assemble, hoping for more of the food that they had enjoyed the day before. They present a challenge to Jesus to lead them from a desire for earthly food to an understanding of himself as the 'Bread of Life'.

In his dialogue and encounter with the crowd, the meaning of this Bread of Life shifts. At times it refers primarily to the bread as God's Word or revelation (Deuteronomy 8:3), the sort of word that God passed on to the prophets (John 6:45); at other times it refers to the bread as the flesh of Jesus, that is to the sacrament of the Eucharist. The verses we read today certainly refer to the Eucharist. They may be John's version of the words that Jesus originally spoke at the Last Supper, where his disciples would be much more likely to understand them than the fickle crowd in Galilee.

Jesus here repeats his claim to the Bread of Life. He so emphasizes the physical reality of this bread as his Body that we must take it in a sacramental sense. We pick out three essential features of eucharistic doctrine. First, the Eucharist is sacrificial. In Paul, the bread is said to be 'for you' (1 Corinthians 11:24). Here it is given 'for the life of the world'. Secondly, the flesh is to be eaten and the blood drunk. The Greek word used, *trogo*, is a particularly emphatic one for the physical act of eating. Thirdly, the references to the last day and living 'for ever' underline the eschatological nature of the Eucharist. It is a sacrament not only for the needs of the present life but also for the world to come. Finally, the Eucharist gives us a share in the life of the Father. Through it, the life that the Son has from the Father is passed on by the Son to the believer.

Year A
The Year of Matthew

THE 34 SUNDAYS OF THE YEAR*

These Sundays are divided into two blocks, separated by the three months of the seasons of Lent and Easter. Some Sundays, which occur between the two blocks, are always omitted. The Feast of the Baptism of the Lord is reckoned as the first Sunday of the Year.

The ***First Readings****, from the Old Testament, are intended to throw light on the Gospel Reading of the day. Never during this period is there any continuous reading from the Old Testament. To concentrate on the Old Testament passage without reference to the Gospel therefore seems inappropriate.*

The ***Responsorial Psalms*** *are designed to help with the understanding of the First Reading, to deepen some significant theme, to clarify its message. They also prepare for the Gospel since the First Reading is related to the Gospel.*

The ***Second Readings*** *are taken from a New Testament letter. They are semi-continuous, which gives a preacher the opportunity to take the congregation through the particular letter. Only coincidentally do these readings have any relationship to the First Reading or the Gospel. No letter is proclaimed in its entirety and sometimes the unit given is incomplete.*

- *The First Letter of Paul to the Corinthians (Part One)*
- *The Letter of Paul to the Romans*
- *The Letter of Paul to the Philippians*
- *The First Letter of Paul to the Thessalonians*

The ***Gospel Readings*** *are taken from Matthew. This Gospel is read throughout the year, except for the Easter season, when John is usually read. We may therefore speak of Matthew as evangelist of the year.*

* See 'General Introduction', *Roman Missal*, nn. 105–107.

Sunday 2 A

Isaiah 49:3, 5–6
Psalm 39:2, 4, 7–10
1 Corinthians 1:1–3
John 1:29–34

The Lamb of God

This week, like last, we hear a Servant Song of **Isaiah**. God has chosen for his servant the weak and timid Israel when it has hardly recovered from the shock of exile. He speaks to the Servant as he spoke to Jeremiah: he knew him even before he was formed in the womb (Jeremiah 1:5). Moses was to deliver the Israelites from Pharaoh (Exodus 3:10); the Servant is to be a light to the nations, to bring salvation to the ends of the earth.

The **Psalm** is a thanksgiving hymn, thanking God for rescue from trouble. It fits well on the lips of the Servant, who worships God not by formal sacrifice but with the dedication of a spirit who delights in generous service (Hosea 6:6).

In the greeting at the beginning of **1 Corinthians**, as in other letters, Paul transforms the literary conventions of the time. He names himself, with Sosthenes, the synagogue official mentioned in Acts (Acts 18:17), as the author, but he insists on his authority as an apostle, which his opponents were rejecting (2 Corinthians 11:4). The recipients of the letter he calls a Church; they are God's assembly, his people, in Corinth (Exodus 19:6). Theirs is a city no better and no worse than many others in that world, but they are called to holiness. He wishes them much more than conventional greetings, namely grace, which includes everything associated with God's free gift in Christ, and peace, which is the reconciliation won by Christ between God and his people and between themselves (Romans 5:1).

The first human being mentioned in **John** is John the Baptist. He has a single function, to witness to the light (1:7). We learn today how he carries out this function. Various others give Jesus titles in the first chapter of John, but the Baptist's is unique—though common in Revelation (5:6), it occurs nowhere else in the Gospels.

John points out Jesus as the Lamb of God. In writings of the time, a lamb was a symbol of power. God was expected to raise up such a lamb to deliver his people from the Romans, who were occupying their country. As a man of his time, the Baptist may have understood the term in this way. The evangelist would have other ideas. In Isaiah's final Servant Song, the Servant is described as a lamb being led to the slaughter (Isaiah 53:7). This passage was applied to the passion of Christ (Acts 8:32). John, however, like Paul (1 Corinthians 5:7), thinks of Jesus in terms of the Passover lamb (Exodus 12). Pilate condemned Jesus to death at the very time when the Passover lambs were being slaughtered for the festival (19:14). When Jesus cried from the cross, 'I am thirsty', he was given vinegar on a hyssop stick, a wood used in the ceremonies associated with the lambs (19:28–29). Once Jesus had died, we learn that not a bone of his was broken. This is an instruction on how the Passover lamb was to be killed (Exodus 12:46; John 19:36). Jesus, as Lamb of God, won liberation from sin just as, in former times, the old Passover lamb brought liberation from Egypt (Exodus 12:31).

The Baptist also witnesses to what he sees at the baptism of Jesus. He hears a heavenly voice and sees the Spirit descend in form of a dove (Mark 1:10–11). This Spirit rests on Jesus. The Baptist has had a revelation of the persons of the Trinity. In his ministry, the Son will perform the works of the Father (5:19) and, once his mission is complete (19:30), will in turn hand on the Spirit to his disciples (20:22).

Sunday 3 A

Isaiah 8:23–9:3
Psalm 26:1, 4, 13–14
1 Corinthians 1:10–13, 17
Matthew 4:12–23

Galilee of the Gentiles

Zebulun and Naphtali are old names for Galilee. These territories had suffered under the Assyrian king Tiglath-Pileser III. **Isaiah** foresees a reversal in their fortunes. They will emerge from darkness into light, rejoice in marvellous harvests and enjoy the spoils of victory. They will be as glad as their ancestors were when Gideon conquered Midian with troops from Naphtali (Judges 7:16–21). For Matthew, the prophecy came true when Jesus came to Galilee.

In the **Psalm**, we join a worshipper in meditation in the Temple. He uses many terms to describe the Lord; this is the only place in the Old Testament where he is identified with the Light. Christ was the light that came into Galilee. In Jerusalem, he described himself as light of the world (John 8:12).

The first problem that Paul has to address in **1 Corinthians** is the division in the community reported to him by Chloe's people. Paul had been the first to bring the gospel to Corinth (3:10), but others have come since, and the lack of Christian maturity in the community is creating factions. They have become fascinated by details of the Christian message rather than its foundation, the cross. Apollos, whom we meet in Acts (18:24), may have been too philosophical; Cephas may have introduced attitudes about meal fellowship for which Paul rebuked him in Antioch (Galatians 2:12). The party that claims to belong to Christ may have no time for fellow-believers. As for Paul, he plays down his role of baptizer; he sees that his priority is to preach Christ crucified.

Jesus' baptism and temptation are over (4:1–11); it is time for his mission to begin. He goes not to the Holy City of Jerusalem (4:5) but to Galilee, the land of Herod Antipas, the ruler who has just arrested John the Baptist. This remote province seems a strange place for the messiah to reveal himself. **Matthew** sees this, like so much else in the life of Jesus, as a fulfilment of ancient prophecy (Isaiah 9:1–2). Light has come into a land of darkness. Soon he will call his disciples the light of the world, whose light must shine out before others (5:14–16).

Jesus begins his preaching as the Baptist had begun his, with a message of repentance and the nearness of the Kingdom (3:2). His activity in Galilee is summarised as proclaiming, teaching and healing. He proclaims what God has done and teaches what the human response must be. He heals to show that the time of the messiah has come (Isaiah 35:5). He is bringing the good news of salvation (Isaiah 52:7). As we listen to what he teaches and witness what he does, we learn what he means by the Kingdom.

His first action is to call disciples. He picks them out from among the people at their business thronging the shore of the lake of Galilee. He summons two sets of brothers who are working in their fishing boats. They respond immediately, leaving behind their father and their livelihood and going after him. The only reward he suggests is that they will be fishers of men. From now on, Jesus will never be alone in his ministry; we must always see him accompanied by disciples. His ministry is a school for discipleship. The ready obedience of the brothers encourages all subsequent disciples to do the same. This first exercise of Jesus' authority prepares us for the Sermon on the Mount, when he will speak with the authority of God himself (5:22). These four disciples are the beginnings of the Church, which will consist one day of 'all the nations' (28:19). Their career shows the way to this Church.

Sunday 4 A

Zephaniah 2:3; 3:12–13
Psalm 145:7–10
1 Corinthians 1:26–31
Matthew 5:1–12

The Beatitudes

Zephaniah lived at a time when Israel was recovering from oppression by the Assyrians and from the wickedness of its kings Manasseh and Amon. He addresses the *anawim*, the humble of the Lord. Such people are not poor through their own fault. They can only put their hope in God. They will make up the faithful remnant which will ensure the survival of the nation (Isaiah 4:3). Typical of these *anawim* were Simeon and Anna, who welcomed the child Jesus in the Temple; they lived exclusively for God (Luke 2:27, 36). The *anawim* are blessed in the Beatitudes of Jesus.

The **Psalm** praises the God who cares for those with no resources of their own. He did not complete creation when he brought the world into being (Genesis 1), but he continues it, as Zephaniah knew, through his exercise and encouragement of social justice (Deuteronomy 24:17).

Paul's converts in **1 Corinthians** want to be outstanding in speech and knowledge (1:5), but they are reluctant to surrender themselves to the preaching and the demands of the cross. Paul reminds them of their origins and background. They are not unlike the *anawim* of Zephaniah. Paul wants them to forget their own achievements and only boast in Christ. Thanks to him, they are justified, as in a law court, declared not guilty before God. They are saved, like their ancestors who were delivered from Egypt, rescued from danger in this life and the next. They are redeemed, as if they had been held in slavery, for they have been bought back from the slavery of sin.

Matthew has prepared his readers for the Sermon on the Mount by his introduction to the ministry of Jesus which we heard last week. In Galilee of the Gentiles, Jesus proclaimed the Kingdom. Accompanied by disciples, he taught, preached and healed. With his disciples, he now goes up a mountain. On this new Sinai (Exodus 19:3), the disciples play the part of Moses and Jesus, addressing them, speaks to them in the person of God.

Originally, as in Luke (6:20), the Beatitudes, with which the Sermon begins, were a summons to the poor, the hungry and those who wept. In Matthew, it is clear that the Kingdom embraces many more than these. It belongs to all who are poor in spirit, all who hunger for justice, and all who weep over the evil in the world and personal sin. The additional Beatitudes that Matthew lists further to Luke find a basis in later parts of the Gospel. The meek are those who make the humility of Jesus in his prayer to his Father (11:29) their own and cultivate his attitude as he entered Jerusalem as a meek king on a donkey (21:5). The merciful are those who imitate Jesus in the mercy he offered the Canaanite woman (15:22), and those who know that God prefers mercy to sacrifice, in Hosea's words (Hosea 6:6; Matthew 9:13). The clean of heart practise a higher righteousness than the Pharisees through their recognition that internal rather than external cleanliness pleases God (15:18). When sent on their mission, the disciples will be peacemakers (10:13). Through the cross of Christ the barriers between peoples will be removed and peace established (Ephesians 2:15). Thus the centurion and those with him confess Jesus as Son of God (27:54).

These beatitudes are sometimes called the constitution of the Kingdom of Heaven. They offer a self-portrait of Jesus. He concludes by directly addressing his hearers, warning them of the cost of living out such ideals. The prophets suffered this cost in the past (23:37). But to those who pay the price, he promises great joy and a great reward.

Sunday 5 A

Isaiah 58:7–10
Psalm 111:4–9
1 Corinthians 2:1–5
Matthew 5:13–16

Salt and Light

The Israelites who returned from exile took their religious obligations, such as fasting, seriously, but God seemed to take no notice. Their piety seemed useless. **Isaiah** explains the reason. They are ignoring the widespread injustice and oppression around them. The poor, the naked, the hungry go without help (Matthew 25:37). If Isaiah's audience will stir themselves to do something about all this, then God will give them favours in abundance. Their light will really shine out in the world.

The **Psalm** offers a character sketch of the just person. Such people reflect in themselves characteristics of God. God is a light in the darkness (Psalm 27:1) and looks after the poor (Psalm 146:7). The people are to make their own the compassion and justice of the God to whom they are bound by the terms of the covenant (Exodus 34:6).

Many philosophers and teachers tried to sell their wares in ancient cities such as Corinth. In **1 Corinthians,** Paul wants to ensure that he is not confused with such charlatans. His preaching does not depend on wisdom and eloquence in the normal sense. His subject is a mystery, that is, a secret of God only now revealed, a crucified Christ (Romans 16:25). Unlike other philosophers, he is not brash and over-confident, but has come among them in fear and trembling (Philippians 2:12; 2 Corinthians 10:1). God's Holy Spirit is his only resource (1 Thessalonians 1:5). This Spirit, not Paul's eloquence, is the foundation of the faith of the Corinthians. Our passage begins and ends with references to God. In its centre, we hear of Christ crucified. Paul knows that the only explanation for any success he had as a missionary is the Spirit of God.

The world portrayed by the final Beatitudes in **Matthew** is a cruel one which persecutes and abuses God's messengers (10:17). The temptation for many good people is to withdraw from such a world, thinking that this is the only way to live out the ideals of the Beatitudes. This was not the mind of Jesus in Matthew. His words are now addressed directly to his listening disciples who, here as elsewhere in this Gospel, represent those for whom the Gospel was written. His followers are to be salt in their world.

Salt had many uses. Not only did it add flavour to insipid food; it was a preservative, it made fuel more efficient, made crops fertile and was a means of healing. The disciples have to be and do all this in their world. Otherwise their discipleship is useless. They will be trodden under foot by men. In Matthew, this term refers specifically to unbelievers.

Light came into the darkness of Galilee with Jesus (4:16). In John, Jesus called himself the 'light of the world' (John 8:12). Paul told his converts that they were 'sons of light' (1 Thessalonians 5:5). In Matthew, the disciples are themselves to be the light of the world. How are they to become that light? The neighbouring hill towns of Galilee suggest the first answer. Just as these cannot be hidden, neither can the real disciple. A second answer comes from the lamps used in houses. A hidden disciple, like a hidden lamp, is useless. A third answer comes from the good works that the disciple performs. Salvation does not come from such works, but they are an appropriate response to the gift of salvation and make sure that it is not endangered. As Paul wrote, faith works itself out in love (Galatians 5:6). Matthew has much to say about social justice and the needs of the neighbour. The climax of such teaching is the parable of the sheep and the goats (25:31–46). Good works are not for self-advertisement (6:1) but for the glorification of the Father, the intimate God whom Jesus knew so well (11:25).

Sunday 6 A

Sirach 15:15–20
Psalm 118:1–2, 4–5, 17–18, 33–34
1 Corinthians 2:6–10
Matthew 5:17–37

Fulfilling the Law

God, who is all powerful and all-wise, created humanity to be responsible and to make choices. **Sirach** teaches that he respects the choice of his creation. God is not responsible for human sin (15:11). In the tradition of Deuteronomy (30:19), Sirach urges his readers to choose life rather than death. Jesus prompts his disciples to choose a life of a higher righteousness than that of the scribes and Pharisees.

The **Psalm**, the longest of all, introduces us to someone thoroughly at home with the person and the teaching of God: one who hears, sees, walks the ways of a caring God. He is a model for the hearer of the Sermon on the Mount in respect for the revelation of God.

Having rejected the wisdom of the philosophers (2:5), Paul in **1 Corinthians** now admits that he is preaching wisdom of a surprising type. Early Christians recognised the teaching Christ as a personification of the Wisdom figure in the Old Testament (Matthew 11:19). Paul identifies the crucified Christ as the Wisdom of God. From now on, there is no Christian wisdom without the cross. Failing to see this, the authorities, whether those of this world who condemned Jesus or the supernatural forces behind them, have no idea what they are doing. This is God's mystery, hidden in the words of Isaiah (64:4) but never understood until now. Thanks to the Spirit (Romans 8:9), we can now understand these depths of God.

The announcement by Jesus that he has come not to abolish the Law and the Prophets, but to complete them, is his first personal statement in **Matthew** about his mission (Luke 4:18). Jesus nowhere insists on the importance of major tenets of the Law such as circumcision, food laws and the Sabbath (Romans 14:17; Galatians 4:10; 5:6), and he speaks here of the first intention of the Law rather than its detailed demands. According to some rabbis, God created the Law before the world itself but, owing to the hard-heartedness of humanity, he gave Moses a compromise version (19:8).

Jesus wants his followers to observe the Law as God intended it. The righteousness of the scribes and Pharisees led them to fence the Law around with many other observances, to ensure that its letter was not broken. The higher righteousness demanded by Jesus does not depend on multiplying regulations but on interpreting the Law in terms of love of God and neighbour (22:37–39). He wants his disciples to practise what God meant in Hosea when he said, 'what I want is love, not sacrifice' (Hosea 6:6; Matthew 9:13; 12:7).

Jesus now reinterprets the Law given by Moses with the authority of God himself. He gives examples of what this higher righteousness means. He protects the unity of the community by declaring that the prohibition of murder also forbids calling a brother a fool. He protects the unity of the family by including under adultery even a lustful look at the wife of another. He forbids the taking of oaths, because truth must be respected for its own sake. These are the commands that the Eleven were to pass on to the nations (28:19–20), as Moses passed on the Law at Sinai (Exodus 24). These are the ethics of the kingdom. They will only be observed in their fullness when the Kingdom is come (1 Corinthians 15:24). Meanwhile, it is the mission of the followers of Jesus to make such observance possible.

Sunday 7 A

Leviticus 19:1–2, 17–18
Psalm 102:1–4, 8, 10, 12–13
1 Corinthians 3:16–23
Matthew 5:38–48

Love Your Enemies

Many readers of the Bible get stuck in **Leviticus**. They cannot cope with what seem endless, at times trivial, regulations. Yet these have a purpose; they aim to make God's people holy as God is holy. The 'holiness code', which we read today, is a version of the Ten Commandments (Exodus 20: 1–17). These concern human relationships, and crucial to understanding them is the command to love our neighbour as ourselves.

The **Psalm** gives thanks for recovery from sickness. Many qualities of God are listed. His name is holy. This holiness expresses itself in his covenant virtues of 'kindness and faithfulness' (Exodus 34: 6) which make him ready to forgive sin (Joel 2: 13); he is a father with compassion for his sons (Luke 15: 20).

Before Paul in **1 Corinthians** sums up his arguments countering the divisions in the community, he introduces a new idea. He has called the community God's field and God's building (3: 9); he now calls it God's Temple. But the behaviour of its members is destroying its holiness. Elsewhere he describes the individual believer as a Temple of the Holy Spirit (1 Corinthians 6: 19). They have been searching for the wisdom of this world (1: 20); they should have learnt from Job (5: 13) and the Psalmist (94: 11) that this was an illusory search. Their boasting, too, is false (1: 31): their only loyalty should be to Christ. They do not belong to the leaders of their factions. Their leaders belong to them, just as Christ belongs to God.

The Law that Moses gave on Sinai was often compassionate and enlightened. In some societies, one crime led to many others. Lamech took 77-fold vengeance on one who struck him (Genesis 4: 24). The Law merely required an eye for an eye and a tooth for a tooth, and there the matter should end (Exodus 21: 24). What the Law demanded was sometimes no more than civilised conduct. 'Love your neighbour', said Leviticus (19: 18). Even the pagans did this and found themselves loved in return.

Jesus in **Matthew** demands more from his disciples. Suppose we offer the wicked man no resistance. Jesus offered none in Gethsemane (26: 52). Suppose we offer the other cheek if we are struck on one, and allow the person who asks for our tunic to have our cloak as well (Exodus 22: 26). Suppose we go two miles when forced to go one? The Law does not forbid these things. Does not another world open up when we do not respond to others in the obvious way? This is the world of the Kingdom, the Kingdom for whose coming Jesus tells his disciples to pray (6: 10).

The followers of Jesus are not simply to conform themselves to the world about them. They are to be like the God whom Jesus calls 'our Father in heaven' (6:9). He does not behave as human beings behave. He does not withhold his sun and rain from the wicked and give them only to the just, but freely makes them available to all. Jesus' final definition of the deeper righteousness that he requires from his disciples (5:20) is to be perfect as the heavenly Father is perfect. This means learning with Peter to think as God thinks (16: 23), understanding with Isaiah that God's 'thoughts are not your thoughts' (Isaiah 55: 8), and knowing with Hosea that God is God and not man (Hosea 11:9). It means accepting the invitation offered to the rich young man to be perfect by selling all he has (19: 21).

Sunday 8 A

Isaiah 49:14–15
Psalm 61:2–3, 6–9
1 Corinthians 4:1–5
Matthew 6:24–34

Images of God

Daily we call upon God as Father in our prayer. We do this because Jesus did so and told his disciples to do the same (Matthew 6:9; 11:25). Israel was called God's firstborn son in the Old Testament (Exodus 4:22; Hosea 11:1); Malachi (2:10) and Tobit (4:3) called God 'Father'. But in **Isaiah** God is also compared to a loving mother. In their exile from land and city, God's people lament how God has forgotten them. God replies, speaking as a loving mother speaks. A mother cannot forget the child of her womb.

Today's **Psalm** is typical of many in addressing God as a rock and a fortress. God has proved himself as a warrior in fighting on behalf of his people in the events of the Exodus (Exodus 15:3) and has given them rest in the promised land (Psalm 95:11). This is the God in whom the psalmist expresses his continued confidence.

We end our readings for this year from **1 Corinthians** with the conclusion to the part of the letter dealing with the disunity that was threatening Paul's converts. Paul states positively what apostles are meant to be. They are not power-seeking leaders of a sect but servants of Christ and stewards of God's mysteries. This is the language of the slavery common at that time. Paul belongs only to his master and is accountable to him alone. It is the language of the Gospels, too. Jesus came to serve (Mark 10:45). His disciples were stewards put in charge of his property awaiting his return (Matthew 25:14; Luke 12:42).

On recent Sundays, we have heard the whole of the first chapter of **Matthew**'s Sermon on the Mount (5:1–48). But we hear little of the remaining two chapters; we have one passage from its second chapter this week and the words that conclude the Sermon next week (7:21–27). Today's text consoles and encourages; next week's will be more one of challenge.

Our passage begins and ends with radical demands typical of the teaching of this Sermon. The deeper righteousness (5:20) that we must practise forbids us from serving two masters at the same time; we have to choose between God and mammon. We are like the rich man invited to follow Jesus (19:16). We must seek only the Kingdom of God and its righteousness, which is the way of life typified by the teaching of Jesus we have heard these last few Sundays.

A good teacher encourages as well as demands and Jesus is such a teacher. He wants his disciples, and the crowd who listen in (7:28), to reflect on their picture of God. Jesus speaks in the tradition of today's readings from Isaiah and the Psalms. At the same time, he gives us a clue that accounts for his own peaceful and dedicated way of life. Like a poet, he knows God as one who cares for all levels of creation. God looks after the flowers of the field and the birds of the sky. These may seem to be much less important than we are but, according to Genesis (1:1–25), God took the trouble to create them before he created human beings. He made man and woman on the sixth day after his labours on the five previous days of creation which he had spent in preparing a home for them (Genesis 1:27). The Psalmist wrote a wonderful commentary on this work of creation (Psalm 104). As for God, he is our heavenly Father who knows all that we need. Earlier in this chapter, in a passage not heard this year, Matthew included the Lord's prayer which tells us how to address this Father (6:9–13).

Sunday 9 A

Deuteronomy 11:18, 26–28, 32
Psalm 30:2–4, 25
Romans 3:21–25, 28
Matthew 7:21–27

The Two Ways

Deuteronomy is presented as Moses' farewell speech. Moses is the one who heard the voice of God on Mount Sinai and delivered God's words to the people. He wants these words to penetrate their hearts; he even urges them to attach the words to their hands and foreheads (6:6–9). These words admit no compromise; they represent two ways. The first leads to a blessing, but the other to a curse. A dramatic narrative of all this can be found at the end of the book of Joshua (chapter 24) where the people, at the foot of another mountain, are called upon to choose whether or not to follow the God who has delivered them from Egypt.

Our **Psalm** passage is a prayer for deliverance from some sort of danger or illness. God is once again, as in last week's Psalm, addressed as the reliable rock. He is the one faithful to his side of the covenant, and repeats again the words given Joshua before the entry into the land—'Be strong'—to those who choose his way (Joshua 1:9).

Today we begin reading the Letter to the **Romans**. We join it at the section where Paul is explaining how God has removed the block to our relationship with him, humanity's universal sinfulness. Struggling to express the richness of what God has done for us through his Son, Paul uses metaphorical language. He speaks in terms of slavery and law courts. When Christ died on the cross, it was as if had bought us back from slavery. He had us declared innocent. In terms of Jewish sacrificial custom, he had made himself, rather than some ritual for the 'Day of Atonement' (Leviticus 16), the means of expiation for sin.

The final chapter of the Sermon on the Mount in **Matthew** is concerned mainly with relationships to others, and includes the Golden Rule: 'always treat others as you would like them to treat you'. But today we read only the conclusion of the Sermon. Like the other discourses in Matthew's Gospel, it ends with a warning (10:34; 13:49; 18:35; 25:45).

The scene is the final judgment, and the members of the Church are being judged. This final judgment is a common theme in this Gospel (13:40, 49; 25:31). The first group is rejected, not for obvious sin, but for doing works that appeared to be good but were not the will of God. They have cast out demons and done miracles, but have not done what God wanted them to do. Jesus was encouraged to do the same during his temptations (4:1–11). At Gethsemane Jesus prayed that he should not do his will only but that of the Father (26:39). Because he had done so in accepting the sufferings of Calvary at the hands of his enemies, he was given authority over all the nations (28:18). Mature believers must not only choose between good and bad but must discern between apparent goods.

The second group is of those who not only listen to Jesus' words, but do them. They bear fruit, like those in the parable of the sower who hear the word of God and understand it (13:23). They are like a house built on a rock, an image we remember from today's Psalm. Such people can weather any storm. The storm may be those that occur in the life of everyone, or it may refer to the storm that Matthew foresaw for the end of time (24:3–6).

Some are unhappy with the Gospel of Matthew because of warnings of judgment such as those we read today. These were directed at members of his community whose faith had grown cold. But these passages are outnumbered by others in this Gospel which stress the continuing mercy of God. Jesus invites all those who labour and are heavily laden to come to him for rest (11:28).

Sunday 10 A

Hosea 6:3–6
Psalm 49:1, 8, 12–15
Romans 4:18–25
Matthew 9:9–13

The Call of Matthew

Hosea agonises over the infidelity of his people to their God; they worship other gods and ignore the obligations of social justice. The love that God lavished on them as a faithful husband they reject; at most they go through the motions of offering sacrifice. True religion means more than this. God says, in apparent exasperation, 'what I want is love, not sacrifice'. He said the same through other prophets. Micah made similar demands, 'to act justly, to love tenderly' (Micah 6:8).

In the **Psalm**, we meet God, the creator of the world, in a law court accusing his people. Here again, as in Micah (6:6–8), he rejects animal sacrifices offered for their own sake. Sacrifice is to be made in the right spirit, in a spirit of thanksgiving, acknowledging God for what he is. God is not like those pagan gods who need human sacrifice because they are hungry.

Last week's passage from **Romans** concluded that 'a man is justified by faith and not by doing something the Law tells him to do' (3:28). Writing to an audience including many Christians of Jewish origin, Paul goes on to show that his teaching is consistent with the experience of Abraham, their ancestor in the faith, as reported in Genesis (15–17). He does this by explaining how faith was Abraham's response to God's promises in an otherwise hopeless situation. How could he and his wife, Sarah, have a child when he was about a hundred years old and his wife was barren? His was a faith that persevered despite all difficulties. God accepted it and it was a model for the faith of all subsequent believers, including those in Rome, and ourselves, too.

Between the Sermon on the Mount and the Mission Discourse, which we begin next week, **Matthew** recounts ten miracles of Jesus. He is teaching us about the messiah in action after portraying the messiah in word. Today's story, of the call of Matthew and the controversy that it caused, provides a break in this series of miracles.

Matthew, sitting in his tax office, responds to the call of Jesus as a good disciple should. Following the example of Peter and Andrew, James and John, he hears the word of Jesus and immediately puts it into practice (7:24). He leaves his place of work and follows Jesus (4:18–22). But his place of work is a scandal for the pious in society; his profession of tax collector is one that respectable folk cannot follow. Jesus will recall such scenes when he reaches Jerusalem and enters into conflict with the high priests and elders in the Temple. He will tell them that tax collectors and prostitutes are going into the Kingdom of Heaven before them (21:31).

The sequel to the call is also an embarrassment, even a shock, for pious apostles such as Peter, because Matthew calls a party for his friends—other tax collectors. They all sit at table with Jesus, an act which, according to Jewish law, puts him in a state of ritual impurity (Luke 15:2; Galatians 2:12). We do not know the full story; the evangelist simply reports Jesus' final words to the Pharisees who criticize him. First he quotes a proverb: only sick people need a doctor. Then he appeals to scripture, to words of Hosea about love rather than sacrifice (6:6), familiar from our first reading—a text which Jesus will use again later (12:7). He adds a definition of his mission, 'I did not come to call the virtuous, but sinners'. This is an example of Semitic hyperbole: we would probably say, 'not only the righteous but sinners too'. By eating with these people, Jesus anticipates the banquet planned for the end of time (Psalm 107:3; Matthew 8:11). Such behaviour earned him the titles of 'a glutton and a drunkard' (11:19).

Sunday 11 A

Exodus 19:2–6
Psalm 99:2–3, 5
Romans 5:6–11
Matthew 9:36–10:8

Sent on Mission

The **Exodus** from Egypt means more than physical liberation from slavery. It is the first stage of a covenant process in which God enters into a special relationship with Israel. God addresses Moses like an earthly king, pledging himself to confer on Israel the dignity of a priestly kingdom and consecrated nation, provided that they remain faithful to the terms of the Law he is about to reveal.

The **Psalm**, from the temple liturgy, celebrates the qualities of the two partners in the Sinai Covenant. God is faithful and merciful (Exodus 34:6); his people are the sheep of his flock, who enjoy the rule and protection of a caring shepherd who is God himself (Ezekiel 34:11; Psalm 23). Sadly, Israel does not observe its side of the Covenant.

According to Paul in **Romans**, the people of Israel, like the Gentiles, became sinners and failed to give glory to God. But this did not cause God to exercise the anger that was bound to be his as a God who is good and just (1:18). Instead, he showed his love for us all, Jew or Gentile, through the death of Christ on our behalf. A martyr will sometimes die for his people, or for a good man. In contrast, Christ died for us while we were still alienated from God. He won redemption for us, atoned for our sins, gained our justification. All of this was the gift of God and his grace (3:21–26). Thanks to him, we are at peace and reconciled with God, and with one another. This is the fruit of our faith (5:1). Through it we have life (1:17). In principle, then, we are already saved. We make sure of our future salvation in so far as we live out this faith in love in our daily living (Galatians 5:6).

Matthew has by now introduced his readers to the teaching of the messiah in the Sermon on the Mount (5–7) and to his healing activity in the collection of miracles (8–9). It is now time for him to involve the disciples whom he has called (4:18–22; 9:9) in his mission for the Kingdom. This mission is in continuity with the Old Testament. Like Moses, Jesus now speaks of the people being sheep without a shepherd (Numbers 27:17). Like Joel, he foresees the harvest of the end time coming to reality (Joel 3:13).

Mark reported separately how Jesus had called the Twelve (Mark 3:9–13) and how he had later sent them out on mission (Mark 6:7–13). Matthew joins the two events together and then follows this up with the Mission Discourse. He tells us less about the summoning of the Twelve than Mark. We learn their names, but are given little information about them. We know that four are fishermen, one a tax collector (a collaborator with the Romans) and one a Canaanite (a fierce nationalist). Jesus gives them authority to exorcise and heal. They are equipped to do some, but not all, of what he himself does (8:16), because they will not teach until after the resurrection when they will have heard all the discourses of Jesus (28:20). The number twelve reminds us of the Twelve Tribes of which Israel had originally been composed and with whom God made his Covenant at Sinai.

Straight away, Jesus sends these Twelve out on a formal mission. Like Jesus himself, they are to go only to the lost sheep of Israel (15:24); only after the death and resurrection of Jesus would they go to all the nations (28:19). Like the Baptist (3:2), and Jesus too (4:17), they are to announce the nearness of the Kingdom. They are to perform the same messianic works that Jesus would recount to John the Baptist (11:2). Mark reports their return after this mission, which enjoyed success. (Mark 6:30); Matthew tells us nothing about a return. Their mission continues to this day.

Sunday 12 A

Jeremiah 20:10–13
Psalm 68:8–10, 14, 17, 33–35
Romans 5:12–15
Matthew 10:26–33

Fear Not

God offered no guarantee of success when he called a person to be his prophet. Isaiah knew that he was sent to a people who would never understand (Isaiah 6:9). **Jeremiah** finds this too difficult and complains to God. Like Isaiah's Servant (Isaiah 50:7), he can only commend his cause to the Lord, confident that God is at his side and will give final victory, as he would to Christ in his passion. This was the experience of the innocent sufferer of the Psalms (Psalm 22).

The **Psalm** is the prayer of an innocent sufferer. It echoes the complaints of Jeremiah and the distress of the Isaian Servant, but concludes by praising God for giving final deliverance. This is a Psalm quoted in gospel accounts of Jesus' passion (Matthew 27:34).

Paul in **Romans** contrasts Adam, the first head of the human race, with Christ, the second (1 Corinthians 15:22). To the first we owe the entrance of sin and death into the world. These were like tyrants, who held every subsequent human being in their dominion. To the second we owe deliverance from this tyranny. Yet the effects of the two cannot be compared. The grace of the free gift that Christ gave us cancels the effects not of Adam's sin only, but of all sins committed since the appearance of the Mosaic Law, which brought an awareness of sin and of its consequences (3:20). The generosity of what God did in Christ cancelled the curse introduced by Adam. This passage has had great influence in Christian tradition, especially with reference to original sin, but its main importance lies in its teaching about the reality of the free gift of God's grace introduced into the world through Christ.

The continuation of the Mission Discourse from **Matthew**, which we hear today, is best understood as addressed by the Exalted Lord of the Church to the disciples sent out on their mission after Easter (28:19). In an earlier part of the discourse, which has been omitted, Jesus has warned them of the opposition they will meet, not just from their own people in their synagogues but from the governors and kings who rule the Gentiles. Three times Jesus reassures his disciples, telling them, 'do not be afraid'. These words resemble those addressed by God to Joshua, Moses' successor: 'Be strong and courageous' (Joshua 1:6, 7, 9). Likewise, the disciples' preaching is to be active and courageous. They can make their own the prayer for boldness of the first Jerusalem Christians in Acts (4:29).

The disciples are not promised success. They have to remember that, though Jesus is with them (1:23), Satan is against them. They are in conflict with the powers of hell (Ephesians 6:12). They are to deal with Satan as fearlessly as Jesus himself did at his own temptations (4:1–11). They will have God at their side. This God is no remote figure, but one whom they, like Jesus himself, are to call Father (6:9; 11:25). The Father has a special knowledge of and care for each of them, as Jesus taught in the Sermon on the Mount. If God looks after the birds of the air, he will surely look after them (6:26). He even knows the number of hairs on their heads.

As Exalted Lord, Jesus is at the right hand of God, pleading for them (Romans 8:34). He promises that the more readily they speak out on his behalf, the more quickly he will intercede for them with his Father. Sometimes persecution makes confession of Christ difficult. It can cost one's life (Mark 8:35). At times, the cost may be no more than harassment (1 Peter 3:15). This cost must be paid; as at the end of the Sermon on the Mount, we glimpse silent, inactive Christians who have lost their enthusiasm for carrying out the will of the Father (7:21).

Sunday 13 A

2 Kings 4:8–11, 14–16
Psalm 88:2–3, 16–19
Romans 6:3–4, 8–11
Matthew 10:37–42

Christian Hospitality

Stories about Elijah and Elisha are echoed frequently in the Gospels. Jesus, like Elijah, raised the son of a widow (Luke 7:15; 1 Kings 17:23) from the dead. Like Elisha, he fed a crowd on barley loaves (John 6:9; 2 Kings 4:42). The story of the hospitality offered to Elisha in **2 Kings** prepares us for the rewards of hospitality towards a holy man that Jesus promises his hearers.

Today's **Psalm** was composed to glorify David, the king of Israel, chosen by God to rule his people. Christians use it to praise Christ. We use it today to praise the love and mercy of God shown in the story of Elisha and the woman.

In **Romans** we read Paul's classic statement about baptism. For Paul, this is no mere sprinkling of water, but a going down into the tomb with Christ, a burial with him, in which we leave the old life and from which we emerge clothed with the resurrection life of Christ. It gives us assurance that in the future we will have our own share in the glory that Christ now possesses with the Father. The career of Christ thus foreshadows our own; he was 'the eldest of many brothers' (Romans 8:29). The world into which he came was under the dominion of sin and death. 'Both Jew and pagan sinned and forfeited God's glory' (Romans 3:23). To remedy this, he became 'cursed' (Galatians 3:13), and God 'made the sinless one into sin' (2 Corinthians 5:21). God raised him from this death. By our baptism, we went into the tomb with him and shared his victory over sin. This is a truth we can celebrate by saying with Paul, 'I live now not with my own life but with the life of Christ who lives in me' (Galatians 2:20).

The Mission Discourse of **Matthew** concludes both with warnings and with encouragement. Jesus warns of the radical demands of discipleship. He does not cancel the duty of honouring parents (15:4), but he warns that, like the tribe of Levi (Deuteronomy 33:9), the Christian disciple may be asked to put God's word and covenant before the duties to parents. Discipleship may mean having to follow in the footsteps of Jesus as he carries his cross (16:24). The disciple may find the way to true life through the loss of this temporary one, as the martyrs are to discover (16:25).

But such warnings and challenges are balanced by words of encouragement. This is a Jesus who offers rest to those who are heavily burdened (11:28). Here the Exalted Lord speaks to the Church of Matthew's time. His words reflect the composition of that Church when the days of formal hierarchy were still some years away. In it would be found 'prophets', 'holy men' and 'little ones'. Though they might differ in title, they do not differ in dignity. In the later Community Discourse, the 'little ones' will be identified with the 'greatest in the kingdom of heaven' (18:4). According to the final Eschatological Discourse (Matthew 25), the reward for those who give these little ones a cup of cold water will be to 'take for your heritage the kingdom prepared for you since the foundation of the world' (25:34). The community has become one great family of God, with the Father welcomed in the Son and the Son welcomed in the disciple. Here we learn another way in which the title of Jesus as 'Emmanuel' ('God-is-with-us', 1:23), is fulfilled in Christian life.

So, like the Sermon on the Mount (7:21), this discourse ends with a call for Christian action through simple hospitality and the meeting of simple needs. If small-scale kindness merits such reward, what should we say about expressions of great generosity for the sake of Christ?

Sunday 14 A

Zechariah 9:9–10
Psalm 144:1–2, 8–11, 13–14
Romans 8:9, 11–13
Matthew 11:25–30

Come to Me and Rest

The second half of **Zechariah** looks forward to the Lord God defeating his enemies and establishing himself as undisputed king of his people. So peaceful will his kingship be that war-horses will be unnecessary. This humble king can ride on a donkey. Matthew uses this passage to describe Jesus' entry into Jerusalem on Palm Sunday (Matthew 21:5). Jesus applies the word 'humble' to himself in today's Gospel.

Our **Psalm** is one of the great psalms of praise, recited three times a day by the Jewish people. It records especially God's covenant qualities of kindness and fidelity (Exodus 34:6) and anticipates Jesus' description of himself in the Gospel.

In **Romans**, Paul compares humanity before Christ and its condition after his death and resurrection. Formerly, the world was dominated by sin, death and the Law, which could indeed point out what was wrong but offered no power to overcome that wrong (7:24). After the death and resurrection of Christ, not sin but the Holy Spirit is the indwelling force in those who believe. Paul gives various titles to this Holy Spirit, such as 'Spirit of God', 'Spirit of Christ', 'the Spirit of him who raised Jesus from the dead'. Thanks to this Spirit, the Christian need not return to the former state of helplessness, a life 'interested only in unspiritual things', depending on unaided human resources, looking only to the self and leading to sin and death. The Christian vocation is to life, and this is the same life that Jesus lived (Galatians 2:20). Deservedly, this chapter of Paul, which is so full of encouragement for the Christian because of its doctrine of the Holy Spirit, is for many the most attractive in the whole letter.

In our readings from **Matthew**, we are now approaching the mid-point and, on a human level, the mission of Jesus seemed to be failing. John the Baptist, so enthusiastic at first (3:1–11), has sent messengers to Jesus, asking whether he is the one who was to come (11:3). Because Jesus does not live ascetically like the Baptist, he is accused of being a glutton and a drunkard (11:19). Jesus has to threaten the cities that are refusing his message with a fate worse than that of Sodom and Gomorrah (Genesis 19:24; Matthew 11:21).

Such is the context of today's gospel passage. The evangelist wants to assure us of three truths. First, Jesus is doing the will of the Father and so he prays to him in praise. He addresses God in Jewish terms as 'Lord of heaven and of earth'. The Father is said to reveal 'these things ... to mere children', which anticipates Jesus' answer when asked who is the greatest in the Kingdom of Heaven (18:1). This reminds us of Paul's words to the Corinthians, that God had chosen the foolish in this world (1 Corinthians 1:27).

Secondly, Jesus knows God as a son knows a father. Some have seen here a little parable portraying the child Jesus in the workshop, learning from Joseph. The Son's mission is to *reveal* the Father, a word used in the New Testament of supernatural revelation (16:17; Galatians 1:12). The language here is close to that which John uses about the Father and Son in his Gospel (John 3:35; 7:29; 17:1–3).

Thirdly, Jesus invites to discipleship in terms of Old Testament 'Wisdom'. Ben Sirach invited his hearers to take up the yoke of his teaching. Those who did so were assured of rest and refreshment (Sirach 51:23–27). Jesus' description of himself as 'gentle and humble in heart' recalls the beatitude in which he pronounced a special blessing on the humble (5:3), and it looks forward to his action in entering Jerusalem as the humble king of Israel in fulfilment of Zechariah (21:5).

Sunday 15 A

Isaiah 55:10–11
Psalm 64:10–14
Romans 8:18–23
Matthew 13:1–23

Parable of the Sower

We owe to Deutero-**Isaiah** a little treatise about the Word of God. The prophet's hearers are to have no doubt about the reliability of God's promises and his prophetic word. This word resembles a trusty messenger who discharges his message and who refuses to return until he has done so. It is like the rain that guarantees a crop for the farmer. The food that comes from this word of God is a source of life. Isaiah's image of God's word as seed prepares us for the gospel parable of the sower.

The **Psalm** is a thanksgiving hymn for the end of drought. It links the Isaiah passage, which compares God's word to rain, and Paul's reflections about the place of creation in the divine plan.

Paul explains in **Romans** how creation itself shares in the destiny won by Christ. We learn from Genesis how 'God saw all he had made, and indeed it was very good' (Genesis 1:31). This creation was damaged because of Adam's sin (Genesis 3:15–17). But it remained part of the covenant between God and the earth that God made with Noah (Genesis 9:12–13). Paul states that in the future it will partake in the redemption won by Christ. It will be no mere spectator of the glory due to the Redeemed and will escape dissolution and death. The Spirit that the believer possesses in the present is but the 'first fruits' of the final deliverance and redemption still in store for creation. Paul's words remind us of our continuing responsibility for and stewardship of creation, encouraging each of us in our concern for ecology and our environment (Genesis 1:28). The Spirit of God fills the whole earth.

On the next three Sundays, we hear in full the Parable Discourse of **Matthew**. This collection of parables from the lifetime of Jesus continues to instruct and challenge the reader. Jesus, besides being the one who preached in Galilee, addresses us as Emmanuel (1:23), the active Lord of the Church, who is to return as Son of Man for judgment (28:20). We are to identify with the disciples who first heard these parables. They represent all who struggle to live as Christian disciples to this day. The crowds to whom the parables were addressed represent indifferent and even hostile outsiders in every age.

First, the parable of the sower sums up Jesus' own experience in Galilee. The various bad soils describe those who failed to respond to his message (chapters 11–12). The good soil represents the disciples, who will go on to bear fruit beyond all expectation.

Secondly, the conversation about the purpose of parables fits into the situation of Matthew's community. Their hostile neighbours have unknowingly fulfilled the prophecy of Isaiah by rejecting Jesus' ministry and the message of his followers (John 12:40; Acts 26:24–25). In accepting the message that Jesus spoke, Matthew's community was indeed blessed. By contrast, according to Mark, the disciples consistently misunderstood the teaching of Jesus (Mark 8:14–21). This difference in the portrayal of the disciples is a major difference between Matthew and Mark.

Thirdly, in the explanation of the parable, we read of struggles in Matthew's Church and among later generations. Many fall away because they fail to understand their faith. They ignore the need to apply their heads as well as their hearts. Others never allow it to put down roots, letting it remain on the level of a child. Yet others are so fascinated by money or driven by the pressures of life that their faith goes the way of the seed among the thorns and is choked. But some, such as the original disciples, bear fruit of astonishing abundance.

Sunday 16 A

Wisdom 12:13, 16–19
Psalm 85:5–6, 9–10, 15–16
Romans 8:26–27
Matthew 13:24–43

Parable of the Weeds and the Wheat

The author of **Wisdom**, who wrote only a few years before Christ, offers God a description of his divine character. He does not portray him as the vigorous and active God of the covenant, whom we know from Israel's history. This author finds God's best manifestation in lenience and patience. The virtuous must follow God's way, a way which stands at odds with the values of an aggressive world. It mirrors the way of the patient farmer in the Gospel.

The **Psalm** reflects on various qualities of God. He is the God of lenience and forgiveness found in Wisdom. He is the God of all the nations such as we find in Deutero-Isaiah (Isaiah 42:6). He is the covenant God described in Exodus (Exodus 34:6).

Paul continues his reflections on the destiny of believers to share God's glory in **Romans**. First, he now enlists the Christian experience of the Holy Spirit to witness to it. This Spirit dwells in the Christian (8:9), although so far only its 'first-fruits' have been received (8:23). This is 'the spirit of sons, and it makes us cry out, "Abba! Father!"' (8:15), in imitation of Jesus himself (Luke 10:21). Every time we recite the 'Lord's Prayer', we put his teaching into practice. Secondly, the same Spirit helps our weakness in prayer by adding his own prayer 'over and above' our own 'in a way that could never be put into words'. God understands the prayer of the Spirit on our behalf and in our company. God does this since he is the 'assessor of mind and heart' (Psalm 7:9; Jeremiah 17:10; Psalm 139:1). This is one of the many qualities of God that were so familiar to Paul.

Today's instalment of **Matthew**'s Parable Discourse has two sections. In the first, Jesus addresses three parables to the crowds. Again, each is to be read on two levels, in the lifetime of Jesus and in the time of the reader. The weeds in the field symbolize a lack of response to Jesus' teaching. But, despite the warning of John the Baptist (3:10), these will not be rooted out quickly by his Father. They will wait to the end. Matthew's community is like a field too. Why does God tolerate their mediocre Christian life, in which the doubts of the Eleven before the Risen Lord (28:17) and Judas' activity before the Passion (26:14) repeat themselves? The answer of the parable is, 'Have patience'.

The mustard seed and leaven parables have double applications too. For the crowds in Galilee, they are warnings: the Kingdom is here, ignore it at your peril. For the community of Matthew, they are encouragement. Although its members may feel themselves worthless, they are not to despair. Greatness awaits them. They will soon recognise in their own story the fulfilment of Ezekiel's vision of the great tree that grew from the tiny seed (Ezekiel 17:23).

The crowds are forgotten in the second part, and Jesus speaks to the disciples privately. They represent Christians of Matthew's day, a far from perfect Church. The topic is future judgment. This will affect not only the 'subjects of the evil one' but also the 'subjects of the kingdom'. Judgment will begin with the household of God (1 Peter 4:17). 'All things that provoke offences and all who do evil' are flourishing. 'Things that provoke offences' signifies conduct such as that of the scribes and Pharisees described in chapter 23. Evil-doing is the behaviour complained of in the Sermon on the Mount. It is not enough to do works of piety. It is the deeper righteousness (5:20) and the practice of the will of God for which Christ will look 'when the day comes' (7:22).

Sunday 17 A

1 Kings 3:5, 7–12
Psalm 118:57, 72, 76–77, 127–130
Romans 8:28–30
Matthew 13:44–52

Three More Parables

It was common practice in biblical times for individuals to sleep in holy places in the hope of receiving some message from God. Jacob did so as he slept at Bethel (Genesis 28:11–19), and so did Samuel at Shiloh (1 Samuel 3:2–18). We read in **1 Kings** how Solomon, David's successor, slept in the sanctuary of Gideon. His reward was a dream in which he spoke with God. His prayer is a model for all who exercise responsibility for others. He does not ask for wealth, power or long life, but for the ability to govern his people well. God is pleased. Here is a person who knows where his treasure lies.

Our **Psalm**, the longest of them all, is a meditation on how one finds the Lord through keeping his Law. This divine Law is worth more than silver and gold. Like Solomon, the Psalmist has the right priorities.

Paul in **Romans** continues to explain our destiny to share God's glory. He distinguishes five stages in the career of those redeemed by Christ. God foreknows them, gives them power to become images of his Son, calls, justifies and finally glorifies them. These believers, for their part, love God and become 'images of his son', so that Jesus becomes their elder brother. Christ is the image of the unseen God (Colossians 1:15) and we are to become images of Christ. This text is not to be understood as implying the predestination of a few and the rejection of many. Introducing the letter to the Romans, Paul had proclaimed how the gospel was the power of God for all who believed, not just a few (1:16).

The audience in this final section of the Parable Discourse is now the disciples alone and not the crowds. They hear four more parables, which all concern the 'Kingdom of Heaven'. The first two are about commitment. The hearers, whether original disciples of Jesus or members of **Matthew**'s Church, are encouraged to imitate the one who found the treasure and the one who found the pearl of great price. The Kingdom is the equivalent of that treasure or that pearl, so their whole existence is to be dominated by their discovery. Let them overcome the scandals and lawlessness about which we heard last week and give their all to finding and doing the will of God (12:50).

The third parable speaks of fishermen dragging ashore a great catch of fish. This is a symbol of future judgment (Jeremiah 16:16). The judgment is both for those outside the Church (since the net catches fish of every kind) and, as in the parable of the weeds and the wheat, for those within it. The angels are to 'separate the wicked from the just'. Matthew does not allow the reader to forget how the Church is a mixed community. Thus this parable discourse follows the pattern of others in ending with a warning to the slack (7:21; 10:37; 18:21–35; 25:31–46). The quality of Christian life is to match that of the Christian message.

The final saying of our passage is its fourth parable. It tells of a 'scribe who becomes a disciple of the kingdom of heaven'. It can be taken primarily as a self-description of Matthew the evangelist, but it is relevant to every faithful believer. All have found a treasure with their discovery of the Kingdom, and it is for each individual to derive the best from his or her old faith and apply it to the new. They are to be like Jewish Christians of Matthew's community who found Christ in their scriptures, 'they put new wine into fresh skins and both are preserved' (9:17). From start to finish, Matthew's Gospel reminds us of the people and message of the Old Testament.

Sunday 18 A

Isaiah 55:1–3
Psalm 144:8–9, 15–18
Romans 8:35, 37–39
Matthew 14:13–21

The Feeding of the Five Thousand

Meals in scripture mean more than eating and drinking together; they are symbols of shared friendship and mutual obligation. Covenants between God and his people are accompanied by sacred meals. A meal celebrated the giving of the Law at Sinai (Exodus 24:11); the Last Supper of Jesus with his disciples was the occasion of the New Covenant (1 Corinthians 11:25). In **Isaiah** God issues an invitation to such a meal. We encounter other invitations in various Wisdom books (Proverbs 9:1–5; Sirach 24:14–20).

In the **Psalm** we praise the God of the covenant for his care for all his creatures in supplying them with nourishment (Psalm 104:27). This prayer has traditionally been sung at meals.

Paul completes the great eighth chapter of **Romans** with a hymn to the love of God. He has dealt with the consequences of faith and hope; now he concludes his description of how 'the love of God has been poured into our hearts' (5:5). Elsewhere, in his so-called 'fool's speech' (2 Corinthians 12:11), Paul listed the physical hardships he had to endure because of the gospel. The secret behind his ability to exercise such endurance is his love of Christ and Christ's love for him. This mutual love also brought to nothing the ten external forces that he lists. Most derive from astrology, and terrified many in the world of his time. When Paul considers how God has made his love visible in Christ, they become insignificant and irrelevant. The last words of the chapter are 'Jesus Christ our Lord'. They echo the verse that began this section of the letter: 'through our Lord Jesus Christ' we are 'at peace with God' (5:1).

After his parable chapter, **Matthew** gives further evidence of the barrenness of the Palestinian soil for the seed of the word that Jesus was bringing. The people of his home town showed astonishment but refused belief (13:53–58). The greatest 'of all the children born of women' (11:11), John the Baptist, was put to death by Herod because he spoke out for God's Law (14:1–12). Jesus' response is to withdraw to a desert place. But the crowds still pursue him and he does not turn them away. Once again he has compassion on them.

The account of the feeding of the five thousand that follows is less detailed and colourful than the same scene in Mark (6:30–44), and lacks a discourse to explain it such as we find in John 6. Matthew, having used it already, omits Mark's image of the crowds being like sheep without a shepherd (9:36). Instead of teaching them many things (Mark 6:34), he simply takes pity on them and heals their sick. In his dialogue with the disciples, he is not asked how he expects them to find so much bread in a desert place. They already know how much food is available. Jesus takes this food, gives it to them and they distribute it.

Matthew's interest here may well lie in the role of the disciples as models for the future leaders of the Church. They see around them a hopeless situation, but they reckon up their resources and give them to Jesus. He transforms what they offer him, and leaves the disciples to get to work. So effective is the transformation that the crisis is decisively overcome. And not only this: there are twelve baskets full of scraps left over. Originally there were twelve tribes of Israel and Jesus chose twelve apostles. The bread left over is available for others who did not originally belong to the people of Israel. It awaits the nations who will respond to the mission given to the Eleven at the end of the Gospel (28:19). The bread that the Eleven will distribute is the Eucharist.

Sunday 19 A

1 Kings 19:9, 11–13
Psalm 84:9–14
Romans 9:1–5
Matthew 14:22–33

Walking on the Water

Elijah is weary after his conflicts with the prophets of Baal. So, according to 1 **Kings**, he sets out for the mountain of Horeb, or Sinai. In a cave, perhaps the same place where Moses had seen God's back (Exodus 33:13–23), Elijah hears the storm, the fire and the earthquake that Moses had heard (Exodus 19:14–19), but this time God passes by in a gentle breeze. This passing of God prepares us for Jesus' passing by his disciples in the Gospel.

The **Psalm** is part of a liturgy in which the people are at prayer, asking for a good harvest. A prophet speaks a message of reassurance from God. The word 'peace' is repeated. God is a God of peace and justice, the same God who passed by Elijah in his cave.

If Paul's gospel in **Romans** is promised 'through his prophets in the scriptures' (Romans 1:2), why do his own Jewish people reject it? Writing 'in union with Christ', 'in union with the Holy Spirit', he compares himself with Moses who, when Israel worshipped the Golden Calf, declared himself ready to forego his own salvation to save them (Exodus 32:32). He lists the privileges of the people of Israel, which culminate in their giving birth to the Christ. In his final doxology, he may be identifying Christ with God, depending on whether a full stop or a comma is inserted after the word 'Christ'. Paul usually expresses his belief in the divinity of Christ by attributing to him what the Old Testament attributed to God the Father, as he does in the well-known hymn in Philippians, where his language closely resembles that of Isaiah (Philippians 2:10; Isaiah 45:23).

Matthew's account of Jesus' walking on the sea reveals the majesty, and even the divinity, of Jesus. It concludes with the disciples confessing their faith in him as 'Son of God'. After he had fed the five thousand, Jesus dismissed the disciples, while he himself went off to pray on the mountain alone. The disciples once again find themselves in a boat, tossed around by the waves (8:23). Early interpreters recognised in this boat a symbol of the Church. Here is Matthew's Church, alone on the sea, and Jesus appears to be absent, despite his promise to be with them always until the end of time (28:20).

But soon, Jesus comes to them walking on the waves, an action which, according to the Old Testament, is something only God can do (Job 9:8; Habbakuk 3:15). No wonder the disciples cry out with fear. Jesus replies in words from the Old Testament, 'Courage! It is I! Do not be afraid'; 'Be strong .... Be fearless' were words God spoke to Joshua (Joshua 1:9). 'I am' was the name God gave to himself at the burning bush (Exodus 3:14).

Adding to the parallel passage in Mark (6:45–52), Matthew relates how Peter asks that he too might walk on the water. In response to Jesus' invitation, he begins to walk. When he then starts to sink, he cries out with the same prayer the disciples had made in the storm, 'save us, Lord' (8:25). It is a model prayer for Christians in distress, recognising Jesus as Lord of the Church. Jesus replies by calling Peter a man of 'little faith', an expression commonly used of the disciples in Matthew (8:26). Their faith is still that of beginners. Peter's zeal and subsequent failure anticipates the Caesarea Philippi incident, when Jesus called him both 'rock' and 'obstacle' (16:18, 23).

Subsequently, in contrast to Mark, where the disciples are said to be 'utterly and completely dumbfounded' (Mark 6:51), they make their own the confession of Jesus spoken by Peter at Caesarea Philippi (16:16) and by the centurion and his companions at the foot of the cross (27:54). Jesus is 'the Son of God'.

Sunday 20 A

Isaiah 56:1, 6–7
Psalm 66:2–3, 5–6, 8
Romans 11:13–15, 29–32
Matthew 15:21–28

The Canaanite Woman

The third section of **Isaiah**, known as Trito-Isaiah, stresses the universality of the mercy of God. The time will come when foreigners will be welcome to share in God's blessings. The behaviour expected of them is defined in traditional Jewish categories of holocaust and sacrifice, of Sabbath and covenant. The final line about a 'house of prayer for all the peoples' looks forward to the words of Christ when he expelled the traders from the Temple (Mark 11:15–19).

A similar universalism is reflected in the **Psalm**. Its opening blessing echoes the Jewish blessing found in the book of Numbers (6:24), but the praise due to God is to come from all nations. God's concern is for all.

Paul in **Romans** comes to the end of his discussion about the salvation of his own people. Because they rejected Christ, the opportunity for salvation has been given to the Gentiles. Thus rejection by some brings salvation for others. How much more, he argues, would blessings come if they accepted salvation through Christ? It would be like a 'resurrection from the dead'. It would equal in significance the resurrection of Christ and the final destiny of the believer. Paul has confidence in two great truths about God. God is faithful to his promises and never takes away his gifts; and his ultimate purpose is to show mercy to all. If he can save the Gentiles from their disobedience, how much more can he save the Jews? This text must never be forgotten in any discussion of Christian–Jewish relations.

Before he fed the five thousand, Jesus had withdrawn to a desert place. The crowd that followed him, he healed and saved from hunger. This week, **Matthew** tells us of another withdrawal by Jesus, this time to the pagan districts of Tyre and Sidon. A woman comes to him, but all she gets is a rebuff. This experience would hardly surprise her. She is a woman, the mother of a possessed girl and a foreigner. But her address to Jesus as 'Lord' and 'Son of David' surprises us.

Since Jesus says nothing, the disciples break in, asking him to send her away. Then he speaks. His mission is to his own people, who are like lost sheep (10:5). Unlike the woman, the disciples on this occasion fail to recognise him as Son of David. She is not discouraged. She worships him, again calling him 'Lord', but the same Jesus who was so full of compassion for the crowds that he fed five thousand of them, even excluding women and children, seems to insult her even more. His ministry is meant for Israel; he will not 'take the children's food and throw it to the house-dogs'.

But the woman can use picturesque language too. She takes up the insulting word of Jesus and claims that dogs are worthy of the scraps from the table. And this wins Jesus over. He compliments her, 'you have great faith'. Because of this, he brings forward the post-resurrection mission to all nations (28:16–20). The restrictions on the ministry are overturned (10:5; 15:21). We have a parallel to the Cana miracle in John: though his hour was not yet come, Jesus anticipated the abundance of the messianic age in the miracle of the wine (John 2:1–10). So Jesus leads the woman by an unusual pedagogy to a full expression of her faith. This woman joins the company of the magi (2:1–12), the centurion who asked Jesus to cure his servant (8:5–13) and the centurion and his companions at the cross (27:54) in anticipating the mission to the Gentiles that was a reality in the time of Matthew.

Sunday 21 A

Isaiah 22:19–23
Psalm 137:1–3, 6, 8
Romans 11:33–36
Matthew 16:13–20

Peter the Rock

In **Isaiah** we glimpse life in an ancient court. The master of the palace under King Hezekiah (716–687 BC) is Shebna, but his behaviour has been unsatisfactory. He has been ordering his tomb and giving too much attention to his chariots. He is to be replaced; in future, Eliakim will hold the keys of the royal palace; he will be a father to the citizens and a 'throne of glory' in the royal palace. The keys presented to Eliakim prepare us for the keys of the Kingdom of Heaven given to Peter in Matthew (16:19) and the keys held by Christ in Revelation (3:7).

The **Psalm** is a hymn of thanksgiving, acknowledging God's faithful love. In the Temple, the psalmist prays a prayer suitable for Eliakim (and Peter) to make after elevation to high office.

Paul concludes the section in **Romans** on the place of the Jews in the plan of God (9–11) with a hymn to God's mercy, rejoicing that God has found a way to deal with the refusal of his own people to acknowledge Christ (9:1–5). He catalogues the attributes of God in language familiar to both Gentile and Jew. God is praised for his riches, his wisdom and his knowledge, divine qualities which were recognised by the best Gentile thought of the time. Then he proves by means of passages from Isaiah and Job that these qualities belong to the God of Israel too. He concludes with a reference to God's omnipotence and transcendence. Paul's God needs no advice or helper; he is a God who is faithful and who can be trusted. He is truly worthy of the hymn of praise, the doxology, that concludes three chapters which remain most important for Christian–Jewish relations even today.

In **Matthew** the people welcome Jesus' mission, but the religious authorities reject it. They demand signs that Jesus refuses to give (16:1); they behave like the Satan of the temptation narrative in looking for miracles (4:3). Jesus has to warn his disciples against the 'yeast' of the Pharisees, by which he means their teaching (16:6). In this situation, God's people need new leaders. To Peter's confession at Caesarea Philippi, reported by Mark (8:27–30), Matthew adds the commissioning of Peter as the rock on which Jesus is to build his Church.

First, Peter gives Jesus a new title. Common views about Jesus did not go beyond conventional ideas from Israel's past. But Peter, because of a special revelation from the Father, confesses Jesus as the Christ, the Son of God. The term 'Christ', or messiah, had a long history in Judaism and was applied to a triumphant figure, probably a descendant of David, whom God would send to deliver his people (2 Samuel 7). As for 'Son of God', this is a favourite title of Jesus in Matthew (3:17). In Mark, no human being gave Jesus this title before his death. Matthew, by contrast, reports that the disciples after the walking on the water (14:33) and Peter on this occasion use it of Jesus.

In return, Jesus gives Peter a new name, 'rock'. In the Psalms (95:1), this was a name for God himself. On this rock, he would build his Church. The word *church* occurs only twice in Matthew, here and in the Community Discourse (18:17). It corresponds to the assembly (*qahal*) of God's people under Moses in the desert (Exodus 16:2). Peter is to be to the new *qahal* what Moses was to the old. He is also to be bearer of the keys, like Eliakim under King Hezekiah. The promise that the gates of hell will not prevail anticipates that of Jesus' own continuous presence at the end of the Gospel (28:20). The scene resembles church founding stories of the post-resurrection period (John 21:15–17).

Sunday 22 A

Jeremiah 20:7–9
Psalm 62:2–6, 8–9
Romans 12:1–2
Matthew 16:21–27

First Prediction of the Passion

Plain talking with God marks the so-called 'confessions' of **Jeremiah**. They must be seen against the background of his call (Jeremiah 1:10), which appointed him to uproot as well as build up. Conflict with the priest Pashhur (Jeremiah 20:1–6) shows how unpleasant such a mission could be for a prophet. So he abuses God, calling him a trap and a seducer. But he also recognises that God is like a fire burning in his bones. Jeremiah is hearing a second call that will lead to a more mature discipleship. His experience anticipates Peter's in the Gospel.

The **Psalm** describes the wandering of David in the desert. Thirst for water puts him in mind of his thirst for God. Life is a valuable possession, yet the love of God can mean even more. We live in the shadow of God's wings (Deuteronomy 32:11), awaiting a final banquet in the house of God (Isaiah 55:1–3).

The final section of **Romans** concerns Christian behaviour. The time for teaching is over; now Paul turns to its consequences for day-to-day life. The general principle that he offers, is simple enough. The Christian is someone whose whole life is a response to God's mercy and grace through Christ. Religion for the Christian is not a matter of animal or other sacrifices limited to a particular time or place. It concerns the whole person, and the whole of life becomes a sacrificial action in union with Christ. The newness of life put on in baptism, when we descend into the tomb with the crucified Christ (6:4), is to be the inspiration for this life and not the values of the world around. Paul rarely gives orders; he much prefers to encourage as he does here.

Last week, **Matthew** related how Peter gave Jesus a new name and was given in return the name of 'rock'. The time has come for Jesus to speak openly of his future death and resurrection. Peter will not listen, even rebuking Jesus. Jesus' response is severe. He no longer calls him 'rock', but Satan. Peter is a scandal, a 'stumbling-stone' such as the Lord had mentioned to Isaiah centuries before (Isaiah 8:14). In his parables, Jesus has warned how the angels would clear such scandals out of the Kingdom at the end of time (13:41). Peter, like Satan in the desert, tempts Jesus to seek the glory of the kingdoms of this world (4:8). His thoughts are human ones and not the thoughts of God.

Jesus has more to say to the disciples. They have to deny themselves, carry the cross and follow him. The cross will take different forms. For some it will be the effort required to live up to the higher righteousness revealed by Jesus in his Sermon on the Mount (Matthew 5:20). It will include the denial of self, inevitable for any who fulfil the demand of Jesus to 'love your neighbour as yourself' (22:39). Yet, to encourage us, Jesus has already taught that his burden is easy and his yoke is light (11:28).

Other severe sayings follow. Jesus speaks about gaining the whole world. By the end of the Gospel, Jesus will indeed have done this (Matthew 28:18), but at the cost of the cross, by following his Father's will rather than his own (26:39) and by ignoring the temptations of Satan repeated on Calvary (27:42). The final picture is of Jesus coming in judgment as the Son of Man (Daniel 7:13). This judgment will concern behaviour. Matthean Christianity is a Christianity of action, defined most vividly in the parables of chapter 25. We learn from the first Letter of Peter that Peter did finally learn Jesus' way of discipleship and taught others about it. 'Christ suffered for you and left an example for you to follow the way he took' (1 Peter 2:21).

Sunday 23 A

Ezekiel 33:7–9
Psalm 94:1–2, 6–9
Romans 13:8–10
Matthew 18:15–20

The Brother Who Sins

We owe the image of the prophet as watchman to **Ezekiel**. He compares a prophet to the watch on duty on the walls of an ancient city, ready to warn of approaching danger. His duty is to inform the people of what is in the mind of God. A watchman who fails to watch and give the alarm is punished. Likewise a prophet who fails to point out the sinfulness of his people makes himself liable to the punishment that sin deserves.

In the **Psalm**, a prophet bids the people heed the message of God. He carries out the mission of watchman given to Ezekiel and anticipates the situation in Matthew's Church when it discovered sin in its ranks.

We read in the Gospels how Jesus, questioned by a scribe in the Temple about the greatest commandment, quoted the words of Leviticus, 'You shall love your neighbour as yourself' (Leviticus 19:18; Mark 12:31). As he approaches the end of **Romans**, Paul recalls this episode. He has explained in this letter how, because of the work of Christ, we have been freed from the debts imposed on us by the powers behind sin and death, and even from the Mosaic Law. But he knows that we can never repay our debt to the love of God, which he defines by referring to obligations included in the Decalogue, the Ten Commandments (Exodus 20:13–17). As Christians, we have certainly been called to freedom (Galatians 5:1), but it is a freedom which brings with it the obligation to love our neighbour by observing such laws as those against adultery, murder, theft and covetousness. Elsewhere Paul teaches how faith must work through love (Galatians 5:6).

The fourth discourse of **Matthew** is often entitled the Community Discourse (18:1–35). It begins with Jesus defining the greatest in the Kingdom of Heaven as the one who makes himself a child (18:1–4). He underlines the worth of such 'little ones' by his parable of the lost sheep (10:42; Luke 15:4–7). The lost one is so valuable that 99 others can be left on the hillside so that the missing one can be found (18:12–14). It is in this context that he addresses the question of how to deal with the brother who sins.

Jesus lays down three stages. The first is to follow the example set by Jesus himself in his confrontation with Peter and deal with the matter in private (16:22). If this fails, two or three others should be brought in. Only at the third stage is the community as a whole to be involved. We can compare directions given in the Law (Leviticus 19:17–18; Deuteronomy 19:15). The responsibility given to an individual is not to be shifted immediately to higher authority. If all fails, then the sinner is to be treated like a 'a pagan or a tax collector'.

We seem to have a formula for excommunication from the community (1 Corinthians 5:5). But the rest of Matthew's Gospel makes us pause. The parable of the lost sheep stressed the worth of the lost one (18:10–14). Jesus himself was called the 'friend of tax collectors and sinners' (11:19). We still have to read the parable of the unforgiving debtor, about the refusal to forgive by one who has been forgiven much (18:23–35).

The community does not live by itself. God is ready to make its decisions his own. God listens to and answers the petitions of even two of them (18:19). When they come together in his name, then Jesus is among them. He is the Emmanuel (1:23) who will remain with them until the end of time (28:20). Yet the decision of the community does not exhaust the mercy of God (Hosea 6:6). The Lord continues to challenge his Church in the teaching of this Community Discourse and the other discourses of the Gospel (5–7, 10, 13, 24–25).

Sunday 24 A

Sirach 27:30–28:7
Psalm 102:1–4, 9–12
Romans 14:7–9
Matthew 18:21–35

The Unforgiving Servant

We all experience resentment and anger. But **Sirach** gives wise advice to his people to help them cope with such emotions. Let them look at the source. The emotions may have their origin in sin. Let them remember the traditional teaching that vengeance is to be left to God: 'Vengeance is mine' says God in Deuteronomy (32:35). Let them ask what their attitude would be on their deathbed. Which of the commandments have they undertaken to observe? And what are the terms of the covenant by which they have committed themselves to the goodness of God (Exodus 34:6)? All this helps to prepare us for the parable we will hear in the Gospel.

The **Psalm** is the prayer of a person recovering from sickness, who has learnt of the healing and forgiving power of God. To experience God like this is to have little difficulty in forgiving our neighbour.

The Roman Church was composed of both Jews and Gentiles. The difficulties that they experienced in forming a stable community are reflected in **Romans**. Some would arise from traditional food laws and the divisions they demanded. Paul states various principles. Each person must learn to accept the other because they share a common heritage and belong to the same Lord. This has not come about by chance, but happened because they have been 'bought and paid for' (1 Corinthians 6:20) by the death and resurrection of Christ. They will share in that resurrection (Romans 6:5) and in the heavenly glory he already possesses. Paul appeals not to the God of the covenant, like Ben Sira in our first reading, but to the work of Christ.

The final and longest section of **Matthew**'s Community Discourse consists of a dialogue between Peter and Jesus about forgiveness, which is completed by the parable of the unforgiving debtor. In this dialogue, Peter shows astonishing generosity by offering to forgive his brother seven times. But Jesus answers by demanding forgiveness up to 77 times, effectively an uncountable number. The figures remind the reader of the 77-fold vengeance threatened by Lamech in Genesis in contrast to the sevenfold vengeance taken for Cain (4:23–24).

The parable follows on from this dialogue. It has elements of both savagery and humour. The savagery reflects the pagan society of the day, in which wives and children were sold into slavery and debtors were tortured. The humour arises from the pathetic promise of the debtor to repay all his debt, even though the amount concerned is ten times the annual income of Herod the Great. But more important than the contingent details are the theological issues. The debtor is pleasantly astonished to discover that the ruler does not run his affairs on the principle of justice alone. He allows mercy to override its demands. He follows the teaching of Hosea (6:6), which Matthew quotes twice in his Gospel (9:13; 12:7). The debtor does not follow his example. He insists on strict justice in the case of the person in debt to him. Whatever Jesus meant by fulfilling every 'little stroke' of the Law (5:18), it is not this.

Earlier in this Gospel, the need for mutual forgiveness was the only petition in the Lord's Prayer to receive commentary (6:15). In the scanty teaching on prayer found in Mark, the same emphasis is repeated (11:25). As for Luke, he shows us Jesus not simply teaching the need for forgiveness, but himself exercising it as his executioners go about their work (Luke 23:34). This discourse on life in the community, like previous ones, ends with a warning (7:21; 10:32–39; 13:49).

Sunday 25 A

Isaiah 55:6–9
Psalm 144:2–4, 8–9, 17–18
Philippians 1:20–24, 27
Matthew 20:1–16

The Workers in the Vineyard

Isaiah gives two requirements for those who want to worship in the Temple. First, they must turn aside from a wicked and sinful life (Luke 18:13). Secondly, they must know the God who invites them. He is a God of forgiveness, but he is also a God whose 'thoughts are not your thoughts'. Job had discovered this (Job 38–41) and Jesus would make the point again in the parable we hear in the Gospel.

The **Psalm** is a meditation on the greatness of God and on the virtues he displays in entering into a covenant with his people (Exodus 34:6). The response that we repeat emphasizes his closeness to all who call on him. He is a God to be sought while he can be found.

We begin the letter of Paul to the **Philippians**. Many find this the most attractive and positive of his letters. Joy and fellowship are keywords. Paul is in prison, perhaps in Rome, more likely at Ephesus or Caesarea (Acts 23:33). The interest of our passage is that it lets us into the mind of Paul on the subject of his own death. In the early years of his ministry he probably thought that Christ would return before he himself died (1 Thessalonians 1:10). But the possibility of execution has concentrated his thoughts. He wants to die because this would allow him an even greater intimacy with Christ than he has already. He had written to the Galatians, 'I live now not with my own life but with the life of Christ who lives in me' (Galatians 2:20). But because it is his special calling, 'a duty which has been laid on me', to preach the gospel (1 Corinthians 9:16), for the sake of his converts and his mission, he is ready to live on.

Having followed Mark closely for the whole of the previous chapter, **Matthew** suddenly slips in a parable found in no other Gospel. It forms a continuation of a discussion about rewards between Jesus and Peter which had ended, 'The last will be first and the first last'. It is a parable about the rewards that await in the Kingdom of Heaven.

Like most parables, it begins with a normal situation. The owner of a vineyard goes out to hire workers for a fair wage. The story soon takes a strange twist. Why should the owner hire three more sets of workers, and why do those without a job turn up late to look for employment? Why, at the end of the day, does the owner instruct his manager to give out the wages beginning with the last to be hired? Does he want to provoke trouble? Trouble certainly comes when the same wage is paid to all. The reader may sympathize with those who toiled all day for the same pay as those who only worked for a single hour. The owner replies by claiming his right to do what he wishes with his money. The sum originally agreed was accepted as 'fair'. How is he 'unjust' in paying the agreed sum? He is 'generous'; it is those who criticize him who are 'envious'. The parable concludes with the slogan from the previous chapter, 'The last will be first and the first last'.

The story is ended without explanation. Matthew resumes following Mark and gives us the Jesus' third prediction of his passion. Many meanings for the parable have been suggested. Those converted late in life are not to be envied by those who converted early. Jews, whose membership of God's people goes right back to Abraham, are not to be jealous of the Gentiles, the late arrivals. But the main point is surely the generosity of God. His righteousness, or justice, leaves room for his generosity too. He asks, 'Do you begrudge my generosity?' Isaiah and Job would have understood.

Sunday 26 A

Ezekiel 18:25–28
Psalm 24:4–9
Philippians 2:1–11
Matthew 21:28–32

Parable of the Two Sons

Ezekiel's great theological contribution in this chapter is his emphasis on personal responsibility. He teaches that each person is liable for his or her own sin, correcting a false understanding of Exodus that speaks of God 'punishing the father's fault in the sons' (34:7). Anticipating the Gospel, he contrasts the upright man who perishes because of his sin to the wicked man who lives because of repentance.

The **Psalm** proclaims God as the great teacher and guide. No one can be self-taught in following the way of God; as for sin, God alone can provide its remedy.

Paul was not blind to the defects of the **Philippians**. Selfishness and conceit were high on the list. As a remedy, he urges humility. This is the only correct way for the Philippians to stand before God (Luke 14:11). Elsewhere Paul has urged his converts to copy him (1 Corinthians 4:16), but here, in this matter of humility, he can offer no better example than Christ himself. Most experts believe that in this passage he is quoting a hymn which can be divided into two sections. In the first (vv.6–8), he describes the humiliation of Christ, in the second his exaltation (vv.9–11). Some understand this hymn as describing Christ as a second Adam, who refused to seek equality with God as the first Adam had done (Genesis 3:5; Romans 5:14); others prefer to find in it a description of his career as the pre-existent Son of God who, through the incarnation, emptied himself of his divine status and 'was humbler yet, even to accepting death, death on a cross'. Paul, too, exercises humility, because he has suffered the loss of all things in order to gain Christ (3:8).

In **Matthew**'s story, Jesus has made his solemn entry into Jerusalem and has gone into the Temple. He has purged it of those who were making it a 'robbers' den' (Jeremiah 7:11). To those querying his authority he makes no answer, but asks a question of his own about the authority of John the Baptist, which his critics have failed to recognise. He then tells three parables. We read the first today. It begins with a question: 'What is your opinion?' This parable is about two sons and about work in a vineyard (20:1–16).

The first son agrees to work in the vineyard, but does not turn up. The second refuses to work, but later changes his mind. The parable is often applied to the leaders of Israel at the time. They have entered into a covenant with God but failed to observe their side of the agreement. Typical is their misuse of the Temple. The sinners who came to Jesus are those who at first refused but later repented and entered into the Kingdom. This interpretation seems to be confirmed by Jesus' comment that 'tax collectors and prostitutes are making their way into the kingdom of God before you'. He reminds them of John the Baptist, who came to them in the 'way of righteousness' (3:15). Then, too, the sinners had repented but their leaders had not.

Others interpret the parable as a picture of Matthew's mixed community (13:37). Some call Jesus by the correct title of 'Lord' and yet, when it comes to action, fall short of putting the will of God into practice (7:21). Others begin with an inadequate view of Jesus, yet end by doing God's will and become members of the family of Jesus (12:50). Those who were formerly known as sinners are now at home in the community for whom the Gospel is written just as, in the lifetime of Jesus, such people had been comfortable in the company of the 'friend of tax collectors and sinners' (11:19). They were practising a righteousness deeper than 'that of the scribes and Pharisees' (5:20), a righteousness prefigured in the life of John the Baptist (3:15).

Sunday 27 A

Isaiah 5:1–7
Psalm 79:9, 12–16, 19–20
Philippians 4:6–9
Matthew 21:33–43

Parable of the Vineyard and the Tenants

In his Song of the Vineyard, **Isaiah** compares God to a farmer who does everything he can to produce good grapes, but all his efforts turn out in vain. Only sour grapes grow. What is he to do? He will surely give up on the vineyard and let it fall into ruin. Isaiah is telling a parable. His audience are to look at themselves and hear Nathan's word to David, 'You are the man!' (2 Samuel 12:7). They are to realise that they are the vineyard that has produced nothing, and that they are God's possession.

In the **Psalm**, Israel, God's vineyard, repents. Under King Josiah (640–609 BC), the northern kingdom had fallen, and the southern kingdom, which Isaiah had warned, was likely to suffer the same fate. The Psalmist responds with a traditional prayer of penitence, so that God can once more make his face shine on them (Numbers 6:24–26).

In **Philippians**, Paul moves from the encouragement of individuals to the exhortation of the community. Paul writes in a way reflecting his origins as a devout Jew who grew up in Tarsus, a Greek centre of learning. He speaks of peace, the valued Jewish quality of *shalom*. His God is the God of peace. Peace is to guard their hearts and thoughts. It is a peace 'in Christ Jesus', which meant for Paul reconciliation between humanity and God and between individuals (Romans 5:1, 11). They are also to seek the 'noble ... good and pure', ideas taught by the best Greek philosophers of the time. Here we glimpse how Paul respects the background and culture of his converts and expects them to influence their own environment with mutually acceptable values.

We continue with **Matthew**'s account of Jesus' teaching in the Temple and his response in parables to the attack on his authority. We heard the first last week and the second we hear now. This parable presupposes knowledge of Isaiah's Song of the Vineyard. Jesus expands the original. In this new version, the owner sends two sets of servants, and finally his own son, to look for its 'produce'. Far from only finding sour grapes, they meet various fates including death.

Just as Isaiah's readers were to recognise themselves in the Song, so the audience of Matthew is to recognise the history of salvation in the parable. The two sets of servants are the 'former' and 'latter' prophets of Israel, and the son is Jesus himself. They may remind us, too, of Matthew's division of Jesus' ancestors into sets of fourteen (1:1–17). Jesus, like the son in the parable who meets his death outside the vineyard, will die outside the city (Hebrews 13:12).

The parable ends with lessons relevant to both christology and ecclesiology. We learn about Jesus. He is the stone that will be rejected but become the cornerstone on which the new community is built (Psalm 118:22; Acts 4:11; 1 Peter 2:4). We learn about the Church, which Matthew distinguishes from the former people of God. In his passion account, the latter reject Jesus with their cry, 'His blood be on us and on our children!' (27:25). Through this, they put themselves in the same situation as the nations to whom the risen Christ sent his Easter mission (28:19). God does not reject his people, even though they have sinned. In former times, because of their infidelity, they lost their Temple and city, but God had raised up King Cyrus to bring them back again (2 Chronicles 36:14, 23). Jesus' blood, which is to be 'poured out for many for the forgiveness of sins', is for them as for all the nations (26:28). 'God never takes back his gifts or revokes his choice' (Romans 11:29). As for 'the fruits of the kingdom', we have heard elsewhere in this Gospel how words without deeds are insufficient (7:21).

Sunday 28 A

Isaiah 25:6–10
Psalm 22
Philippians 4:12–14, 19–20
Matthew 22:1–14

Parable of the Wedding Feast

Israel in exile was familiar with starvation, sadness and death. **Isaiah** foresees God's intervention, bringing destruction for God's enemies and salvation for Jerusalem, built on Mount Zion. He describes salvation in terms of abundant food, and of the end of death and mourning. It was against this sort of background that Matthew wrote in reporting the deeds and words of Jesus.

The **Psalm** of the Good Shepherd includes the image of the banquet as an expression of God's care for his people. In former times, those newly admitted to the Eucharist would enter singing this Psalm.

Paul wishes to acknowledge the gift he has received from the community in **Philippians**. He does this in a roundabout way, as if reluctant to accept it. He appreciates their generosity (2 Corinthians 8:2), but his preference is to work for his own living (1 Corinthians 9:18; 1 Thessalonians 2:9). At this stage of his life, after years of labour, he has attained a state of indifference. He knows how to live on little or much. His language resembles that of the Stoic philosophers of the time, but the difference between them is that he finds his strength in Christ and in the grace of God (1 Corinthians 15:10). His contentment, for one in prison and mortal danger, may well amaze us (1:7). He may soon be facing execution on charges for which he can admit no guilt. The generosity he really appreciates is that of God, and of Christ who, in that generosity, became poor for our sake (2 Corinthians 8:9). He concludes by praising God's glory. A share in this glory is for him the summit of his ambition and destiny (Romans 8:30).

The third parable taught by Jesus in the Temple and reported by **Matthew** is about a wedding banquet. This time a king, rather than a householder, takes the initiative. This king gives a banquet for his son's wedding. But the people whom he invites refuse the invitation, making various excuses. He therefore sends two sets of servants to summon them, but not only do they ignore the message but they kill the servants. Then he makes a general invitation to everyone to fill the empty places.

Again we have an allegory of salvation history. Marriage in the Old Testament symbolizes the relation of God to his people (Hosea 2:4–7), and in the New Testament the relation of Christ to his Church (2 Corinthians 11:2). The banquet in the story recalls the banquet in Isaiah. The two sets of messengers correspond to the prophets of the Old Testament and the apostles of the New. Those who reject the invitation are the leaders of Israel who rejected Christ. The destruction of the city refers to the destruction of Jerusalem by the Romans in AD 70, which would be well known to the readers of this Gospel, having happened a generation before.

The addition of the man without a wedding garment has puzzled many. Surely his fate is unfair? The Church of Matthew was a mixed group of good and bad (13:48). The bad had not achieved the deeper righteousness (5:20), had not produced in their lives the fruits of the Kingdom (21:43). The man without a wedding garment may represent Gentiles invited after the refusal of those originally called. They have failed to meet the obligations that go with the invitation. His fate of 'weeping and grinding of teeth' is also the fate of the subjects of the Kingdom who find their places at the feast taken by 'many ... from east and west' (8:11). This is the lot of those excluded from the Kingdom (13:42, 50; 24:51; 25:30). If we list such apparently threatening passages in Matthew, we will find they are much outnumbered by verses of encouragement (10:26–31; 11:28–30).

Sunday 29 A

Isaiah 45:1, 4–6
Psalm 95:1, 3–5, 7–10
1 Thessalonians 1:1–5
Matthew 22:15–21

Paying Taxes to Caesar

The prophets taught Israel the universality of the power of its God, who could use other nations and kings as his instruments. Thus he summoned Assyria as the 'rod of my anger' to punish Israel (Isaiah 10:5) and takes Cyrus, king of Persia, by 'his right hand' to restore Israel to her land. (For his part, Cyrus mistakenly thought that Marduk, the Babylonian god, held his right hand!) In **Isaiah**'s view, God arranges the history of the world for the sake of his own people.

The **Psalm**, with its origin in temple liturgy, is a summons to worship God as the true king of Israel and of the whole world. Other gods do not even exist. He, not Cyrus, possesses the qualities of a true king.

When Paul wrote **1 Thessalonians**, he had already been a Christian and a missionary for fifteen years. In writing a letter he is doing something new, because a personal visit is impossible and the efforts of his assistants have proved inadequate (3:2). Following the conventions of his time, he has to build up to the real topic of the letter. He first names himself and two collaborators; Paul's missionary effort is no one-man show. Instead of thanking pagan gods, as contemporary letter-writers often did, he thanks the living God, the Father of the Lord Jesus Christ. He encourages his converts by congratulating them on the quality of their Christian life of faith, hope and love 'in our Lord Jesus Christ'. He recalls that the 'gospel' he preached is not his own but one that came from God with the power of God's creative and prophetic Holy Spirit. Centuries before, Isaiah had used the word 'gospel' to describe the good news of deliverance from exile (52:7)

After reporting the three parables that Jesus spoke in the Temple, **Matthew** relates a series of encounters between Jesus and leading groups among the Jews. The first is a hostile one between Jesus and the Pharisees, who want to trap him. Addressing him as 'Master' (the form of address used by unbelievers in Matthew), they put a trick question, intended to embarrass him whatever his answer. Jesus recognises again the hypocrisy he meets so often in this Gospel (6:5; 23:13).

His reply, in action and word, surprises and disconcerts his questioners. Accepting the coin he is offered, which has Caesar's imprint on it, he points out that by using it, they are already paying Caesar tribute. But they also have to pay tribute to God, and the second part of Jesus' saying, give 'to God what belongs to God', is the more important for those who, at worship in God's Temple, are in debt to him. Jesus passes the test set him.

This passage is one of those biblical texts that is used to encourage support for existing political structures (Romans 13:1; Titus 3:1). But, like all biblical texts, it is to be understood in context. When a government protects human dignity, supporting it becomes part of the daily worship of a Christian whose whole life is a sacrifice to God (Romans 12:1). At times, life for Christians could be difficult enough without provoking the wrath of the civil power (1 Peter 2:12). But there is also a biblical basis for opposition to civil authority when God's law is flouted. In the Old Testament, Daniel and his friends opposed royal decrees ordering false worship (Daniel 3); Elijah was one of the leading opponents of King Ahab (1 Kings 18). In the New Testament, Peter and John replied to the Sanhedrin, 'Obedience to God comes before obedience to men' (Acts 5:29), and in Revelation, Caesar was described as a beast, soon to meet defeat in combat with the Lamb who was Christ (13:17). Jesus and the early Church wanted to restore the primacy of God in daily life. God can work through Caesar as he worked through Cyrus (Isaiah 45:1), but he is the sovereign king of both.

Sunday 30 A

Exodus 22:20–26
Psalm 17:2–4, 47, 51
1 Thessalonians 1:5–10
Matthew 22:34–40

The Great Commandment

After he had spoken the words of the Ten Commandments, or Decalogue (20: 1–17), God in **Exodus** went on to give further instructions for the life of a people bound to him by covenant. Today's reading offers a sample of them. Israel, as the chosen people, liberated from slavery in Egypt, are to demonstrate in their daily existence the kindness and concern for others that a compassionate God has displayed towards them. They are to care for the alien and the widow (Jeremiah 7:6; Deuteronomy 24:19). They are not to deprive a poor man of his cloak (Mark 10:50).

In the **Psalm**, a grateful king invokes God with a litany of titles. Such a king, supremely conscious of God's presence and protection, would have no problem in meeting the demands made by God in Exodus.

In **1 Thessalonians**, Paul continues his prayer of thanksgiving. Usually we look in the Acts of the Apostles (2:42–47) for descriptions of the life of early Christians but this passage is much earlier and more detailed. We note their joy, said to be a fruit of the Holy Spirit (Galatians 5:22). They experience affliction, a reference both to opposition from non-Christians and to the problems that befall those who embrace a new life, once the first novelty has waned. They become an example to others. The quality of their lives inspires others to copy them. The news has spread of their abandonment of idols for the living and true God whose Son is soon to return. Expectation of the return runs right through this, the earliest of Paul's letters. The word that keeps recurring is 'God': Paul's God is a real presence in their lives and affairs, not a distant abstraction.

The Jewish Law, a sample of which we have read in Exodus, is a complex affair and, by the time of Christ, the lengthy written sections we find in the Pentateuch, the first five books of the Bible, were complemented by extensive oral commentaries. The Pharisees, who in **Matthew** continue their encounters with Jesus in the Temple, believed that this oral law deserved the same respect as the written. It put a fence around the Law so that it would not be broken. One of them, a lawyer, questions Jesus directly about this Law.

The question he asks Jesus, about the greatest commandment of the Law, is a good one, because by this time it was reckoned that there were 613 of them. And Jesus is well qualified to answer it. He has not come to abolish the Law or the prophets (5:17). The reader has seen him reinterpreting the Law in the Sermon on the Mount (5:21–48). To the rich young man who wanted eternal life, he had repeated the demands of the Decalogue, adding to them the commandment of love of neighbour from Leviticus (19:18–19).

Jesus gives a prompt and personal reply, in which he combines two Old Testament texts. No teacher is known to have made such a combination before Jesus. He joins the commandment of Deuteronomy on the love of God (6:4–5) with another from Leviticus on the love of neighbour. Jesus knows it is impossible to separate the two. His own life is a demonstration of such love in practice. He lays down the practical consequences in his final discourse, in the parable of the sheep and the goats (25:31–46).

The early Church remembered this teaching, stressing love of neighbour in particular. In letters written years before Matthew, Paul summed up the whole law in a single commandment, 'You shall love your neighbour as yourself' (Galatians 5:14; Romans 13:8–10). In his parallel version, Luke inserted the parable of the good Samaritan in order to explain the meaning of the commandment to love your neighbour (Luke 10:29–37).

Sunday 31 A

Malachi 1:14–20; 2:8–10
Psalm 130
1 Thessalonians 2:7–9, 13
Matthew 23:1–12

Leaders Condemned

On their return to Jerusalem after the exile, Haggai and Zechariah provided Israel with leadership, the Temple was rebuilt and the survival and expansion of Judaism seemed assured. But, a century later, **Malachi** is addressing a miserable situation. The priests are failing to perform regular sacrifice and to offer solid teaching. God threatens to turn the blessings they pronounce into curses. The people are not only estranged from God but also divided. They have forgotten that they are the creation of a common Father.

The **Psalm** was sung by pilgrims on arrival at the Temple. The sentiments of humility and repentance it expresses are those that Malachi demanded from the corrupt priests of his time.

Paul in **1 Thessalonians** writes in self-defence about himself and his work. His converts are being told that he is no different from other wandering teachers common in the Greek world. Many of these were charlatans, only interested in self-promotion and financial advantage. So Paul is forced to clarify the nature of his work and its motivation. He cares for his converts like a mother; they are his brothers and sisters. Together they form a new family. He takes no money from them but works 'night and day', exercising his trade as a tent-maker in the workshop of Jason (Acts 17:5–6). As for his message, it comes from God and carries a power of its own for those ready to believe it. As he put it in his letter to the Romans, it is 'the power of God saving all who have faith' (Romans 1:16). Malachi would have found nothing to criticize in the activities of Paul.

Jesus concludes his Temple activity with a long denunciation of the scribes and the Pharisees, seemingly hard to reconcile with the Jesus found elsewhere who is 'gentle and humble in heart' (11:29). In **Matthew**, it is important to remember that the Pharisees represent not only the Pharisees of Jesus' time, but also the leaders of hostile synagogues at the time when the Gospel was written, and even members of Matthew's community whose Christianity has become tired and turned sour.

Our passage opens with apparent approval of the teaching, if not the example, of the Pharisees, who were earlier called 'blind guides' whose instructions should not be followed (15:14; 16:6). The disciples of Jesus have heard that they are to practise a deeper righteousness than that of the Pharisees (5:20). What is spoken must be endorsed by what is done (7:21; 21:29). The Pharisees are criticized on three grounds. First they have, through their teaching, distorted the Law, which should have been a delight, 'a lamp to my feet, a light on my path' (Psalm 119:105), easy and light like the yoke of Christ (11:30), into a burden (Acts 15:10). Secondly, they wear their phylacteries and tassels with their quotations of the Law in order to win admiration rather than provide edification (Deuteronomy 6:4–9; 11:13–21; Exodus 13:1–16). They are like the hypocrites who perform the traditional works of piety—prayer, almsgiving and fasting—for ostentation (6:1–18). Thirdly, they love titles that obscure the one Fatherhood of God and the one brotherhood and sisterhood of God's family.

This section reflects the egalitarianism of Matthew's Church. Though Peter has been given the keys of the Kingdom, (16:19), the greatest in it are the little ones (18:1–6). The only Father the disciples have in the Gospels is their Father in heaven (Mark 10:29–30; Malachi 1:6). The only greatness they are to seek is measured by the quality of their service (20:27). In all these respects, Jesus himself provides the example.

Sunday 32 A

Wisdom 6:12–16
Psalm 62:2–8
1 Thessalonians 4:13–18
Matthew 25:1–13

Parable of the Ten Maidens

Isis, the Egyptian goddess of culture, was an influential figure in the world around Israel. She may well have contributed to the portrait of Lady Wisdom in the **Wisdom** of Solomon and other wisdom books (Proverbs 8; Sirach 24). The exhortation in this passage to love Wisdom and to watch out for her prepares us for the bridesmaids who look out for the bridegroom.

The **Psalm** continues the theme of watching. The speaker's only ambition is to find God; in comparison, ordinary human needs such as food and sleep are secondary. Such a person will be ready when the bridegroom comes.

The **Thessalonians** are worried. They believed in the imminent return of Christ, but what of those who had already died? Will they miss out on salvation? The first point in Paul's answer is to remind his converts of the death and resurrection of Christ. If Christ rose, the Christian dead will rise, too. God will bring them to himself in a new exodus. To express this, he uses what is, for us, strange apocalyptic language, about archangels and trumpets, and clouds transporting the faithful to heaven. These traditional descriptions of God's power are not to be taken literally; they are poetic expressions designed to assure the Thessalonians that, whether they are alive or dead, they will be 'with the Lord for ever'. Like the penitent thief in Luke's Gospel, they will be with Christ in paradise (Luke 23:43). They can comfort one another with this knowledge. Let them meanwhile be like those looking for wisdom and those awaiting the bridegroom. To this day, Paul's words are regularly read to bring consolation at funeral Masses.

Over the next three Sundays, we hear the final section of the Eschatological Discourse of **Matthew**, which deals with the period between the departure of Christ through his death and resurrection, and his return in glory at the end of time. Such farewell speeches are common in scripture. They were spoken by leaders of God's people to prepare their followers for the time when, because of impending death, those followers would no longer enjoy their company. Thus Jacob spoke to his sons (Genesis 49), Moses to the people of Israel (Deuteronomy 33), David to Solomon (1 Kings 2) and, in the New Testament, Paul addressed the elders of Ephesus (Acts 20: 18–35). The difference between these speakers and Christ is that none of them expected to return.

Matthew adds three parables to the description of the coming of the Son of Man he found in Mark (13: 24–36). These all deal with the topic of delay. Early Christians expected a swift return of Christ (1 Thessalonians 4: 13–18; 2 Peter 3: 4). The first parable is that of the ten maidens, which we read today. It takes up themes familiar in this Gospel. The bridegroom represents the returning Christ. Jesus had earlier called himself the bridegroom who would be taken away, and his disciples the bridegroom's attendants (9: 15). The reader would recognise the scriptural imagery of God being married to his people (Jeremiah 2: 2). The maidens who cope with the delay by buying sufficient oil represent Christians who practise a life of responsible discipleship as they wait. The ones who allow their lamps to run out portray those who do not value the time allowed them. Their plea to the bridegroom on his arrival is identical to the complaint of those rejected at the end of the Sermon on the Mount. They too cried out, 'Lord, Lord' (7: 21). The idleness and lack of preparation condemned in this parable earn the same rejection as the foul behaviour of the steward described in the preceding passage (24: 49–51). Christian life demands activity, alertness and preparedness (Romans 13: 11–14; 2 Thessalonians 3: 10–11).

Sunday 33 A

Proverbs 31:10–13, 19–20, 30–31
Psalm 127:1–5
1 Thessalonians 5:1–6
Matthew 25:14–30

Parable of the Talents

The woman described in **Proverbs** may be compared to the Lady Wisdom whom we met last week (Wisdom 6:12). She is down to earth, the ideal mother of a family, a perfect wife, strong, competent, responsible. Does this mean that those who accept Wisdom will exercise the qualities of such a woman? Or is she simply a model of the activity, concern and reliability looked for in today's Gospel?

A temple official promises prosperity to recently arrived pilgrims in the **Psalm**. This is defined in terms of a large family and material abundance. The simple theology treats earthly success as a reward for virtuous living. The Book of Job gives us another such approach.

Paul turns to another question about the end in **1 Thessalonians**, one perhaps brought to him by Timothy after his visit (3:2). When would the Parousia, the 'Day of the Lord', take place? He identifies what the prophets called the 'Day of the Lord' (Amos 5:18; Zephaniah 1:7) with the second coming of Jesus. His reply parallels the saying of Jesus in Matthew about a thief in the night (24:43–44). It also reminds us of his words in Mark: 'as for that day or hour, nobody knows it, neither the angels of heaven, nor the Son; no one but the Father' (Mark 13:32). For those who reject Christ, the day will bring destruction, but for believers it will bring salvation. They already share in the divine qualities of light and brightness that will then be revealed (2 Corinthians 3:18). They are already children of light. As such, they are to shine as lights in the world (Philippians 2:15). Paul echoes the words of Jesus in the Sermon on the Mount, 'You are the light of the world' (Matthew 5:14).

The parable from **Matthew** is his third about Christian life between Jesus' resurrection and his return. Jesus speaks in it of a man going abroad who gives various numbers of talents to his servants. 'Talent' has not yet acquired its meaning of personal ability, but refers to the amount of money a labourer would earn in fifteen years (Matthew 18:24). Three servants are given different sums according to their ability. Two trade with the money and make as much again, while the third hides his and makes nothing. If the parable stopped here, we could admire the care shown for property. There is no irresponsible behaviour here, like that of the servant who 'sets about beating his fellow servants and eating and drinking with drunkards' (24:49).

The story continues with a shock for the reader. The servant who was so prudent in keeping his talent safe is condemned as wicked and lazy. A first reaction might be that he is being treated unfairly by his master, like the labourers in the vineyard who worked all day in the heat (20:1–16). His excuse corrects this first impression when we learn how unfair he is to his master. He accuses him of being a hard man, reaping where he has not sown. How could a hard man have given out such enormous sums of money at such a risk? Like the labourers in the vineyard and the steward who refused to forgive his debtor (18:23–35), here is another character who thought he knew what God was like and how God ought to act.

The two others are rewarded, because, entrusted with property, they use it to earn more. They put their resources to work, like the disciples with the loaves and the fishes (14:16–17). This is how Christians are to spend the time of waiting. This story of trading with the talents has nothing to do with business practice or commerce. These are not Matthaean interests. The parable teaches us to take the ethical and religious message of this Gospel seriously, which urges its hearers to do the will of the Father (7:21), to bear fruit in the life of the Kingdom (13:23), to seek the deeper righteousness (5:20).

Christ the King A

Ezekiel 34:11–12, 15–17
Psalm 22:1–3, 5–6
1 Corinthians 15:20–26, 28
Matthew 25:31–46

The Judgment of the Nations

Before Jerusalem fell in 585 BC, **Ezekiel** warned about the catastrophe to come (33:7), but afterwards he became a prophet of restoration. He blamed the disaster on the wickedness and incompetence of the people's rulers rather than the sin of the people. In future, God promises that he will himself be their shepherd and king (Isaiah 40:11). He will assure good government and, as a wise judge, separate the good sheep from the bad, the rams from the he-goats.

God is praised as shepherd and ruler in the **Psalm**. Ezekiel's promise is a reality. God is source of rest and food for the pilgrim journeying through life to the final destination, the house of God.

In **1 Corinthians**, in his chapter on the resurrection, Paul modifies the thought of his time, which conceived of world history as divided into two ages, this age and the age to come. For Paul, there is now a third age, that between the resurrection of Christ and his return in glory. In this age, Christ reigns. He has won this status through his death and resurrection, when he defeated the powers of sin and death, but it is only when, in the words of the Psalm (8:6), he has put all such enemies 'under his feet', that he will hand over his Kingdom to his Father. This will constitute his final victory, which, like the resurrection, does not belong to him alone, but to all who are with him. Long ago, Israel was called a 'kingdom of priests' (Exodus 19:6), a description applied to the Church in 1 Peter (2:9). This feast of Christ the King reminds us of our royal status as the People of God.

The final discourse of Jesus in **Matthew** concludes with a picture of the Last Judgment. Here we find the most vivid appeal in the Gospels for an active, caring Christianity. In the Sermon on the Mount, Jesus demanded of his disciples the greater righteousness (5:20). Here Jesus calls righteous those who have recognised him in the hungry, the thirsty, the stranger, the imprisoned, the naked, the sick. These he identifies as the 'least of these brothers of mine'.

We learn first about Jesus himself. No longer speaking as the one who is 'gentle and humble in heart' (11:29), he is the Son of Man who judges, the one to whom all authority on earth and in heaven has been given (28:19; Daniel 7:13). He speaks as king, the title given him at the beginning by the magi (2:2) and at the cross by his enemies (27:29, 37, 42). Like Ezekiel's shepherd, he separates the sheep from the goats (Ezekiel 34:17). He calls God his Father (11:26; 26:39). He is addressed as 'Lord', the title that reflects his dignity as the Exalted One (8:25; Philippians 2:11). Nowhere else do we learn that his identity as Emmanuel, 'God-is-with-us' (1:23; 18:20; 28:20) is exercised in his presence in the least of the brethren.

Secondly, we learn about discipleship. His discourses began with the Beatitudes (5:3–10) and end with these words on the Last Judgment. They are the climax of his final teaching on discipleship, which has stressed the vigilance of the bridesmaids (25:1–13) and the activity and opportunism of those who doubled their talents (25:14–30).

Thirdly, we learn about Christian ethics. The disciple is to go beyond even the humane provisions of the Law (Exodus 22), is not to neglect 'the weightier matters of the law—justice, mercy, good faith' (23:23). In Luke, Jesus explained the commandment to love the neighbour by the parable of the Good Samaritan (Luke 10:25–37); in Matthew, he interprets this great commandment (22:39) in terms of his vision of the End.

YEAR B
THE YEAR OF MARK

MARK MAY BE REGARDED as the elder brother among the evangelists. His is the shortest of the Gospels, just 16 chapters with 661 verses but, paradoxically, he often gives the longest accounts of incidents in the life of Jesus. His Jesus speaks of the mystery of the kingdom of God (Mark 4: 11). But he himself is the real mystery of the Gospel. The one whose ministry begins with such success, ends it with the cry, 'My God, my God, why have you forsaken me?' (Mark 15: 34). The story that begins with the confident announcement of good news in the first verse (Mark 1: 1) concludes with the fear of the women expressed in the last verse (Mark 16: 8). The disciples who responded to their initial call with such generosity (Mark 1: 16–20; 3: 13–19) turn out to have ears that do not hear and eyes that do not see (Mark 8: 14–21). Their leader's last word is to deny with an oath that he even knew Jesus (Mark 14: 71). But the reader can pray with the father of the epileptic boy, 'I believe; help my unbelief' (Mark 9: 24), may respond with Bartimaeus, 'Rabbuni, let me see again' (Mark 10: 51), and confess with the centurion at the foot of the cross, 'Truly this man was the Son of God' (Mark 15: 39). Full of paradox and mystery, those who know Mark have good reasons for calling it not only the oldest of the Gospels but the best.*

* Edmonds, *Rediscover Jesus*, 24.

Year B
The Year of Mark

THE SUNDAYS OF ADVENT*

*The **First Readings**, taken from the Old Testament, are described as 'prophecies about the messiah and the messianic age, especially from Isaiah'. They have therefore an importance of their own apart from the gospel readings.*

*The **Second Readings** 'from an apostle serve as exhortations and proclamations in keeping with the various themes of Advent'. In this Year B, we have three readings from different letters of Paul and one from the second letter of Peter.*

*The **Responsorial Psalm** is designed to help with the understanding of the First Reading, to deepen some significant theme, to clarify its message.*

*In the **Gospel Readings** we reflect on the three comings of Christ: at the end of time, in his public ministry, in his birth. The evangelist selected is the one whom we will hear for the remainder of the year.*

THE CHRISTMAS SEASON

The readings for Christmas and Epiphany are taken 'from the Roman tradition'. On other days, we learn by means of the readings about Jesus' childhood, the virtues of family life, the mystery of the Incarnation, the Virgin Mother of God and the mystery of the Baptism of Jesus.

* Quotations from 'General Introduction', *Roman Missal*, nn. 93–95.

Advent I B

Isaiah 63:16–17; 64:1, 3–8
Psalm 79:2–3, 15–16, 18–19
1 Corinthians 1:3–9
Mark 13:33–37

The Final Day

On their return from exile, the people of Israel found their land and city in a wretched condition. The lamentation that we read in **Isaiah** mirrors this situation. Having lived without God, they now, in a spirit of repentance, acknowledge God as their Father and Redeemer. He is the potter who has formed the clay that is his people (Jeremiah 18: 1–12); let him intervene and rescue them as he had done long ago in the events of the Exodus and Sinai (Exodus 15:4–10; 2 Samuel 22:15).

The **Psalm**, a prayer for restoration, asks God to visit his people. Certainly he is a God of majesty, enthroned between the cherubim (Exodus 25:22), but he is still Israel's shepherd and vinedresser. In the past they have forsaken him, but now they implore him to return and tend his vineyard.

Paul begins 1 **Corinthians** by giving thanks for the past and praying for the future. His converts have responded well to the gospel that he preached, but they still need the grace of Christ. He writes ironically. He compliments them on their progress in word and knowledge but, in the rest of the letter, he corrects their misunderstandings of what they have heard and of what they know. They lack the dispositions of humility and repentance of Isaiah and the Psalmist, which they need to meet Christ on his return. They may fall short of their destiny of fellowship with Christ. The coming of Christ will fulfil the expectations of God's intervention looked for in ages past. Paul no longer looks forward to the 'Day of the Lord' (Amos 5:18) but to the 'day of our Lord Jesus Christ'.

Beginning a new liturgical year, we start with a fresh Gospel, that of **Mark**. This year, we are invited to see Christ through Mark's eyes, as we explore with him the meaning of discipleship and his understanding of Christianity. His readers were probably a group of persecuted Christians in Rome some thirty years after the death and resurrection of Christ.

We begin our reading of Mark with the final words of Jesus to his disciples before the passion story, which conclude his farewell discourse. We have read a much fuller version of this discourse over the last few Sundays in Matthew. In reply to a question from the four disciples whom he called first (1:16–20), he has been speaking of the coming destruction of Jerusalem and the Temple (which took place a few years after Mark wrote, in the year 70), and the fulfilment of Daniel's prophecy of the coming of the Son of Man (Daniel 7:13).

In contrast to other predictions of the Final Day, then and since, no date is given. Not only do the hearers not know it; it is unknown even to the Son (13:32). The message to the disciples, and their successors, is a simple one. They are to think of themselves as servants of a householder who has gone abroad and is to return at some unknown time. Each has been given work to do. They are to get on with it. The person at the door must keep awake. This expression, 'keep awake', is repeated four times in the short passage.

Matthew expanded the message with his three parables of delay (24:45–25:30). Likewise Paul, in Romans and elsewhere, called for responsible and sober living (Romans 13:11–14; 2 Thessalonians 3:10). The precision of the temporal references at the end of our passage ('evening, midnight, cockcrow, dawn') is unusual. But each corresponds to an event in Mark's account of the passion of Jesus (14:17, 41, 71; 15:1). Is Mark telling his readers, as they watch and work, to call to mind the sufferings of Jesus on their behalf when he gave his life as a ransom for many (10:45)?

Advent 2 B

Isaiah 40:1–5, 9–11
Psalm 84:9–14
2 Peter 3:8–14
Mark 1:1–8

John in the Desert

At his inaugural vision in the Temple (6:1–13), **Isaiah** learnt of the punishment in store for a people that refused to change its ways. In contrast, the opening of Deutero-Isaiah, which we hear today, brings comfort and consolation for a nation weary of suffering. A message comes from God's throne room. Not only is the time of punishment over, but God will again lead his people in a new Exodus (Exodus 15:13–18). Jerusalem hears the good news (the *gospel*), that God will fight for it as a warrior and as take care of it as a shepherd.

A temple prophet announces God's intentions in the **Psalm**. He is a God of peace, mercy, faithfulness and justice, who provides fruitful land. In the past, he revealed himself in the Exodus (Exodus 34:6–7); he will again rescue Israel, leading them into peace.

When **2 Peter** was written, probably the last of the New Testament books, hostile, false teachers were scoffing because the second coming of Christ had not arrived (1 Thessalonians 1:10). The author explains the delay in two ways. First, he proves from a Psalm that God's concept of time differs from ours (Psalm 90:4). Secondly, he recalls the prophetic teaching that the merciful God gives time for repentance (Ezekiel 18:23). Christian faith looks to the future; the second coming has not been cancelled. He confirms the teaching of Jesus in the Gospel (Matthew 24:43), repeated by Paul (1 Thessalonians 5:4), that Christ would come like a thief in the night. He avoids allowing Christianity to cut itself off from its Jewish roots by using poetic terms from Jewish apocalyptic. Meanwhile, while we wait, we are to live lives that please God (Romans 13:11–14).

Mark calls his work the good news, or *gospel*. The biblical background of this word takes us back to the preaching of Deutero-Isaiah, who announced that God would comfort his people (Isaiah 40:1). He would deliver them from their sufferings in a new Exodus (Isaiah 40:9; 41:27). In the secular world, the word meant good tidings, as of the birth of an heir to the ruler. The story of Jesus is good news for a suffering Christian community in Rome. Mark lets his reader into the secret about Jesus from the beginning: he is the Christ and the Son of God. Peter would acknowledge Jesus as the Christ at Caesarea Philippi (8:29) and the pagan centurion would accept him as Son of God after his death (15:39). Mark says nothing about the infancy of Jesus. He follows an earlier tradition, reflected in Peter's speech to Cornelius (Acts 10:37), of beginning the story of Jesus with the Baptist.

The Baptist and his activity do not happen by chance. His coming is the result of God's initiative, an initiative hidden in Old Testament writings. So Mark begins his story of the Baptist with a quotation derived from Isaiah (40:3), Malachi (3:1) and Exodus (23:20). The Baptist is the messenger of Malachi, the voice of Isaiah, the angel of Exodus. He show he is a prophet by wearing the clothing of Elijah (2 Kings 1:8).

Mark tells us least of the evangelists about what the Baptist did. He preaches repentance and announces the coming of one more powerful than he who will baptize with the Holy Spirit. His preaching causes all Judaea and Jerusalem to accept baptism as a symbol of their repentance. Pious Israelites would consider baptism as appropriate for foreigners, but not for themselves. Jesus, too, would preach repentance (1:15). but crowds would come to him from every corner of the Holy Land (3:7–8). Eventually, the Baptist would die alone, the victim of an unjust ruler (6:14–29). In his death, as in his life, the Baptist was the forerunner of Jesus. For Mark, this was his significance.

Advent 3 B

Isaiah 61:1–2, 10–11
Luke 1:46–50, 53–54
1 Thessalonians 5:16–24
John 1:6–8, 19–28

The Witness of the Baptist

Solomon was anointed king (1 Kings 1:39); Aaron was anointed priest (Exodus 29:7). The prophet of Trito-**Isaiah** announces that he too has been anointed as he proclaims his mission to the poor. The poor in the Bible are sometimes the lazy (Proverbs 13:18), but usually they are victims of social factors (Amos 8:4). God hears the cries of the poor (Psalm 12:5), especially in delivering his people from Egypt (Exodus 2:23–24). Luke tells us that these words of Isaiah were Jesus' first public announcement (4:18). Our passage concludes with thanksgiving; new life from God is like the new life that nature enjoys after winter.

Verses from the Magnificat of Mary from **Luke** take the place of the Psalm. Mary speaks on behalf of the *anawim*, the poor who know that their salvation comes from God. She praises God for his care for the poor in general and his mercy to herself in particular.

Mary's joy, prayer and gratitude in her canticle are the will of God for all, writes Paul to the **Thessalonians**. He wants a community, already an example to all believers (1:7), to advance ever further in its quality of life. A remark about the Spirit and prophecy anticipates his teaching in 1 Corinthians (12–14). A God of peace calls them to a life that is complete and holy (1 Thessalonians 4:4). Meanwhile, they are to wait for the Christ's coming, as persons totally dedicated in body, soul and spirit. These are not descriptions of the different principles in a person, but the person in its totality. Worship of God involves the whole being (Romans 12:1).

Last week, we heard in Mark how John the Baptist preached a baptism of repentance and behaved as forerunner of the one to come. **John** gives us another view of the Baptist. In the trial of Jesus that extends throughout this Gospel, the Baptist's role is simply that of witness to the Word (1:1). He claims no importance for himself. He is the voice foretold by Isaiah. While the Word will increase, he himself will decrease (John 3:30). And even in our passage his answers grow shorter and shorter.

This Gospel, unlike Mark, gives no account of all Jerusalem flocking to John. Rather, the authorities send priests and Levites to enquire about his identity. Their questions show us the type of deliverer they expect. God cannot allow his people to suffer the domination of Roman power indefinitely.

They enquire first whether John is the Christ. This word means 'anointed', used in Israel for kings such as Solomon and priests such as Aaron. The most important 'Christ' was David himself, so the question means *Are you the new King David who is coming, in fulfilment of the prophecy of Nathan* (2 Samuel 7)? Secondly, they ask him whether he is Elijah. Elijah was the great prophet who, according to tradition, had not died but had been taken directly to heaven (2 Kings 2:11). Thirdly, is the Baptist the prophet? Moses had spoken of a prophet like himself who would come in the future (Deuteronomy 18:15). So we learn from these questions of the common expectation of a figure such as David, Elijah or Moses to deliver Israel from the rule of the unclean. All this prepares us for the portrayal of Jesus in John's Gospel. The identity of Jesus goes beyond all these categories. For Peter, he is the Holy One of God (6:69), for Martha, the messiah, the Son of God who is coming into the world (11:27), for Thomas, 'My Lord and my God' (20:28). For the evangelist, he is equal to God himself and bears the divine name, *I am* (Exodus 3:14; John 8:58; 18:5).

Advent 4 B

2 Samuel 7:1–5, 8–12, 14–16
Psalm 88:2–5, 27, 29
Romans 16:25–27
Luke 1:26–38

The Annunciation to Mary

Once David is established in Jerusalem, he remembers that God had no Temple for his dwelling. He still lives in the Ark of the Covenant, housed in a tent (**2 Samuel** 6:17). David decides to build God a Temple. He sends for the prophet Nathan, who encourages him in the project. But then Nathan receives a message: God is not interested in such a house, but he promises David to build him a house instead, by which he means a dynasty. This will last for ever as a symbol of God's love for Israel. The apparent disappearance of David's dynasty explains the New Testament emphasis on Christ being a son of David (Matthew 1:20; Romans 1:3).

The Psalmist meditates on the covenant qualities of God, especially as revealed in the promises made to David through Nathan. Peter quotes this **Psalm** at pentecost (Acts 2:30) as does Paul in Antioch (Acts 13:22).

Paul concludes **Romans** with a hymn of praise to God, which recalls major themes of the letter. In it he has proclaimed his gospel (1:16) of how the righteousness of God (1:17) has brought liberation to a humanity trapped in the chains of sin and death (3:21–26; 7:24). God has not ignored the past, but has brought the writings of the prophets to fulfilment (1:2). (Here he would include the prophecy of Nathan.) Paul's gospel is to bring about the obedience of faith among all the nations (1:5). Previously he had extolled the wisdom of God (11:33); now he writes for the first time of the wise God whom he praises for his glory, the glory that the reader knows is the destiny of those who believe in Christ (8:30).

Luke devotes his first chapter to events that precede the birth of Jesus. Gabriel, the angel of the end times (Daniel 8:16), appears to Mary. The scene follows the pattern of the birth announcements we read in the Old Testament as, for example, that of Isaac (Genesis 17:16–21) or of Samson (Judges 13:3–7). The announcement of John the Baptist's birth to Zechariah is of the same type, and is to be contrasted with the annunciation to Mary (Luke 1:5–15).

Luke's primary interest is to inform us about the child to be born. He is to be great; he will be called what God himself was called in the Psalms (47:2; 135:5). He will be of the house of David, fulfilling the prophecy of Nathan (2 Samuel 7:9–16). He will also be the Son of God. The descriptions of him given by Gabriel anticipate what would be proclaimed about the Risen Jesus in the apostolic preaching (Romans 1:3; Acts 13:33). The child will be born through the direct intervention of God. The Holy Spirit, God's creative power (Genesis 1:2), will come upon Mary. The birth of this child will mean a new beginning for the world, a new creation.

Luke is also interested in Mary. On a human level, there seems no reason why God should choose such an obscure, unsuspecting person for such a destiny. But through the grace of God, she is highly favoured. In turn, she shows herself fully responsive to the plan of salvation that God wants to work out in partnership with her. Her 'let it be with me according to your word' anticipates the later saying of Jesus: 'My mother and my brothers are those who hear the word of God and do it' (Luke 8:21). On her first appearance in the gospel story, Mary shows herself a perfect Christian disciple as she prepares for the birth of her son. She continued this role in her final appearance in Luke, when, with the Eleven and the brothers of Jesus, she waited and prayed for the outpouring of the Holy Spirit at pentecost and the birth of the Church (Acts 1:14).

Holy Family B

Genesis 15:1–6; 21:1–3
Psalm 104:1–6, 8–9
Hebrews 11:8, 11–12, 17–19
Luke 2:22–40

The Presentation in the Temple

The first family histories in the Bible are the stories of the patriarchs. And the first and most important of these is Abraham. At his call, God promised him family and land (**Genesis** 12:1). But he was old and his wife Sarah beyond the age of child-bearing. How could one who was childless become the father of many nations? God merely confirms his promise: let him look at the stars in the sky; such will be the number of his descendants. Abraham believes and is justified. According to Paul, the quality of Abraham's faith made him the father of all believers (Romans 4:11).

The **Psalm** is a call to thanksgiving and belief that the God who called Abraham and gave him Isaac remains faithful to his promises. Despite its own past infidelity, Israel can always call on him and hope to be heard.

The author of **Hebrews** is writing to Christians in crisis. He mingles lofty doctrine with practical warnings and exhortations. He appeals to the example of the great ancestors of Israel. They found themselves in situations where human resources were insufficient. But God remembered them and these blessings were proof of realities that we cannot see. Abraham and Sarah could only rely on God. Though the outcome seemed impossible, Abraham obeyed God's call (Genesis 12:4). Sarah, though past the age of child-bearing, believed in the power of God to give her a child (Genesis 21:2). Although Isaac was his only son and his only hope for the fulfilment of God's promise, Abraham was still prepared to sacrifice him if God commanded it (Genesis 22:3).

We find few stories about the infancy of Jesus in the canonical Gospels. **Luke**'s account of the presentation in the Temple is one. In obedience to the Law, Jesus' parents take him to the Temple, either for the purification of Mary (Leviticus 12:2–8) or for the presentation of Jesus (Exodus 13:1–2). An action inspired by a desire to fulfil the requirements of God's Law concludes with a double manifestation of his prophetic Spirit.

In the Temple, Mary and Joseph meet two aged Israelites, representatives of the *anawim*, the poor of Israel who trust in God alone. Their sanctity and age remind us of Abraham and Sarah (Genesis 17). The Spirit prompts Simeon to prophesy about the future of the child, of Israel and of Mary herself. In the language of Deutero-Isaiah (46:13; 52:10), he declares that the child personifies the salvation God intends for all the nations. For Israel, his message mixes comfort and lament, since, though this child will bring about the 'rising of many', it will be a sign of contradiction and rejection for others. Jesus' first preaching in Nazareth (4:16–30), and indeed the rest of Luke's Gospel and Acts, demonstrates the truth of this prophecy. As for Mary herself, Simeon sees how in the future a sword will pierce her heart. Her role in the life of Jesus was not only that of mother but of follower. As a disciple, much would happen to her that she would not understand—such as the next incident in the Gospel, when her child was lost in Jerusalem and she failed to grasp what his explanation meant (2:41–50).

Often in Luke, a story about a man is followed by another about a woman (15:4–10). Once Simeon has uttered his prophecy, an aged widow and prophetess, Anna, meets Jesus. She too typifies Luke's respect for the Old Testament and the piety of old Israel. But she is also a link between the old and the new. Like a good Lucan Christian, she prays, praises God and speaks of Jesus and the deliverance of Israel. She is the first of the devout widows in Luke (18:3; Acts 9:36).

Baptism of the Lord B (Sunday I B)

Isaiah 55:1–11
Isaiah 12:2–6
1 John 5:1–9
Mark 1:6–11

Jesus the Beloved Son

Last week (*see Epiphany Year A*), **Isaiah** looked to the rebuilding of a city and the Psalmist to the future coming of a king; this week, Deutero-Isaiah writes of the restoration of the nation after its exile in a foreign land. 'Come to the waters', it is told, and you will have all the gifts that God's Wisdom offers in her banquet (Proverbs 9:1–6). The favours once promised in covenant to David (2 Samuel 7:25) are offered to a whole people. All this will come about, once wickedness is abandoned and God's ways are adopted. If God has spoken, nothing can cancel his decree, just as nothing can wipe away the effects of rain on a thirsty land.

A hymn from **Isaiah** replaces the Psalm. It, too, is concerned with water. As in every good prayer, we praise God for the past and look with confidence to the future. God is not a figure far away in heaven (as we might understand from Isaiah 6:1–4), but a Saviour in the midst of his people. He is the well from which saving water can be drawn.

In **1 John**, we again read of water. Some have left the Johannine community because they cannot accept the humanity of Christ (2:19). For them, he was the Son of God who had come down directly from the Father. In reply, our author insists that it was Jesus, the man from Nazareth, who was Son of God. He came by water; he was one with the people of God in accepting baptism in the waters of the Jordan. But he came by blood too; he really died as Lamb of God (John 1:29), a sacrifice on the cross to liberate us and make us children of God. This is how he overcame the world and, through believing in him, we overcome the world too.

Jesus came to the water (Isaiah 55:1) as a result of the preaching of John the Baptist. In his description of the Baptist, **Mark** refers to his dress, his activity and his words. His dress puts him in the line of desert prophets such as Elijah (2 Kings 1:8). His activity of baptism for the remission of sins associates him with other preachers of the time, such as those at Qumran, who called for purification by water as a sign of cleansing from sin. His words of proclamation point to the powerful one who is coming after him, whose baptism will be one of judgment (Malachi 3:1).

That this powerful one should present himself for baptism was a source of embarrassment for the early Church. Why should Jesus come for a baptism for the remission of sins? A conversation between Jesus and John is added in Matthew to explain (3:14–15). Luke subordinated the baptism to the descent of the Holy Spirit (3:21–22) and John does not mention it at all directly (1:32). Acts calls it his anointing (10:38).

This is the first of many paradoxes in Mark's Gospel, that the one who was 'to give his life as a ransom for many' (10:45), should accept baptism. Certainly he did not need it for himself. There is no suggestion in Mark, or anywhere in the New Testament tradition, that Jesus was a sinner (2 Corinthians 5:21; Hebrews 4:15; John 8:46). His acceptance of baptism shows his willingness to identify with the people of God who need to 'seek the Lord' (Isaiah 55:6). With him, a sinful people pass through the Jordan a second time (Joshua 3:14–17) before entering a new promised land, the Kingdom that Jesus is to preach (Mark 1:15). The heavens, closed for so long, open again (Isaiah 64:1). The Spirit, which had swept over the earth at creation (Genesis 1:2), appears once more, in the shape of a dove. And God speaks, identifying Jesus as his Son, with words that the temple priest used anointing a new king (Psalm 2:7), and that God spoke about his Servant (Isaiah 42:1), words which would not 'return to me empty' (Isaiah 55:11).

Year B
The Year of Mark

THE SUNDAYS OF LENT*

The ***First Readings*** *take us through the 'history of salvation':*

Sunday 1	*The covenant with Noah*	*Genesis 9:8–15*
Sunday 2	*Abraham and Isaac*	*Genesis 22:1–2, 9–13, 15–18*
Sunday 3	*Moses and the Decalogue*	*Exodus 20:1–17*
Sunday 4	*The exile*	*2 Chronicles 36:14–16, 19–23*
Sunday 5	*Jeremiah and the new covenant*	*Jeremiah 31:31–34*
Passion Sunday	*The Suffering Servant of Isaiah*	*Isaiah 50:4–7*

Second Readings: *'The reading from the letters of the apostles have been selected to fit the gospel and the Old Testament readings, and, to the extent possible, to provide a connection between them'.*

Sunday 1	*Noah and the Ark*	*1 Peter 3:18–22*
Sunday 2	*God and his Son*	*Romans 8:31–34*
Sunday 3	*The folly of the cross*	*1 Corinthians 1:22–25*
Sunday 4	*God's work of art*	*Ephesians 2:4–10*
Sunday 5	*The prayer of Jesus*	*Hebrews 5:7–9*
Passion Sunday	*Jesus humbled and exalted*	*Philippians 2:6–11*

The ***Responsorial Psalms*** *are designed to help with the understanding of the First Reading, to deepen some significant theme, to clarify its message.*

The ***Gospel Readings*** *of* ***Sundays 1 and 2*** *are always about the temptations and transfiguration of Jesus, this year according to Mark.* ***Sundays 3 to 5*** *are texts from John: the cleansing of the Temple (John 2), Jesus and Nicodemus (John 3), the coming of the Greeks (John 12). On Passion Sunday (****Sunday 6****), the passion story according to Mark is read.*

[On Sundays 3 to 5, the Gospels of year A may be repeated: the Samaritan woman (John 4), the man born blind (John 9) and the raising of Lazarus (John 11). If not, they should be read during the week.]

* Quotations from 'General Introduction', *Roman Missal*, nn. 97, 100.

EASTER AND THE SUNDAYS AFTER EASTER

The **First Readings** *are always from the Acts of the Apostles, about 'the life, witness and growth of the primitive Church'. Every year, we hear on Easter Sunday about the preaching of Peter to Cornelius, on Ascension Day the story of the Ascension and on Pentecost Day the descent of the Holy Spirit. We learn about the life of the early Christians in Jerusalem. In this Year B, we hear other samples of Peter's preaching, about the call of Paul and about Peter's acceptance of Cornelius into the Christian community.*

The **Second Readings** *form, a semi-continuous reading of the First Letter of John, which is an appropriate accompaniment to the readings of the Gospel of John at this period. This letter fits 'especially well with the spirit of joyous faith and sure hope proper to this season'.*

The **Responsorial Psalms** *are designed to help with the understanding of the First Reading, to deepen some significant theme, to clarify its message.*

The **Gospel Readings** *are always the same on* **Sundays 1 and 2***: they are taken from John and tells of the three persons at the tomb on Easter Day and the story of Thomas on the second Sunday.* **Sunday 3** *introduces Luke's account of the appearance of the Risen Lord to the disciples in Jerusalem.* **Sunday 4** *always provides a passage from John 10, the shepherd chapter.* **Sundays 5, 6 and 7** *provide extracts from the Last Supper discourse in John—on the vine and the branches, on mutual love and an passage from the final prayer of Jesus to the Father.*

[Ascension Day and Body and Blood of Christ are often celebrated on the Sunday following rather than the traditional Thursday; hence they are included here.]

Lent I B

Genesis 9:8–15
Psalm 24:4–9
1 Peter 3:18–22
Mark 1:12–15

In the Desert with Satan

On this Sunday each year, we hear a key passage from the book of **Genesis**. This year, the topic is Noah and the flood story. This concludes with a new start for humanity. Noah is a second Adam. Thanks to his obedience, which contrasts with the disobedience of the first Adam (Genesis 3), the world survives a crisis of sin. God binds himself to Noah by a covenant which foreshadows the promises he will make to Abraham (Genesis 12: 1–3) As a sign of this covenant and of his commitment never to destroy creation by flood again, he causes the rainbow to appear. According to Revelation, a rainbow still encircles the throne of God (4:3).

The **Psalm**, the prayer of a person committed to God, acknowledges God's mercy in forgiving sins and the grace of God that makes a good life possible. It would have been a good prayer for Noah to pray during the flood and for Jesus during his temptations.

The readers of 1 **Peter**, living in a hostile world, poor and persecuted, need encouragement. The author first reminds them how Christ, though innocent, had suffered and died—and been raised to life again. He then adds that he 'made a proclamation to the spirits in prison'. These spirits may have been the rebellious angels who provoked the wickedness that led to the flood (Genesis 6: 1–2). Noah was saved, not by his ark, but by the flood waters themselves, prefiguring the waters of baptism that save the Christian. Through baptism, Christians share in the victory of Christ over every power in the universe, including those now persecuting the readers. What power can these have, compared with Christ, in glory at the right hand of God?

Mark's version of the temptation of Jesus is brief, but it should be interpreted as it is, without reference to the fuller accounts found elsewhere. The temptation immediately follows the baptism. The Spirit that had descended on Jesus (1: 10), drives him into the desert. The temptations are somehow, therefore, part of God's salvific plan. Long before, God gave permission for Satan to test Job (1: 12). The desert, as the place of temptation, has many associations in the Old Testament. In the desert God was betrothed to his people (Hosea 2: 16); there Israel proved unfaithful (Exodus 15:24), there Moses and Elijah each spent forty days and forty nights (Exodus 34: 28; 1 Kings 19: 8). In the Old Testament, Satan was a member of God's court, a sort of prosecutor (Job 1–2; Zechariah 3: 1–2), but in the New Testament he is the embodiment of evil, identified with the serpent that tempted Eve in Genesis (Revelation 20: 2).

Mark relates how Jesus is among the wild beasts and the angels look after him. He knows, as Paul knows, that God will never allow us to be tempted beyond our strength (1 Corinthians 10: 13). He remembers the Psalmist who wrote that God would protect his own, that 'he will put you in his angels' charge to guard you wherever you go', so that 'you will tread on lion and adder' (Psalm 91: 11–13). He recalls the prophecy of Isaiah about the day when the wolf would live with the lamb (11:6). He may have been aware of the old tradition that while Adam lived in Paradise the angels brought him his food.

In Jesus' first clash with his opponents, the scribes from Jerusalem complained that 'it is through the prince of devils that he casts devils out'. Jesus replied, 'no one can make his way into a strong man's house and burgle his property unless he has tied up the strong man first' (Mark 3:22–27). This was the result of Jesus' meeting Satan in the desert and, by this means, he made it possible for his hearers to repent and believe in the gospel when he began his ministry.

Lent 2 B

Genesis 22:1–2, 9–13, 15–18
Psalm 115:10, 15–19
Romans 8:31–34
Mark 9:2–10

Transfigured on the Mountain

Last week we heard of the temptation of Jesus by Satan; this week, in **Genesis**, we hear of the testing of Abraham by God. Every year on this day, we hear a biblical passage about Abraham. God promised Abraham land and many descendants (13:14–16). But now God demands that Abraham sacrifice his son. Abraham's faith in God is so firm that he does not hesitate. He obeys, certain that God will remain faithful to his promise. He assures his servants, 'we will ... come back to you' (22:5). He is right. At the last moment, God provides a substitute victim, a ram caught in the brambles near the mountain top. God repeats his promise. The God who demands obedience is the God who grants blessings without limit.

The **Psalm** is a prayer of a faithful Israelite from late in Israel's history. This poet is a person at peace with God, whose trust nothing can break and who understands even death as precious in God's sight. In his gratitude, he will refuse God nothing. Abraham could have prayed this prayer.

In the New Testament, God the Father is compared to Abraham and Christ to Isaac. John writes that God loved the world so much that he gave up his only Son (3:16). In **Romans,** Paul uses terminology from the law court to describe our relationship with God. God is our judge, but he is on our side. He has given up his Son on our behalf. And Christ, his Son, is on our side too since, when he rose from the dead, he took upon himself the new role of interceding on our behalf. If the Father is the judge who has already acquitted us and the Son our advocate, how can we fail to win final salvation?

After Peter had confessed Jesus as the Christ, Jesus spoke openly to his disciples for the first time in **Mark** about his coming suffering and the rigorous demands of discipleship (8:29–37). They found this doctrine very difficult. The vision of the Jesus transfigured is to encourage them in the trying times ahead.

Three select disciples see Jesus as if he were already glorified, wearing dazzlingly white clothes like the Ancient of Days in Daniel (7:9). They see with him, authenticating his message, Elijah the prophet, who was taken up into heaven rather than dying (2 Kings 2:11) and Moses the law-giver, whose grave had never been found (Deuteronomy 34:6). Peter reacts as if he has forgotten Jesus' warnings about future trials. He wants to build tents to celebrate a perpetual Feast of Tabernacles (Leviticus 23:40), as if Heaven had come already and the way of the cross had been cancelled. But his words are prompted by fear rather than understanding. The vision fails to enlighten the disciples and terrifies them instead. It is the storm on the lake all over again, when Jesus, using the authority of God (Psalm 107:29), had calmed the storm (4:35–41), but the disciples failed to recognise who he was.

Then God himself breaks the silence from a cloud, the place of divine presence (Exodus 16:10). He repeats the words that had identified Jesus at his baptism (1:11). But for the disciples he adds, 'listen to him'. The original baptismal words are quotations from a Psalm (2:7) and from Isaiah (42:1). The additional ones come from Deuteronomy, concerning the future prophet like Moses (18:15). God has added his voice to those of Elijah and Moses. Then they see 'only Jesus'. The only way open to the disciples is to follow the way of the cross behind Jesus (8:34). On the way down the mountain, Jesus speaks about the resurrection. The cross is not to be the end of the story even if, at that moment, they do not know what is meant by resurrection.

Lent 3 B

Exodus 20:1–17
Psalm 18:8–11
1 Corinthians 1:22–25
John 2:13–25

The Cleansing of the Temple

The **Exodus** from Egypt and the covenant of Sinai are the events that made Israel a people. The terms that God expects his treaty partner in the covenant to observe are the Ten Words or Commandments that he gives to Moses. The God who has defeated Pharaoh and Israel's enemies is a God who liberates. His commandments are words of liberation, not oppression (Psalm 118). To understand them as a burden is to reintroduce the slavery from which our ancestors in faith were freed (Acts 15:10). They concern, first, our relationship to God, and then our relationships to one other. The Gospel sums them up in terms of love of God and neighbour (Matthew 22:37–39; Galatians 5:14). The petitions of the Lord's Prayer reflect the same pattern (Matthew 6:9–13; Luke 11:2–3).

In the **Psalm**, we meditate on the qualities of God's Law. These are really the qualities of God himself, since his commands mirror his own ideals and character. God is to be trusted; God is holy, true and pure.

Through his conversion experience, Paul had met the crucified Christ (1 Corinthians 9:1) and had realised how this Christ is the unique means of salvation. He still respects the Law of Sinai as a holy, just and good (Romans 7:14) guide to human conduct. But he knows that it cannot give life to its hearers, nor does it possess power to enable them to observe what it commands. This can only be done by Christ, through his death and resurrection. This is his message to the **Corinthians.** It is far more important than the incidentals of religion, such as the miracles for which the Jews are looking or the worldly wisdom that the Greek world values so much.

John's account of the ministry of Jesus begins with two significant incidents. The first is the wedding feast at Cana, a domestic, family scene which, because of the water become wine, was a sign of the messianic abundance that Jesus brought (2:1–12; Amos 9:13). The second is the cleansing of the Temple at Jerusalem, a public action located in the most sacred place of the Holy City, the Temple, performed at its most solemn festival, the Passover.

In the past prophets had attacked the institution of the Temple, complaining that its external rites obscured the internal piety and the social responsibility that should mark genuine religion. Jeremiah had stood at the Temple entrance, denouncing the emptiness of its worship (Jeremiah 7:1–15). The words and actions of Jesus also recall words of Malachi, prophesying that the Lord would suddenly come into his Temple (Malachi 3:1), and of Zechariah, who foresaw the time when there would be no more traders in the house of the Lord (Zechariah 14:21). The disciples are reminded of a line from one of the Psalms about the righteous sufferer: 'zeal for your house devours me' (Psalm 69:9). This Psalm will be quoted in accounts of the death of Jesus (Matthew 27:34).

The Jews in John represent Jesus' enemies and, like those in 1 Corinthians, they asked for a sign. They understand Jesus' answer, 'Destroy this sanctuary, and in three days I will raise it up', in its literal sense. The evangelist wants the reader to grasp it in the spiritual way in which the disciples later understood it. The body of Jesus is the real Temple. At his death, from the side of his body came the living water that Ezekiel in his vision saw flowing from the side of the Jerusalem Temple (19:34; Ezekiel 47:1–12). John places this incident at the beginning of his Gospel to alert the reader that, from now on, the persons and institutions of the old religion will find their fulfilment in Jesus. Through Moses and Abraham, Passover Lamb and Temple, God is preparing for his final word, which is Christ.

Lent 4 B

2 Chronicles 36:14–16, 19–23
Psalm 136:1–6
Ephesians 2:4–10
John 3:14–21

God's Love for the World

The beginning of the Bible, which tells of the creation of the world by God, is well known (Genesis 1). Much less familiar is the end of the Bible in the form known to Jesus and his contemporaries: the conclusion of **2 Chronicles**, which we read today. It tells of the disaster that leads to the loss of city, Temple and nationhood by God's people; it attributes the cause to their sin and infidelity. But the anger of God never lasts; though his messengers have been ignored, God has not spoken his last word. He is to raise up Cyrus, a foreign king, who will rebuild his Temple in Jerusalem. Out of death will come resurrection.

The **Psalm** is a funeral lament of Israel suffering exile in Babylon. The river that flows through the city reminds them of the streams formed by their tears. They cannot sing songs of joy in a foreign land; they cannot forget Jerusalem, their home. The Christian who understands what sin is cannot forget the real home and the destiny God intends.

Key points in early Christian preaching were the resurrection of Jesus from the dead and his exaltation by God into the glory of heaven (Ephesians 1:20). The author of **Ephesians** believes that the Christian has been through the same experience. Sin brought death but, through baptism, our incorporation into Christ, this sin has been cancelled and already we have a place in heaven. This salvation is a sheer gift from God out of love. Our good works are a grateful response to what we have been given in Christ. We must not throw away this salvation that God has given us, as God's people in Chronicles did.

Last week, we heard **John**'s account of Jesus in the Temple, the most sacred place in Israel. This week, we read of a secret encounter between Jesus and a ruler and scholar, Nicodemus. He comes by night, a symbol in John of ignorance and sin. Jesus tries to teach him, step by step, how a person must be born from above to see the Kingdom of God. This comes about by water and Spirit (a reference to baptism), and is possible only through the lifting up of the Son of Man, that is, through the cross and ascension of Jesus (3:3–5). Our reading begins at this point.

Nicodemus, despite his learning, takes no further part in the conversation. Indeed, it is not clear whether we are now listening to the words of Jesus or to the evangelist. They range over key points in salvation history. Remarks about the serpent in the wilderness recall the desert journey of Israel and Israel's grumbling (Numbers 21:9). The lifting up of the serpent echoes the lifting up of the Servant in Isaiah (52:13). The mention of God giving his only Son reminds us of the patriarch Abraham, who was prepared to sacrifice his son Isaac (Genesis 22). The comparison of light and darkness suggests the light that God separated from the darkness at the creation (Genesis 1:4). God's love for the world brings to mind the loving God of the prophets (Hosea 11:1). A later Johannine writing identifies God with love (1 John 4:8, 16).

Nicodemus would expect judgment in the future, but we learn here that with Christ judgment has already taken place. In his presence, people divide for him and against him (11:45–46). For those who receive him (1:12), eternal life is already available. Those who sin choose darkness. Because the light of Christ is in the world, they can no longer conceal their sin and so they condemn themselves. Silent now, Nicodemus appears twice more in this Gospel. He appeals for Jesus to be allowed a hearing before being condemned (7:50) and, with Joseph of Arimathea, another secret disciple of Jesus, he gives him a royal burial (19:39).

Lent 5 B

Jeremiah 31:31–34
Psalm 50:3–4, 12–15
Hebrews 5:7–9
John 12:20–30

The Coming of the Greeks

On the second Sunday of Lent, we heard about the covenant that God made with Abraham. On the third Sunday, we heard the terms of the Sinai covenant, the Ten Words. Now, we hear **Jeremiah**'s prophecy of the new covenant, inaugurated by Jesus at the institution of the Eucharist (1 Corinthians 11:25). The difference between this Covenant and those earlier ones is that the obedience demanded by them all is now possible. By writing his Law on the heart rather than on stones (Exodus 34:1), God has brought about a new creation (2 Corinthians 5:17).

The **Psalm**, the best known of the Penitential Psalms, is a powerful prayer of repentance. Its opening shows a profound understanding of sin and the need for forgiveness that results. It proposes that the true remedy for sin is a new heart and a new spirit, the new creation spoken of by Jeremiah which, according to Paul, came about through Christ (2 Corinthians 5:17).

The understanding of Christ that dominates the letter to the **Hebrews** is of Christ the priest. A priest shares the humanity of those for whom he mediates. This letter stresses the humanity of Christ. He had to be made like his brethren in every respect (2:17). In our passage, Jesus prays his Gethsemane prayer before his passion (Mark 14:32). The Sinai Covenant had failed because the people had not obeyed its terms. Christ was one who learnt to obey. The author may be quoting here an ancient hymn about Christ which was designed to encourage his readers in their own difficulties and to lead them to a more profound understanding of Christ.

The coming of the Greeks in **John** marks a new stage in the mission of Jesus. He had come to his own and his own had not received him (1:11), but others, symbolized by these Greeks, do receive him and are given power to become children of God (1:12). Truly, already the whole world is following him (12:19), because he is to die, not for the nation only, but to bring into one the scattered children of God (11:52). The Greeks send their message to Jesus through Philip and Andrew, the two disciples with Greek names introduced at the beginning of the Gospel (1:40, 43).

Jesus does not reply directly to these Greeks, but in a short discourse indicates the significance of what is soon to happen, now that his long-awaited hour of death, resurrection and return to the Father is upon him (2:4; 7:30; 8:20). His words are optimistic and challenging. He does not deny the reality of his own coming death, of the loss of life that awaits his followers, of the trouble that even now makes his own soul shudder. He knows that these things are the way to a rich harvest, to eternal life and to glory.

For the first time in John, the voice of the Father is heard. (John omits the stories of the baptism and transfiguration.) The voice confirms that the works Jesus has done in the story so far manifest glory from the Father (2:11) and guarantee that the coming events of the hour will also be part of his salvific plan. The passion of Jesus, for John, was not a disaster but a further revelation of the glory of God (17:1). The scene concludes with the last of the three 'lifting up' sayings of John (3:14; 8:28). This lifting up of the Son in death and ascension will bring about the end of the power of Satan, the prince of this world. All people will be drawn to Jesus. This does not mean that we can no longer sin (1 John 1:8) or that others do not yet belong to his sheep (10:16). The Easter mission given to the disciples is to bring about in practice what Christ has established in principle (20:21).

Passion Sunday B

Isaiah 50:4–7
Psalm 21:8–9, 17–20, 23–24
Philippians 2:6–11
Mark 14:1–15:47

The Passion of Jesus

During the events that culminated in the exile, many Israelites were rebellious. But others remained faithful. In the Servant Song from **Isaiah**, we learn the form that this fidelity took, and its cost. It consists in attentiveness to the word of God and a readiness to proclaim it. Its hearers do not welcome this word. Their blows and insults anticipate the mockeries offered to Christ (Mark 14:65). The servant remains faithful because he knows that the Lord is with him in his suffering and will deliver him.

Our **Psalm** is one of the Psalms of the 'righteous sufferer'. Like the Servant Song, it anticipates the passion of Christ, where its mocking bystanders and the divided garments also appear (Mark 15:24–29). Jesus spoke its first words as his last; he may have prayed the rest in silence as he died (Mark 15:34). In its triumphant conclusion it looks forward to the glory of the resurrection.

In **Philippians**, Paul uses a hymn about the sufferings of Christ to restore the mutual respect and unselfish behaviour in the community that are essential for those called through love to be servants of one another (Galatians 5:13). Christ, like Adam, was in the image of God (Genesis 1:26). Unlike Adam, he did not grasp at equality with God, but accepted the status of a slave, so that he died on a cross. Adam, through wanting everything, lost everything (Genesis 3:17). Christ, because he gave up his claim to everything, was exalted by God. The dignities that belong to God, according to Isaiah (45:23), were paid to Jesus. He is now the Lord Jesus Christ and all this gives glory to God.

Each Gospel presents its own account of the passion and death of Christ. In general terms they agree, but they differ in particulars and in emphasis. We can divide **Mark**'s into three parts. In the first, Jesus is in full charge of events, as he prepares himself and his disciples for what is to come. In the second, he is silent and seems to succumb to hostile forces. In the third part, after his death, we realise that, in fact, he was the victor. The first part extends from the plotting of the priests until Gethsemane. Despite the conspiracy of Judas and the priests, Jesus continues to exercise the initiative shown during his ministry. He defends the woman who anoints him. He warns of his betrayal by Judas and the imminent denials of Peter. He informs his disciples, at his institution of the Eucharist, of the significance of his death in which his blood would be 'poured out for many'.

The mood of the second part is set by his struggle in Gethsemane. He looks for comfort from his disciples and finds them asleep. From now on, like the Suffering Servant of Isaiah (53:7), he is almost silent. He makes the fullest revelation of his person in the entire Gospel to the priests, but this wins for him only abuse and condemnation. Cynically exchanged for the guilty Barabbas by Pilate, he is sentenced to a death reserved for rebels and slaves. Dying, he is mocked by all in sight; he dies with the terrible opening words of Psalm 21 on his lips, 'My God, my God, why have you deserted me?'

In the third part, the reader is to see that Jesus died victorious over his enemies. Two events follow his death. The Temple veil is torn, a symbol of the destruction of the Temple (11:17; 13:2; 14:58). A pagan centurion suddenly confesses Jesus as 'Son of God', something that no apostle in Mark had done. The boldness of Joseph of Arimathea in going to Pilate for the body and the presence of the women who had come from Galilee tell us that the story is not over.

Easter 2 B

Acts 4:32–35
Psalm 117:2–4, 15–18
1 John 5:1–6
John 20:19–31

The Confession of Thomas

In **Acts**, Luke presents the first years of Christianity in Jerusalem as a golden age, an ideal to which every later generation of Christians is to aspire (Acts 2:42–47). Readers from a Greek background would be impressed by the unity of the newly converted, which fulfilled the Greek ideal of friendship, while those of Jewish origin would notice with delight how their care for the poor met the requirements of the Mosaic Law, which demanded that there be 'no one poor among you' (Deuteronomy 15:4). Jesus in the Gospel had insisted on repudiation of possessions by those who wanted to be his disciples (Luke 14:33).

The **Psalm** is an expansion of the *hallel* song of thanksgiving used last week (*see Easter Sunday Year A*). Verses that once formed the grateful prayer of a person recovered from sickness sit easily on the lips of the Lord risen from the tomb. His resurrection proved that he was truly the rejected stone of which Isaiah spoke (Isaiah 28:16).

1 John probably dates from after the Gospel of John. It repeats the doctrine of the Gospel, though often with a different emphasis thanks to believers' changing circumstances. Because of the teaching of this Gospel, we believe that the Jesus who came from Nazareth is the Son of God (John 20:31), but we must not forget the reality of his humanity. We know that he was anointed by the Spirit in water (John 1:32), but we must not forget the importance of the blood that he shed. We know that we must love God, but we must also express this love by keeping his commandments, which means we are to love one another (John 15:12). Such faith will enable us to overcome the world as he did (John 16:33).

At his final meal with his disciples in **John**, Jesus had promised not to leave them as orphans (14:18). His resurrection appearances are part of his fulfilment of this pledge. When he shows himself to them as they hide behind locked doors in Jerusalem, he makes real the joy (16:20) and the peace (14:27) of which he had spoken at the Last Supper. His words then were preparing them for this future.

They are to continue his mission (8:42). Just as he has never been alone, since the Father is with him (16:33), neither will they be alone. He solemnly breathes the Spirit over them (Genesis 1:2). John the Baptist had seen this Spirit coming down on Jesus and remaining on him at the beginning at his baptism (1:31–32). He had spoken of this Spirit during his ministry (7:39). He had described it in detail as the paraclete at the Supper (14:15–17, 26; 15:26–27; 16:7–11, 12–15). It had been symbolized in the water from his side at his death (19:34). When, in their turn, the disciples pass it on to others, sins will be forgiven.

Jesus had performed many signs during his lifetime, with the purpose of producing belief (2:23). In the new age of the Spirit, faith is no longer to depend on such signs. Thomas seeks for the reassurance of touch and feeling as the price of his belief in the Risen Lord. Jesus refuses to give such reassurance. There are two beatitudes in John's Gospel: one is concerned with mutual service at the foot-washing (13:17) and the other with belief that does not depend on sight.

It is easy to identify with Thomas. He was the pessimist among the disciples. He regarded an invitation go to Jerusalem with Jesus as an invitation to death (11:16). Thomas bluntly said, when Jesus called himself the 'Way', 'How can we know the way?' (14:5). As a good shepherd, Jesus sought Thomas out. He knew him as one of his own (10:15) and enabled him to make a confession of Jesus surpassing all others in the Gospel, 'My Lord and my God!'

Easter 3 B

Acts 3:13–15, 17–19
Psalm 4:2, 4, 7, 9
1 John 2:1–5
Luke 24:35–48

The Lord with the Eleven

The missionary speeches of Peter in **Acts** follow a common pattern. They first refer to the situation, here the cure of the lame man in the Temple (3:12). They then give a brief account of the life, death and resurrection of Jesus. Finally, they call for repentance, so that the sins of the hearers may be wiped out. There is often an appeal to the Old Testament, to reassure the listeners that it is no new God that is being preached, nor is his plan of salvation a new one. The God of Jesus is the God of the prophets; Jesus is to be identified with the prophet 'like myself' of whom Moses spoke (Deuteronomy 18:15).

Our **Psalm** is a traditional evening prayer. In it, a temple priest who has been delivered from distress gives thanks. It is easily applied to Christ, whom God released from anguish, so that he could find his joy in God his Father alone. Christians, who know that salvation is only found in Jesus, can make the prayer their own.

Some of those in the community to which **1 John** was sent believed themselves incapable of sin because their sin had been wiped out through Christ. They misunderstood words they read in the Gospel, such as, 'You are pruned [like a vine] already, by means of the word' (John 15:3). They need reminding that Christian life demands continuous obedience to the commandments of Christ, particularly the law of love. Christ did not finish his work when he offered himself as an expiation for our sins and those of the whole world. He continues even now as our paraclete, or advocate, with the Father, to defend us from our sins.

In his account of the career of the disciples of Jesus, **Luke** stresses his care and concern for them at key moments. Peter, after the great catch of fish, said to Jesus, 'Leave me, Lord; I am a sinful man'. Jesus reassured him, 'Do not be afraid' (Luke 5:8–10). Before he called the Twelve, Jesus spent a night in prayer on their behalf (6:12). Before his own suffering, Jesus prayed for Peter that his faith might not fail (22:32). It is no surprise, then, that before sending them out on their post-Easter mission to all nations, Jesus appears to them, eats with them and instructs them.

He finds the Eleven in the same state of alarm and fright in which he had encountered the two walking to Emmaus earlier in the day (24:17). First, he reassures them of his identity, by pointing to his wounded hands and feet but, though joy begins to break in, they are still incredulous and doubting. Next, he shares food with them. To share table fellowship with Jesus was a privilege eagerly sought during his ministry, especially by 'the tax collectors and the sinners' (15:1). The climax of these meals was the Supper the night before his death (22:14). The Eucharist represents the continuation of these meal encounters with Jesus in the life of the Church.

At this Easter meal with his disciples, the Risen Lord not only eats food with them, but also broaches the word of Scripture, explaining how the story told by Moses, the Prophets and the Psalms has been continued in his sufferings, death and resurrection. We read in the speeches in Acts the arguments he uses. This same divine plan will continue in the preaching of repentance and the forgiveness of sins by the disciples. Their future task is to be witnesses (Acts 1:8). They will not be alone but will be accompanied by the Holy Spirit. Luke's Gospel concludes with two blessings: Jesus blesses the disciples (24:50) and they, in turn, in the fullness of their joy, bless God (24:53).

Easter 4 B

Acts 4:8–12
Psalm 117:1, 8–9, 21–23, 26, 28–29
1 John 3:1–2
John 10:11–18

Portrait of the Shepherd

In **Acts**, Peter addresses the Jerusalem leaders, the same rulers, elders and scribes who had condemned Jesus (Luke 22:52). They have questioned by what authority he healed the lame man at the Golden Gate of the Temple (3:1–10)—a question also asked of Jesus after his cleansing of the Temple (Luke 20:2). Peter's reply is simple: it was through the name of Jesus, the name that is now the only means of salvation, that the man has been healed. As in his other speeches in Acts, he quotes a scriptural text in support, this time about the stone that was rejected (Matthew 21:42). The times are over when salvation could be sought through Law and Temple. Peter speaks these brave words because he is full of the Holy Spirit. He thus learns the reliability of Jesus' promise that the Spirit would tell his followers what to say when they were in trouble for their belief (Luke 12:12).

The **Psalm** was originally sung by pilgrims on their entry into the Holy City. It is an appropriate resurrection song. Besides its repeated exhortations to thank the Lord, it twice greets the Lord as Saviour, the title that Peter in his speech in Acts applies to Jesus.

Some of those to whom **1 John** was addressed had a wrong understanding of the future. Because the Christian was a child of God (John 1:12; Romans 8:16) and already in possession of eternal life (John 5:24), they were saying that there was nothing more for the believer to expect. The author denies this. Though he cannot picture the precise nature of our future existence, he does know that we shall be like God and see God. In similar circumstances, Paul assured the Thessalonians that we shall always be with the Lord (1 Thessalonians 4:17).

At the end of **John**, the Risen Lord ordered Peter to feed his lambs and tend his sheep, that is, to exercise the duties of a Good Shepherd (21:15). In 1 Peter, the author instructs his fellow elders to shepherd the flock of God (1 Peter 5:2). The obligations of a Good Shepherd are made clear in our chapter of John. Jesus is defending himself against the blind leaders of Israel, who, like the wicked shepherds of Ezekiel 34, failed to look after the flock put in their care. Jesus has just healed a man who was born blind; his opponents, instead of rejoicing over this victory of the light over darkness, denied that the cure had ever taken place (9:19) and became spiritually blind themselves (9:41).

Three characteristics of the Good Shepherd may be distinguished. First, he is ready to lay down his life for his sheep, in contrast to the hireling who runs away at danger. Jesus repeats this three times. These predictions of the death he was himself to die include the reassurance that he will lay down his life in order to take it up again. Secondly, the Good Shepherd knows both his sheep and the Father. John has given us examples of how Jesus knows his own (6:70), at times even before they have met (1:48). Jesus knew the Father before the world was made (17:5). His followers will know the Father if they know Jesus (14:7). As their leader, Peter is to know those whom he is to serve. Thirdly, the Good Shepherd is to be a principle of unity. There are other sheep to come into the fold. These may be those whom the apostles will later convert (17:20). They may be people such as the Greeks who were soon to come seeking Jesus (12:20). They may be those who belong to other Christian groupings, perhaps including those who have broken away from the original one (1 John 2:19). The self-description of Jesus as the Good Shepherd not only informs us about how he understands his own relationship to his followers but also offers a challenging model to all those who would exercise authority in the Christian community in the future.

Easter 5 B

Acts 9:26–31
Psalm 21:26–28, 30–32
1 John 3:18–24
John 15:1–8

The Vine and the Branches

Paul was converted, we are told in **Acts**, on his way to Damascus as an agent of the Jerusalem authorities sent to persecute Christians. His return to Jerusalem would be a tense occasion which, according to Galatians (1:18), did not happen until three years later. He finds himself unwelcome, even among the Jerusalem Christians, probably because he has admitted Gentiles as Christians without insisting on the Mosaic Law (Galatians 2:4). The greatest threat to him comes from Greek-speaking Jews, perhaps those who killed Stephen (Acts 6:9). He flees back to Tarsus, his home town. His rejection by his own people corresponds to the experience of Jesus when he proclaimed the Kingdom in Nazareth (Luke 4:16–30).

Our **Psalm**, the conclusion of the Psalm that Jesus prayed on the cross (Mark 15:34), fits the situation of Paul after his conversion since, through him, peoples of many nations came to hear what God had done in Christ.

In 1 **John**, the faith of Christians is summed up very simply: 'that we believe in the name of his Son Jesus Christ and that we love one another as he told us to'. Our belief is in the human Jesus as well as the divine Son who fulfilled the messianic expectations of his people. Our mutual love will guarantee a Christianity that is active and caring. Such belief and behaviour will assure the indwelling of God in the believer. This indwelling is a favourite doctrine of John (14:23). It is a reality known through the Spirit (John 14:26). We notice how the author thinks of God in terms of Trinity, though he nowhere gives us a formal treatise about a doctrine which will take some centuries to be defined.

One difference between **John** and the other Gospels is the absence of the parables. The closest John comes to parables is comparisons or figures of speech. After the sign of the man born blind (9:1–41), Jesus compared himself to the Good Shepherd. Israel called its kings shepherds, but they fell short. God promised that he would make up for the shortcomings of the kings by becoming their shepherd himself (Ezekiel 34:11). For John, Jesus alone is shepherd and king (19:37). Earthly rulers must take second place.

To his disciples, gathered at the Last Supper, he compares himself to a vine. They would be familiar enough with vines. Not only were these a common feature of the landscape, but the Old Testament compares the people of Israel to a vine (Psalm 80:8; Jeremiah 2:21). Israel proved unfruitful (Isaiah 5:1–7). But Jesus, the obedient Son of the Father (4:34), is the true vine on which the Father, the farmer, will find the fruit for which he is looking. By identifying himself with the vine, Jesus also identifies himself with the true Israel.

Traditionally, John has been called the spiritual Gospel. The various 'I am' sayings, of which 'I am the vine' is one, indicate how this is to be understood. He called himself the Bread of Life (6:35) and the Light of the World (8:12). What the ordinary person finds in bread, the disciple finds in Christ: he gives true nourishment through his word and his flesh (6:35–58). The role that light plays in the world, Christ plays. More important than physical healing for the blind man was the spiritual sight that he found through true belief in Christ (chapter 9). If Jesus is the true vine, then it is more important to belong to him, the true Israel, than to belong to a particular nation. The image of abiding in Jesus runs throughout the Gospel (8:31). The comparison of the believer and the branch of the vine clarifies the image. A good branch produces fruit: an active and caring Christianity. Good growth implies pruning and gives a hint of the place of the cross in Christian life.

Easter 6 B

Acts 10:25–26, 34–35, 44–48
Psalm 97:1–4
1 John 4:7–10
John 15:9–17

Mutual Love

The meeting of Peter with Cornelius and his conversion form one of the turning points in **Acts**: here a Gentile receives the Holy Spirit just as the first Christians at pentecost had done (2:1–11). Peter has to learn to imitate God and make no distinction between Jew and Gentile. Formerly, he was horrified at the prospect of eating unclean food (10:14), but his vision told him to do so. Thus God teaches him to treat no person as unclean, whatever his or her origin (10:28). However amazed believers are at what God is doing, they cannot refuse to go the way the Holy Spirit, the main actor in this book, intends them to go.

The **Psalm** celebrates not only the 'kindness and faithfulness' God shows to Israel (Exodus 34:6) but also the salvation that he offers to all the nations (Isaiah 52:10). It is a song that Cornelius would have gladly sung after his meeting with Peter.

The key word in **1 John** today, as in the Gospel reading, is *love*. The Psalmist (and Exodus) knew about the steadfast love (*hesed*) of God in history. In his Gospel, John spoke about God's love in sending his Son into the world (John 3:16) and about the love shown by the Son in going to his death (John 13:1). In the entire Bible, this is the only chapter where God is identified with love. Because he made humanity in his image (Genesis 1:26), believers are to love one another and by doing so, they exercise a God-given gift. The greatest expression of God's love was his sending of his Son. But the incarnation, of itself, did not achieve our salvation. This came about through the death of Christ. Through his blood he cleanses us from sin (1:7), and this atonement is for the whole world (2:2).

One way of approaching the words reported by **John** in his account of Jesus' discourse at the Last Supper is to consider their relationship to the activities and teaching of Jesus during his ministry. When he speaks of a man showing no greater love than to lay down his life for his friends, we recall Jesus as the Good Shepherd, who lays down his life for his sheep (10:11). When he claims to make known what he had heard from the Father, we remember Jesus' role as revealer (1:18). He made his fullest statement of this claim before Annas (18:19–23). When he tells his disciples that he has chosen them, not they him, we remember how he called them at the beginning of the Gospel (1:35–51).

We can also explore parallels elsewhere in the discourse. The mention of the fruit the disciples are to bear returns us to the figure of the vine (15:5). The promise that the Father will give them anything for which they ask calls to mind Jesus' insistence that they must let his words find a home in them (15:7). His words about joy anticipate his description of joy to come (16:20–22), as well as his meeting with them on Easter Day (20:20).

Sometimes in the discourse a key word is repeated again and again. Such a word, in today's passage, is *love*. During his ministry, Jesus taught mostly about life (10:10), but once the Supper begins, it is love that he emphasizes (13:1). We learn how this love is shown by the Father to the Son, how the disciple must not only abide in Jesus, as a branch in the vine, but must also abide in the love of Jesus. Surprisingly, the disciples are not told to love Jesus but to keep his commandments. The only commandment found in John is that of mutual love, to be limited only by death. Hence, the disciples of Jesus become no longer servants but friends, as Moses had been a friend of God (Exodus 33:11). This is what Jesus meant when, at the beginning of the Supper, he had washed the feet of the disciples and told them to wash one another's feet (13:14); they are to love each other as he has loved them.

The Ascension B

Acts 1:1–11
Psalm 46:2–4, 6–9
Ephesians 4:1–13
Mark 16:15–20

Final Commission

The opening of **Acts** solemnly describes the start of the third stage of world history for Luke. The time of Israel and the time of the earthly Jesus are past, and the time of the Church begins. Moses was prepared for his mission by a forty-day stay on the mountain (Exodus 24:18). Elijah (1 Kings 19:8) and Jesus spent forty days in the desert (Matthew 4:2). At the end of a similar period, the disciples were promised the same Holy Spirit that had anointed Jesus as he began his mission (Luke 3:22) and they were appointed his witnesses to the ends of the earth. This mission was symbolically completed by the arrival of Paul in Rome but meanwhile the disciples are to cease gazing upward into heaven and devote themselves to the continuation of Jesus' ministry in this world.

The **Psalm** was probably first sung after some great military victory. The Ark of the Covenant was solemnly carried through Jerusalem to the Temple, where God was greeted as the Lord Most High (Genesis 14:18) and as Great King. On Ascension Day we apply it to Christ, now exalted in heaven as the Lord of all creation.

We find the word *ascended* in **Ephesians**. The author is quoting a Psalm which he applies to Christ, and is reflecting on the consequences of the ascension in terms of its significance for the Church. The Church is now the body of Christ; each of its various members contribute to its growth. These are, as it were, the farewell gifts that the Risen Lord left his disciples when he ceased his earthly presence with them. Thanks to these gifts, the Church moves towards the fulfilment of its destiny, named as the fullness of Christ.

The Gospel of **Mark** almost certainly originally ended with the commissioning of the women to tell Peter to go to Galilee (16:8). What we read today is canonical scripture, but by another writer, that reflects the history of the Church as told in Acts. First, there is Jesus' commission to the ends of the earth (Acts 1:8); here they are to preach the gospel—a word found only in Mark (1:1, 15)—to the whole of creation (Romans 8:20). Peter in Acts calls for repentance and baptism (2:38); the risen Lord here calls for belief and baptism. When he sent them out during his ministry, he prepared them for acceptance and rejection (Mark 6:10–11). Paul had a taste of both at Antioch in Pisidia (Acts 13:46). Their message will be a source of division, as Simeon warned Mary at the beginning of Luke's story (Luke 2:34).

Secondly, the Lord promises signs for those who believe. We find examples in Acts. When Ananias laid his hands on Paul, he was given back his sight (9:18) and, in Malta, the same Paul picked up a deadly snake and came to no harm (28:5). The Church of Corinth prided itself on the gifts of healing and the ability to speak in tongues (1 Corinthians 12:9–19). By contrast, Paul in his letters made little of the marvels that accompanied his preaching, only referring to them in passing (Romans 15:19); he preached Christ crucified (1 Corinthians 2:2) and strove to build up charity and mutual love (1 Corinthians 4:21). This contrast is also the pattern of Mark's Gospel. In the first part, it emphasizes the miracles of Jesus, while in the second it has few to report. There is even a warning about seeking signs and Jesus refuses to give them (8:12).

Mark concludes with the Ascension itself. Jesus is given his Easter title of Lord. Like Elijah, he is taken up to heaven (2 Kings 2:11) and, like a newly appointed king of Israel, he takes his place at God's right hand (Psalm 110:1). Jesus' final words became a reality as the gospel spread out from Jerusalem to all nations in the Holy Spirit and in power (1 Thessalonians 1:4). The Church continues the mission of its Lord.

Easter 7 B

Acts 1:15–17, 20–26
Psalm 102:1–2, 11–12, 19–20
1 John 4:11–16
John 17:11–19

Prayer for the Future

Luke reports how, at the Last Supper, Jesus told Peter to confirm his brethren (Luke 22:32). We read in **Acts** an example of how he did this. God's salvific plan is for the renewal of Israel. To achieve this, the Twelve apostles, who are to judge the twelve tribes of Israel (Luke 22:30), have to be brought up to their full number after the defection of Judas (Luke 22:3). In this, Peter sees the fulfilment of scripture (Psalm 69:25; Psalm 109:8). The qualifications listed for apostleship are interesting. The candidate has to have been with Jesus from the time of John the Baptist and to have been witness to the resurrection. He has to provide a direct link between the earthly Jesus and the Church. Matthias, otherwise unknown, is chosen.

The **Psalm**, a thanksgiving for recovery from sickness, makes an appropriate Easter hymn. The court of heaven is invited to join in expressing gratitude. God has shown his love in forgiveness and healing.

We hear again from **1 John** that God is love (4:8). The consequence emphasized here is not that we must love God but that we are to love one another. Jesus said the same thing in the Gospel about our response to his love for us (John 15:12). This time, no commandment is mentioned (3:23). We love one another because of what God has done and is doing for us. He has given us his Spirit (John 7:39), and he has sent his Son as Saviour (John 3:16). Thanks to this love, God dwells within us (John 14:23). If we love each other as he wants us to, there will be no need to see God. Those who recognise the fullness of Christian dignity see God already, as Jesus told Philip that those who saw him, saw God (John 14:9).

Each year on this Sunday, we hear part of the prayer Jesus said in **John** when his hour had come (17:1). Jesus, at supper with his disciples, is already on his way out of the world, but they remain in it. The world represents everything hostile to Jesus and his message. Earlier in this discourse, we heard Jesus' promise to return to them in a new type of presence by sending them the paraclete (14:16) and dwelling within them together with the Father (14:23). To equip them further for their future without his physical presence, he makes three requests of his Father. He prays first for unity among his followers: that they be one. He wants them to be as united with each other as he is with the Father, as close and dependent as the branches on the vine (15:4). As Good Shepherd he has kept them all together, apart from Judas, until now (10:14). The seamless tunic on Calvary (19:23) and the net at the sea of Galilee that was not torn (21:11) may be symbols of the unity for which Christ prayed.

His second request is that they may possess the joy that found its fulfilment in himself. This would be a fruit of the Resurrection (16:14), the first effect of their seeing him on Easter night (20:20). Through making the joy of Jesus their own, they will be able to live on in the world which hates them and resist the evil one, whose power will be broken through his raising up on the cross and in his ascension (12:31).

The third element of his prayer is for them to be sanctified in the truth. Such sanctification usually came about through correct ritual (Exodus 28:41) or sacrifice (Exodus 13:2). Jesus promises that it will come about through his word. We know from his washing the feet of the disciples that his word purifies (15:3). This word is the truth, or revelation, that he brings from the Father. Pilate was not interested in such revelation, dismissing it (18:38). Jesus promised the Samaritan woman that the time was coming when 'true worshippers will worship the Father in spirit and truth' (4:23).

Pentecost B

Acts 2:1–11
Psalm 103:1, 24, 29–31
Galatians 5:16–25
John 15:26–27; 16:12–15

The Spirit Poured Out

Thanks to forty days' preparation by the Risen Lord (Acts 1:3), earnest prayer by the disciples and the mother of Jesus (1:14), and the election of Matthias, which restored the college of the apostles to its full number (1:26), all is ready in **Acts** for the solemn inauguration of the renewed Israel which became the Church. The agricultural festival of pentecost had been transformed into a commemoration of the giving of the Law at Sinai. Once more, fire and wind come from heaven (Exodus 19:16) but this time, God gives his Spirit rather than the Law. The Spirit through whom the world was created recreates Israel and empowers the apostles to proclaim the works of God in many languages. Babel is cancelled (Genesis 11:9).

The **Psalm** is a meditation on the creation account of Genesis, in which the Spirit of God took part. This Spirit is also a Spirit of renewal, like the Spirit that Ezekiel saw bringing life to the dry bones (Ezekiel 37:1–14).

For Paul, without Christ humanity could only live according to the flesh, which is Paul's way of describing unaided human nature. The result was a life of sin. But the person living in Christ was supported by the Spirit of God (Romans 8:9). Concluding **Galatians**, Paul gives his list of the fruits that the Spirit produces in the life of Christians. The first is love, the gift described so eloquently in 1 Corinthians (13:1). The other gifts in Paul's catalogue are consequences of this first one. Paul helps us to see that the Holy Spirit is more than the external force so emphasized in the Acts of the Apostles; it is a vital principle that dwells in the believer.

We find a special emphasis on the Holy Spirit in **John**. Jesus spoke to Nicodemus of the need for rebirth through water and Spirit (3:5), but this Spirit could not be given until Jesus was glorified (7:39). The hour of glorification came when he died and rose. The Spirit was first given in symbol by through the water that came from the side of the crucified Christ (19:34) and later more solemnly when the Risen Jesus breathed the Spirit on his disciples on the evening of Easter Day (20:22).

Our gospel reading consists of two passages from Jesus' Supper Discourse where he speaks about the Spirit or Advocate who is to come. He gives this Spirit a special name in Greek, one which is difficult to translate: the paraclete. The basic idea in the Greek word is of one who 'stands alongside'. Just as Jesus was never alone, since the Father was always with him (16:32), neither will the disciples be alone, though Jesus will be absent physically. Jesus came from the Father (17:21); so will the paraclete. Among his roles will be that of witness. During Jesus' ministry, the Father bore witness about him (5:37); in future, the paraclete will do the same. The Baptist bore witness about Jesus because of the word of the one who sent him (1:33); when they are sent into the world to witness (20:21), the disciples will be accompanied by the paraclete.

The paraclete is also the Spirit of Truth, who will interpret in the future the words of the one who was the Way and the Truth (14:6). Before the glorification of Jesus in death and resurrection, the disciples failed to understand the meaning of all that he had said and done; they did not understand his words when he cleansed the Temple (12:22) or why he entered Jerusalem on a donkey (12:16). As their teacher, the paraclete will make clear to them what they could not understand before. He will take the place of Jesus, who had taught them what he had heard from his Father (15:15). Thanks to the paraclete, they will not be bereaved by the earthly departure of Jesus.

Trinity Sunday B

Deuteronomy 4:32–34, 39–40
Psalm 32:4–6, 9, 18–20, 22
Romans 8:14–17
Matthew 28:16–20

The Three Persons

Idolatry and polytheism characterized the religions of the nations surrounding ancient Israel. Our passage from **Deuteronomy** celebrates the superiority of the God of Israel to other so-called deities. He is unique; he has not only created the world, he has chosen a people for himself. He has delivered them from slavery in Egypt and revealed himself to them in the majesty of Sinai. All he wants in return is for them to live a life that is faithful and obedient to his commandments, so that he can continue to show his favours to them.

The **Psalm** reflects the same picture of God. God is praised for the creation effected through his word (John 1:1). He is faithful and loving (Exodus 34:6). He keeps them alive in famine (11:3). He delivers from evil (Matthew 6:13).

Paul's apostolic experience has revealed God to him as Trinity. We read in **Romans** how his readers address God as intimately as Jesus had done, calling him Abba, Father (Luke 10:21; 22:42). They can do this because the Holy Spirit is living within them (Romans 8:9); when the believer prays, the indwelling Spirit prays too. As children of God, Christians now belong to the family of the God who is Trinity. As the Son of God, Christ now has many brothers and sisters (Romans 8:29). They all share in the inheritance belonging to him as the eldest, and this is a share in the glory of God. The Son has entered this glory through suffering (Luke 24:26). Paul had suffered many things in his life as an apostle (2 Corinthians 12); this was an assurance to him that he was living the way of Christ (2 Corinthians 4:8–11). When Paul wrote about God, he did not use the expression 'Trinity', but he could not but think of God in Trinitarian terms.

Matthew ends his Gospel with the Risen Jesus' command to his disciples to baptize in the name of the Trinity. Baptism is an incorporation in the family of the Trinity. The Trinitarian formula he uses occurs nowhere else in the gospel tradition, but the individual members of the Trinity have been distinguished and active throughout Matthew's story.

Baptism is to be in the name of the Father. For Matthew, this is the God of the Old Testament, whose providence ensured the birth of Jesus at the end of a long line of ancestors (1:1–17). He is the Father who makes his sun shine on the just and the unjust (5:45), who knows the Son and is known by him (11:27). He hides his revelation from the wise and the prudent but reveals it to the little ones (11:25). In Gethsemane, he had the power to send twelve legions of angels to defend his Son (26:53). He is the Father to whom the disciples are to pray (6:9).

Baptism is also to be in the name of the Son. This Son is the one whose birth came about through the Holy Spirit (1:20). During his life, he lived in intimacy with the Father (11:27). Before his death, he prayed to the Father, pledging himself to the Father's will rather than his own (26:39), an example to the disciples who would be judged on how far they had done the 'will of my Father' (7:21). His name was Emmanuel, because he would be God with us until the end of the time (1:23; 18:20).

Baptism will be in the name of the Spirit. This Spirit, active at the creation (Genesis 1:2) and in the lives of the prophets (Isaiah 42:1, Matthew 12:18), descended on Jesus at his baptism (3:16), enabling him to cast out demons and make the presence of the Kingdom a reality (12:28). In time of persecution, this Spirit of the Father will speak through the troubled disciples (10:20). Matthew did not speculate about how God could be three and one. He was content to tell his readers what the individual members of the Trinity did.

Body and Blood of Christ B

Exodus 24:3–8
Psalm 115:12–13
Hebrews 9:11–15
Mark 14:12–16, 22–26

Institution of the Eucharist

Exodus describes how Moses acts as a mediator between God and his people when Israel become a people at Sinai. He tells them what God requires of them as their part of the covenant. They signify acceptance of these conditions by performing rites familiar in religions of that age and culture. They build an altar, sacrifice animals and sprinkle blood. They publicly declare their commitment to obey the commandments of God. This obligation is ratified when Moses casts over them the blood of the animals their young men have slaughtered.

Our **Psalm** is a thanksgiving song. The sacrifices in the Temple were an expression of gratitude for God's goodness. The cup of thanksgiving anticipates the cup used in the Eucharist. The death of the faithful one, precious in the eyes of the Lord, looks forward to Jesus' death and the positive attitude to death he made possible (2 Corinthians 5:1).

The special insight of the author of **Hebrews** concerns the priesthood of Christ, which surpasses in effectiveness all Old Testament priesthood and is the root of all priesthood in the Church. Our reading takes up and transforms themes mentioned in Exodus. The mediator is not now Moses or a priest, but Christ himself, who has entered not Sinai but the sanctuary of heaven. There is now no need of the blood of animals, because the blood of Christ is eternally effective in dealing with sin. There is now no talk of a covenant needing renewal because of human infidelity, but of a new covenant which lasts forever because of the perfect sacrifice of Christ.

Our gospel reading consists of two passages from **Mark**. The first concerns the arrangements Jesus makes for a final Passover meal with his disciples. The narrative is relatively detailed, and the fourfold repetition of the word *Passover* is noteworthy. Originally a nomadic feast of thanksgiving, Passover was celebrated at the time of Jesus to commemorate Israel's liberation from bondage in Egypt. Important events in Israelite history had taken place at Passover, such as the entry into Canaan (Joshua 5:10–12); and a special celebration of the feast had taken place at the time of Josiah's reform (2 Kings 23:21–23). For the evangelist, the events to take place at this Passover will far surpass what has happened in the past.

The second passage describes the institution of the Eucharist at this final meal. The account falls into three parts. First, Jesus takes bread, blesses it in accordance with custom, and then gives it to his disciples, describing it as his body. Secondly, he takes a cup, saying 'This is the blood of the covenant', the same words that Moses used in Exodus of the animal blood with which he had sprinkled the people as a sign of their commitment (Exodus 24:8). To take the blood of Christ is to commit oneself to live according to his teaching. This blood will be 'poured out for many', words reminiscent of an Isaian Servant Song (53:12). 'Many' here means 'all', a fact shown clearly from a parallel in Paul (Romans 5:14, 17). Jesus has previously identified himself with the Servant when he described his death as a ransom for many (10:45). Thirdly, he adds a saying about drinking new wine in the Kingdom of God. This reminds us that the Eucharist is an eschatological gift; it is for the last times. With the death of Jesus, the final days have begun and will end with his return (Mark 13:26). The new wine is now a reality (2:22). The joy of this new kingdom is anticipated in the joyful *hallel* psalms that Jesus sang with his disciples on their way to the Mount of Olives (Psalms 113–118).

Year B
The Year of Mark

THE 34 SUNDAYS OF THE YEAR*

These Sundays are divided into two blocks, separated by the three months of the seasons of Lent and Easter. Some Sundays which occur between the two blocks, are always omitted. The Feast of the Baptism of the Lord is reckoned as the first Sunday of the Year.

The **First Readings**, *from the Old Testament, are intended to throw light on the gospel reading of the day. Never during this period is there any continuous reading from the Old Testament. To concentrate on the Old Testament passage without reference to the Gospel therefore seems inappropriate.*

The **Responsorial Psalms** *are designed to help the understanding of the First Reading, to deepen some significant theme, to clarify its message. It also prepares for the Gospel since the First Reading is related to the Gospel.*

The **Second Readings** *are taken from a New Testament letter. The reading is semi-continuous, which gives a preacher the opportunity to take the congregation through the particular letter. Only coincidentally does it have any relationship to the First Reading or the Gospel. No letter is proclaimed in its entirety and sometimes the unit given is incomplete.*

- *The First Letter of Paul to the Corinthians (Part Two)*
- *The Second Letter of Paul to the Corinthians*
- *The Letter of Paul to the Ephesians*
- *The Letter of James*
- *The Letter to the Hebrews (Part One)*

The **Gospel Readings** *is taken from Mark. This Gospel is read throughout the year, except for the Easter season when John is usually read. We may therefore speak of Mark as the evangelist of the year.*

* See 'General Introduction', *Roman Missal*, nn. 105–107.

Sunday 2 B

1 Samuel 3:3–10, 19
Psalm 39:2, 4, 7–10
1 Corinthians 6:13–15, 17–20
John 1:35–42

Disciples Witness

The books of **Samuel** begin with the story of Eli and Samuel. Eli is priest at the shrine of Shiloh, but he is old and blind. He is blind, too, to the wickedness of his scoundrel sons, and he thinks that God has nothing to say in those days. But he is wrong. Israel's God is still a God of initiatives, preparing to work through a new prophet, Samuel. He calls Samuel while he is still a child. Asleep in the temple, Samuel hears a voice. He does not realise it is God calling him, as he runs back and forth to Eli. But once he does realise, he replies with words to be used by all those who hear God calling, 'Speak, Yahweh, your servant is listening'.

The **Psalm** calls for a personal knowledge of God and willing response. Religion is more than Temple and cult. True believers say, 'Am I not commanded to obey your will?'. According to the Letter to the Hebrews, Christ himself used these words as he came into the world (Hebrews 10:5–7).

At the beginning of **1 Corinthians** (a letter read at the start of each liturgical year), Paul commended his readers on their eloquence and knowledge (1 Corinthians 1:5). But the eloquence and knowledge were immature. So clever do some think themselves that they have concluded that, being in Christ, they are superior to ordinary morality. 'For me there are no forbidden things', they claim. They apply this even to fornication. Paul tells them in return that their bodies are temples of the Holy Spirit. No longer does God need temples such as Shiloh for a dwelling. He dwells within the believer who has been bought for him at the price of the death of his Son 'who loved me and who sacrificed himself for my sake' (Galatians 2:20).

Thanks to **John**, we know that John the Baptist's disciples became disciples of Jesus. Continuing his function of witness (1:7), the Baptist points Jesus out to his followers as the Lamb of God. By this he may have meant no more than that Jesus was the one to set his people free. Contemporary writers described the liberator of God's people as the leader, or ram, of his flock. The evangelist would want us to think of the Passover lamb offered in sacrifice (19:37), or of Isaiah's Servant of God led to death as a lamb to the slaughter (Isaiah 53:7).

As a result of the Baptist's witness, two of his disciples follow Jesus. Meeting them, Jesus asks the question addressed to every reader of the Gospel: 'What do you want?' They reply, perhaps surprised by the question, 'Where do you live?' They are invited to 'Come and see', and spend the day with Jesus. The evangelist is playing with words here. A single word in Greek may be translated as 'stay', 'abide', 'live' and 'spend the day'. The disciples think they are asking Jesus where he lives in the ordinary sense. John knows that God lives in Jesus (14:10), that these two live in the believer (14:23), that the perfection of the believer is to live, abide, dwell in the Father and the Son (1 John 2:24).

How does one come to be a disciple of Jesus? Usually through the witness of another: Andrew and his friend come through the Baptist, Simon through Andrew. But for Philip (and Samuel), the call is direct (1:43). The one called is to stay with Jesus, abide with him. This experience teaches more about Jesus. The two who are called first address Jesus as 'Rabbi' but, thanks to his stay with Jesus, Andrew tells his brother Simon that he has found not a rabbi, but the messiah. A disciple cannot keep the news of Jesus to himself but seeks to share it with another. Jesus knows about the one called. When he meets Peter, he already knows him and had plans for him. John has given us a second prologue to his Gospel about vocation.

Sunday 3 B

Jonah 3:1–5, 10
Psalm 24:4–9
1 Corinthians 7:29–31
Mark 1:14–20

Call of the Four

To bring the great city of Nineveh to repentance, God chooses the prophet **Jonah**. The first time Jonah is called, he disobeys God. He takes a ship in the opposite direction, is shipwrecked, and survives only because God sends a great fish to save him. A second time God sends him on mission to Nineveh. Unlike Jonah, this mighty heathen city obeys God's word and repents as soon as it hears Jonah's preaching. God repents too, and changes his mind about the punishment he had intended for the city. God's concern for the sinner proves much stronger than that of his prophet.

In the **Psalm**, classified as a Wisdom psalm, the poet ponders his need for divine guidance. His prayer is suitable for all who answer the divine call, whether they be Ninevites, Jonah or the disciples in the Gospel.

In 1 **Corinthians**, Paul is replying to questions sent to him about Christian marriage. The whole institution is despised by some, while others are being too demanding in their attitudes. Paul teaches that both marriage and celibacy are gifts from God (7:7). His advice is that each should remain in the state in which he or she was called (7:17). Among his reasons is his belief, which we read today, that the end of all things is at hand. This is what he taught in his earliest letter (1 Thessalonians 1:10); later, he thought he might die before it happened (Philippians 1:20). But whether Christ is soon to return or not, his teaching has been valued because of the warning it gives not to treat this world as the only reality. God has other plans for us; we are 'to stay with the Lord for ever' (1 Thessalonians 4:17).

Mark begins his account of Jesus' ministry with his initial proclamation and his call of four fishermen. His first words—'The time has come ... and the kingdom of God is close at hand. Repent, and believe the Good News'—are important for understanding the story of Mark. The reader has always to question how far this initial summons is being obeyed. As for the Kingdom, Jesus does not define its meaning; the reader has to work this out by listening to his teaching, particularly in the parables (4:1–34), and watching his actions. Ultimately, Jesus himself is the Kingdom.

Jesus' first action is to summon his first four disciples. He directs his call to four fishermen, hard at work in their boats, and they probably do not even see him coming. The invitation appears suddenly. Without hesitation, they obey it, leaving behind their families, their employees, their future. They do not volunteer for the task of disciple of Jesus. They obey a call. Their prompt response can only be explained by the attractiveness of the person of Jesus. He offers no prospectus or hint about the way that leads ahead, apart from the strange promise that he will make them 'fishers of men'. Jesus himself will be their trainer. These four form the nucleus of those who will later become the Twelve (3:13), and, later still, the worldwide Church (13:10).

In this way Jesus opens his school of discipleship. He has to bring these four first to the repentance and belief in the gospel that he requires of all. To them he will reveal the 'secret of the Kingdom' (4:11). Their thoughts have to become the thoughts of God and not those of men (8:33). They are to follow Jesus to Jerusalem, the city of his enemies, the city of his death and resurrection (10:32). Readers are invited to identify with them and to 'be his companions' (3:14) as he preached to the 'neighbouring country towns', for 'that is why I came' (1:38). Catechumens in Rome who asked for baptism were to join these four in the school of Jesus.

Sunday 4 B

Deuteronomy 18:15–20
Psalm 94:1–2, 6–9
1 Corinthians 7:32–35
Mark 1:21–28

Conflict in the Synagogue

There were many soothsayers, sorcerers and necromancers in the world in which **Deuteronomy** was written. But, according to Moses, who speaks in this book, God only wants one sort of prophet. This prophet must be called by God, belong to Israel, proclaim God's word, make intercession for the people and teach God's Law. In the time of the Baptist, the people longed for such a figure (John 1:21). Peter preached that Jesus was the one who finally fulfilled the role. He was 'a prophet ... from among your own brothers' (Acts 3:22).

The **Psalm** would be sung during processions to the Temple. On arrival, a temple prophet addresses the worshippers, urging them to listen to the voice of God. They are not to harden their hearts as their ancestors did when they refused the word of Moses at Meribah (Exodus 17:7).

In **1 Corinthians** Paul continues his discussion of marriage. Some in Corinth are too lax, forgetting that marriage is a gift of God (7:7) and a means of sanctification (7:14); others, like the false teachers in 1 Timothy (4:3), claimed that a Christian should have nothing to do with it. Paul agrees that it can be good not to marry. Lack of family commitments leaves him free to be devoted to the affairs of the Lord. A person can remain unmarried 'for the sake of the kingdom of heaven' (Matthew 19:12). But Paul is the apostle of Christian freedom (Galatians 5:1). He does not want to put a halter round their necks. And he himself was grateful to married couples such as Prisca and Aquila, who were 'his fellow workers in Christ Jesus' (Romans 16:3).

Today we hear **Mark**'s account of the first public manifestation of Jesus. In baptism, he has been anointed with the Spirit (1:9–11) and in his temptation, he had tied up Satan, the strong one; he can now break into his house (1:12–13; 3:27). This he proceeds to do. In the synagogue at Capernaum, which is still shown to visitors, he found an agent of Satan. Synagogues were used as schools during the week and for worship and hearing the Law of God on the Sabbath (Acts 13:15).

Jesus' activity begins with teaching, admired both for its content and for its authority, which is acknowledged as greater than that of the recognised teachers, the scribes. For the present, the latter make no move, but their final answer to him will be a plot to kill him (14:1). The immediate response to Jesus' activity comes from the possessed man. His words sum up the aim and the issue of Jesus' ministry. As the Holy One of God, Jesus has come to destroy the power of Satan. The conflict has begun.

Jesus' reply is swift. His retort to the spirit uses a word that means muzzling like an animal, 'Be quiet. Come out of him.' He will use it again to calm the storm (4:39). Such power is in the word of Jesus that, with a great shudder and mighty cry, the spirit leaves the man. We are not told of the feelings of the disciples, so soon after their call (1:16–20), but the crowd react with fear and astonishment. We are not informed that they repent or welcome the presence of the Kingdom (1:15).

The news of this new teaching and of the defeat of the evil spirit spread all over Galilee. So Jesus begins his ministry. The reader is to join his disciples, encountering his exciting teaching and fearsome activity. They may well have felt a hint of the risk that went with following this Jesus. The scribes, who have been humiliated by his teaching, and Satan, whose house has been broken into by the expulsion of the spirit (3:27), will want to get their own back.

Sunday 5 B

Job 7:1–4, 6–7
Psalm 146:1–6
1 Corinthians 9:16–19, 22–23
Mark 1:29–39

A Day in Capernaum

There is no easy answer to the problem of human suffering. **Job**'s friend Eliphaz had a simple philosophy, 'Can you recall a guiltless man that perished?' (Job 4:6) Job himself, in his affliction, compares human life to being a soldier compelled to serve in a tyrant's army, and to being a labourer, a slave, someone looking for release and never finding it. Job's own sufferings exceed all of these. He had in the end to bend down in humility before a mystery he could not solve, before a God whose thoughts he could not grasp, and admit, 'I am the man who obscured your designs with my empty-headed words' (42:3).

The optimism of the **Psalm** contrasts with the pessimism of Job. Though the people have suffered exile and loss, God has brought them back and healed them. He is in charge of his creation and no one can measure his wisdom. He raises the lowly and humbles the wicked.

As an apostle to the Gentiles, Paul lived a life on the move; he had no permanent home or income. We know from the Acts that he could earn his own living as a tentmaker (Acts 18:3), and at times he did. He boasted to the Thessalonians that he worked night and day so as to be a burden to nobody (1 Thessalonians 2:9), but at another time he had to thank the Philippians for the help they sent him 'more than once' (Philippians 4:16). He had to judge how to behave in different situations. He tells the **Corinthians** that he has to make himself 'all things to all men'; such adaptation was part of his whole approach to misison He was charged with being fickle and vacillating (2 Corinthians 1:17), and replied that the glory of God was his only motive (2 Corinthians 1:20).

The exorcism in the synagogue that we heard last week was the first event of a long day. Today, we hear in **Mark** the other events of this day in Capernaum. After overcoming Satan's agent in a synagogue, a religious setting, Jesus continues his assault on evil in the private house of a disciple and the public places of the town. At this opening stage of the gospel story, no evil, demon or disease can resist Jesus.

We meet Simon for the first time since his call (1:16–20). Jesus, accompanied by his four disciples, goes into Simon's house. His mother-in-law is sick. Jesus cures her, with none of the noise or commotion that marked his recent exorcism. He simply takes her by the hand and raises her, anticipating his own future resurrection. In response, she ministers to them all, her service foreshadowing so much future service and ministry in the Christian family.

Late in the day, the Sabbath over, all are free to move and to labour again. The whole city comes to the house where Jesus is, bringing the sick and the possessed. This time, the demons are not allowed to speak. All are cured. The bustle and confusion of the scene is reflected in confusing language, which both Matthew and Luke take care to tidy up.

Night falls; early in the morning, Jesus makes for the desert where he had battled with Satan before the angels came to feed him (1:12–13). He wants to speak with the Father, but instead, he meets Satan again, in the shape of 'Simon and his companions'. At Caesarea Philippi this same Simon would urge him to reject the way of suffering and would be called Satan (8:33). In his naïveté, Simon wants Jesus to be content with the popularity as a miracle-worker that is his for the asking, and forget his search for repentance and belief (1:15). But Jesus has not come out just to heal the sick. He will go to other towns to preach repentance. All have to learn, with Peter, not to seek a Jesus who is a mere exorcist and miracle-worker. There is more to him than this.

Sunday 6 B

Leviticus 13:1–2, 44–46
Psalm 31:1–2, 5, 11
1 Corinthians 10:31 – 11:1
Mark 1:40–45

A Cure of a Leper

The laws of **Leviticus** against the skin diseases that we commonly translate as leprosy were very severe. The community had to be protected against such dangerous and ill-understood afflictions. Hence clothing is worn torn, hair dishevelled, and the victim has to cry out 'Unclean'. The community has no place for the victim. The disease was presumed to be the effect of sin (John 9:3).

The **Psalm** is one of seven Penitential Psalms. The psalmist rejoices because he has confessed his sin and received forgiveness. If we accept leprosy as a symbol of sin, then it fits well on the lips of the man cleansed by Jesus in the Gospel.

The exclusion of the leper was one way of protecting the community. Paul in **1 Corinthians** offers more positive methods. He has been dealing with the problem of meat sacrificed to idols. The Mosaic Law put great stress on food laws. Paul urges his readers to turn from the letter to the spirit of these laws. Food and drink must not be an end in themselves, but a means to God's glory (Romans 14:17). At the same time, each must be sensitive to the conscience of others. If some people cannot bring themselves to eat certain foods, then they are to be respected. For this reason, Paul declared he would never eat meat (8:13). He did not want his conduct to trip anyone up on their way to salvation. He offers himself as a model of behaviour because he is confident of his role as an apostle, an officially appointed representative of Christ (9:1). He does everything for the glory of Christ and he urges his readers to do the same.

The story of Jesus curing the leper in **Mark** is a transitional one between two types of activity. So far Jesus has attacked the kingdom of Satan directly by casting out demons and healing the diseases attributed to Satan (1:34). Soon he will confront sin when he cures the paralytic (2:1–12) and find himself embroiled in various controversies with his critics (2:13 – 3:6). Leprosy was popularly taken to be a symbol of sin, so by cleansing the leper Jesus is already hinting at his power to forgive sins, which he would shortly exercise (2:5). Leprosy was among the most terrible of diseases in isolating a person from the human society.

Jesus' authority (1:22) is sufficient to effect a cure immediately. He gives two orders to the man who has been cured. He is to tell no one. This is the first mention of the so-called messianic secret in Mark; Jesus did not want misinformed rumours of his identity to spread. If it was said he was the Christ, his mission would be endangered in those times of political instability. Only once we know Christ as the crucified and risen one are we to share our knowledge of him. The one cured disobeys Jesus. Like a newly baptized member of the Christian community, he goes around preaching the word. Jesus' second instruction to the man is that he should report his cure to the priests. When the Law did not contradict the spirit of his mission (10:5), Jesus upheld it. The priests would put the seal on the man's restoration to the community and ordinary human life.

This is the only report in Mark of Jesus cleansing a leper. According to Matthew, it is one of his messianic works (11:5). In Luke, on one occasion he healed ten at once, including a Samaritan (17:12). We should not fail to notice the last words of Mark's report. Jesus found himself unable to enter a town; he, like the leper before his cure, has to stay outside in the countryside. Here is a hint of the cost to Jesus of his ministry of healing, foreshadowing his giving of himself as a ransom on the cross for many (10:45).

Sunday 7 B

Isaiah 43:18–19, 21–22, 24–25
Psalm 40:2–5, 13–14
2 Corinthians 1:18–22
Mark 2:1–12

A Cure of a Paralytic

Our passage from **Isaiah** probably dates from the time of Israel's exile in Babylon. It is as if the people are on trial before God and God is speaking. Their sin has brought them to their present condition and, even now, they are failing to worship God as they should. But, in terms that recall the desert journeys of Exodus, God promises them restoration and forgiveness of sin. He will find for them a way out of the wilderness and chaos in which they struggle (Isaiah 40:3; Mark 1:3).

Our **Psalm** may originally have been a prayer of thanksgiving by one who had recovered from sickness. Our liturgy applies it to the sickness that a whole people suffered because of exile. But it also prepares us for the recovery of the paralyzed man in the Gospel, who is cured by Jesus.

In the course of his second letter to the **Corinthians**, Paul has to defend himself against numerous charges. Here, at its beginning, he is being criticized for apparent inconsistency. In his previous letter (1 Corinthians 16:5–7), he had announced certain travel plans, but has not carried them out. He had promised the Corinthians a visit and has failed to turn up. Paul answers, as always, in theological terms. He works as an apostle for God. Just as Christ was always the 'Yes' to God's promises, so whatever Paul does is a 'Yes' to Christ. It is the same 'Yes' (*Amen*) they all pronounce in worship. It is also pronounced at their anointing in baptism. Paul reminds us how, for him, God is not only a living and true God, in contrast to the idols so common in his time (1 Thessalonians 1:9), but a God who is faithful to his promises. Christ is the personification of these promises.

Mark now introduces a series of five stories of conflict in the life of Jesus, after his description of the day in Capernaum, in which Jesus demonstrated his authority in his healings, exorcisms and teaching (1:21–39). In the story of the paralytic, Jesus continues to display his authority over disease and he shows that it extends even to the forgiveness of sin. But he meets criticism and opposition from an unexpected quarter. Scribes, learned and respected people, accuse him of blasphemy, the charge on which the leaders of his own people will eventually condemn him (14:64).

The miracle is a response to the faith of the four men who bring the paralytic to Jesus by letting him through the roof of the house. Jesus demanded faith in his initial proclamation (1:15). Their faith contrasts with the lack of faith of the people in Nazareth, where Jesus could do no miracle (6:5), and with the failure of his own disciples' faith when they found themselves in danger from the storm (4:40). Such faith culminates in the praise of God expressed at the end of the story. The woman with the haemorrhage and Bartimaeus will also find healing through faith (5:34; 10:52).

This story also gives us a glimpse of the insightful personality of Jesus. He knows that the real need of the paralyzed man is forgiveness of sin. This reminds us of the appeal for repentance he made when he began his ministry (1:15). The scribes, despite their learning, cannot see this. Somehow they are paralyzed themselves. Their deafness to the teaching of Jesus prevents true sight. For the first time in the Gospel, Jesus claims authority as the Son of Man, an expression found fourteen times in Mark, used in three ways. First, as Son of Man, Jesus has authority on earth, as he instructed his critics (2:28); secondly, he is to undergo suffering and rejection, as he taught his disciples (8:31), but thirdly, he will complete his destiny (as foretold by Daniel [7:13]) of coming on the clouds of heaven for judgment, as he informed the High Priest (14:62).

Sunday 8 B

Hosea 2:16–17, 21–22
Psalm 102:1–4, 8, 10, 12–13
2 Corinthians 3:1–6
Mark 2:18–22

Christ the Bridegroom

Israel's prophets struggled to find adequate images to describe the relationship of God with his people. The one that fascinated **Hosea**, and other prophets too (Isaiah 62:5; Jeremiah 3:1–3; Ezekiel 16:8), was that God is the husband of Israel. But, like Hosea himself, God has married an unfaithful wife. Israel has gone after the Baals, the gods of neighbouring peoples. But God is a faithful husband who lives out the covenant, those virtues of mercy and faithfulness that define his nature (Exodus 34:6; Numbers 14:18). He is ready for a new beginning; he will take back his unfaithful bride. He will bring Israel to Egypt and the desert once more, the places where long ago their marriage began.

The **Psalm** is a very personal song of thanksgiving, perhaps celebrating recovery from sickness, articulating consciousness of sin forgiven. Like every good prayer, it is God-centred, using the same language to describe the covenant virtues of God that we find in Hosea and other prophets (Joel 2:13).

In the Greek world where Paul carried on his mission it was very useful for travellers to have letters of recommendation with them. Paul himself recommended Phoebe to the Roman Church (Romans 16:1–2). In **2 Corinthians**, Paul replies to those who objected that he carried no such letter himself. As usual, his answer, is theological. His converts themselves are all the letter of recommendation he needs. He does not need some patron to write one; God himself plays this role, because he has sent Paul. Paul works in the world of God's Holy Spirit. He is engaged in the ministry of the new covenant (Jeremiah 31:33).

We omit **Mark**'s account of the call of Levi and the controversy it caused (2:13–17), and move into the third of the five conflict stories in this section of the Gospel. The issue at stake is why Jesus' disciples do not fast. Fasting was a traditional work of piety for the devout Jew (Joel 2:15; Matthew 6:16–18), and the Pharisees and John the Baptist's disciples practised it.

In reply, Jesus first appeals to the language of the prophets. These prophets, including Hosea, thought of God as married to his people. Jesus calls himself the bridegroom. He has come to claim his people for his own and his disciples know it. That is why they cannot think of fasting. John expresses this image dramatically in his account of the marriage feast at Cana (John 2:1–11). The closing chapters of Revelation make much of the marriage of the Lamb of God with his people, and pronounce a blessing on all those invited to the marriage (Revelation 19:9).

But the time of celebration will come to an end. Just as John the Baptist has been arrested (1:14) and will soon be put to death (6:14–29), so will Jesus. The bridegroom, like the Servant of Isaiah (Isaiah 53:8), will be taken away. So fasting became a practice of Christians as they waited for his return, till this day (Mark 13:35; Acts 13:2).

This difficulty about fasting is part of a wider problem: the relation between the patterns of the old religion that Jesus is encountering and the new way that he is bringing. The people reacted to Jesus' initial activity in their synagogue with the cry, 'Here is a teaching that is new ... and with authority behind it' (1:27). To help his hearers think out the consequences of such novelty, Jesus speaks about new garments and new wine. The caution against mending old garments with new cloth, which shrinks, and in putting new wine, which ferments, into old wineskins, is a warning about the radical demands that the ministry and message of Jesus will always make on his followers. Old ways have to be thought through.

Sunday 9 B

Deuteronomy 5:12–15
Psalm 80:3–8, 10–11
2 Corinthians 4:6–11
Mark 2:23–3:6

The Man with the Withered Hand

We find the Ten Commandments (the Decalogue) listed in Exodus (20:1–17) and in **Deuteronomy** (5:6–21). The observance of the Sabbath day stands out as the main religious duty. This seventh day of the week is to be a day of rest from work. In Deuteronomy it is linked to God's deliverance of his people from Egypt. In Exodus, it recalls the rest that God himself took after his creation of the world in six days (Exodus 20:11; 31:12–17). This rest also has a social dimension; it applies to everybody, even to domestic animals.

In the **Psalm**, we are to place ourselves at the celebration of a liturgy in which the people commit themselves once again to observe the terms of the covenant of Sinai, where the commandments were given. The words that God speaks about bringing the people out of Egypt are close to those we find at the beginning of the Decalogue.

2 Corinthians contains some of Paul's most powerful and challenging language. His critics were asking what sort of an apostle he could be in view of the chaos that marked his efforts in Corinth. He first appeals to his own divine call. God's creative light has shone on him, too, as it had shone on the world at its creation. Secondly, he reflects on his apostleship. He is an apostle according to the model of the crucified Jesus. From this cross of Christ came the power of Christ. To human eyes, he might be no better than a fragile clay pot, but that pot contains treasure. And that is the force behind his apostleship. It is 'to shame what is strong that [God] chose what is weak by human reckoning' (1 Corinthians 1:27).

Mark concludes his five accounts of Jesus' conflicts with his opponents with two centred on Sabbath observance, a practice that distinguished Judaism in the first-century world. Jesus never abrogated the Sabbath commandment (3:4; 6:2). Even Easter Sunday could not begin before the Sabbath was over (16:1). But Jesus always asked what God's original intention was in giving his commandment (10:6). We have learnt this in our Deuteronomy reading. Here his final word is to stress how its purpose is to serve rather than oppress humanity .

In our first story, the institution of Sabbath is not called into question. The problem addressed is what sort of work is permitted on the Sabbath. Jesus appeals to an incident in the life of David. The point seems to be that human need overruled religious regulation. But the evangelist puts a stronger argument from the authority of Jesus. He is greater than David (12:37), and as Son of Man has authority not only in teaching (1:27) and in forgiving sins (2:10), but in interpreting the Sabbath.

The second story, like the first conflict of the five, combines both miracle and controversy (2:1–12). It is the bleakest of the series. Jesus alone breaks the silence. In contrast to other miracle stories, in which others speak and react, the sick man, the crowd and Jesus' opponents are all dumb. Jesus displays his anger at the hardness of heart he encounters. The conclusion of the story is a plot to destroy him. We are already on the road to the cross (14:1).

In this series of five conflict stories (2:1–3:6), we have seen something of the newness that Jesus is bringing (2:22). He is not contradicting the ways and institutions of the old religion, but demonstrating what God's real intentions had been in establishing them. In the words and actions of Jesus 'the kingdom of God is close at hand'; repentance and belief are the response for which he is looking (1:15).

Sunday 10 B

Genesis 3:9–15
Psalm 129
2 Corinthians 4:13–5:1
Mark 3:20–35

Jesus Accused

The opening of **Genesis** informs us about the introduction and progress of sin in the world (Romans 5:12). Our first parents want to know good and evil, and so disobey God. They learn instead about their own helplessness and dependence, symbolized by shame at their nakedness. The man blames the woman and the woman blames the serpent. God has words for each. He foretells the future enmity between Satan and the woman's descendants, and how her offspring will crush the serpent's head. Christian tradition understands this to apply to the conflict between Satan and Christ. Mary, the mother of Jesus, is the successor of the first woman and her offspring breaks Satan's power.

Our **Psalm** is one of the seven Penitential Psalms (Psalms 6, 31, 37, 50, 101, 129 and 142). The worshipper does not deny responsibility for sin, but knows that he prays to a God ready to forgive (Jeremiah 31:34). Comparing himself to a city watchman (Jeremiah 31:6), three times he repeats how he waits for the Lord. Left to himself, he cannot cope with his sin and guilt.

Paul in **2 Corinthians** has been under attack for making false claims to be an apostle (1:1). He continues his reflections on the marks of a true apostle. An apostle must believe in Christ and must proclaim him to others as his representative. He must also share in both Christ's death and his resurrection. Paul's missionary hardships have already brought him a share in the death of Jesus (Galatians 6:17), so he is confident of a part in the future resurrection. His destiny is a heavenly home and a spiritual body (1 Corinthians 15:44) when the earthly tent in which he now lives comes to its end.

Mark has prepared his readers for Jesus' encounters with his relatives and with scribes from Jerusalem by his story so far. Crowds have come to Jesus from every corner of the Holy Land (3:7–8), who far surpass in numbers those attracted by John the Baptist from Judaea and Jerusalem (1:5). Out of this crowd Jesus summoned Twelve to be with him (3:13–19). We learn today of their first experience of life in the company of Jesus. They have to watch him being accused by his relatives of being out of his mind and charged by the most learned authorities in the land, the scribes from Jerusalem, of performing his miracles in league with Satan.

The story of Jesus and his family is told in two parts. In the first, they wish to seize him (the word used of his later arrest in Gethsemane [14:44, 46, 49]), because they claim he is crazy. Practically all of Mark is reproduced in other Gospels; this incident is not, as if it was a tradition too embarrassing and better forgotten. In the second part, Jesus speaks of his own true family, a new family for which the qualification is to do the will of God, as Jesus himself did (14:36). Peter will later learn more about this new family (10:29–30).

The scribes from Jerusalem accuse Jesus of being an ally of Satan. He replies in parables. First, he tells a proverb about a divided household. Common sense makes it clear that such a kingdom cannot survive. Next he speaks about a burglar. Jesus himself is the burglar in the story: before attacking the power of Satan (1:25) he has first tied him up in their struggles in the desert (1:12–13). His final saying is a solemn Amen saying, the first in Mark. He promises forgiveness for every sin, even for the apostasy which was probably common during the persecution of Mark's time, but he solemnly warns about a sin that cannot be forgiven, a sin against the Holy Spirit. Such a sin occurs when someone attributes to evil what comes through the power of God. Such was the sin of the scribes from Jerusalem.

Sunday 11 B

Ezekiel 17:22–24
Psalm 91:2–3, 13–16
2 Corinthians 5:6–10
Mark 4:26–34

Parables of the Kingdom

Ezekiel was the prophet of restoration. At the time of Israel's exile, he looks forward to the return of the Davidic dynasty and to the fulfilment of the prophecy of Nathan (2 Samuel 7:5–16). He expresses this hope in his allegory of the cedar tree. God himself will plant this tree, which will become a shelter and a refuge for all the birds. Like Jerusalem on Mount Zion, it will be planted on a mountain. All the nations of the world, symbolized by the birds, will find a home in it (Isaiah 2:1–3).

In the **Psalm**, we are at prayer in the Temple, praying the prayer that the aged Simeon might have made morning and evening (Luke 2:25). The tree of the Psalm does not stand for the nation, but for the faithful Israelite who flourishes in his old age because of his fidelity and trust in his God (Psalm 1).

For Paul, the believer lives a life in Christ (Romans 6:11) as a result of faith and baptism. The final destiny and vocation of the Christian is to be 'with Christ', a state attained only through death (Philippians 1:23; 1 Thessalonians 4:17). In **2 Corinthians**, Paul describes the present state of the believer as exile from the Lord, an exile to be ended by the judgment that awaits every believer (Romans 14:10). In principle, we are already saved (Romans 5:1), but we have to ratify this salvation by living the sort of life appropriate for those whose bodies are instruments of righteousness (Romans 6:13). If this were not so, Christian hope would be meaningless, since 'Christians are told by the Spirit to look to faith for those rewards that righteousness hopes for' (Galatians 5:5). Our behaviour in this life does matter (John 5:29).

Although the teaching of Jesus was admired, according to **Mark**, right from the beginning of his ministry (Mark 1:22), so far we have heard little of its content. This is remedied by his parable chapter (4:1–34), which concludes with the two seed parables read today. Each offers an image of the Kingdom of God (1:15), a concept never defined in the Gospels, but only described obliquely through Jesus' deeds and words, among which we include these parables.

In the first parable, the contrast is between the day-to-day activity of the farmer and the silent but persistent growth of the seed. The farmer wakes and sleeps, the seed puts up shoot and ear, and is finally ready for harvest. Then it is time for the farmer to resume his work. The parable can be understood in various ways. It could be a warning to Jesus' enemies (such as the Pharisees and the Herodians [3:6]), that nothing can stop the growth of the Kingdom. It could be a reassurance to his friends (such as the Twelve whom he has recently called [3:13]). Though they seemed to be achieving little, God's work has begun and, despite opposition, will continue. It could be a challenge to impatient members of Mark's Church: God is taking his time and they cannot hasten the conclusion of his work.

The second parable concerns a mustard seed, said to be the smallest of all the seeds on the earth. We ignore its period of growth and move straight to its final state, when it has become the greatest shrub of all; now all the birds of the air nest in its branches. This fresh version of Ezekiel's allegory could be a message to their enemies not to be deceived by the apparent helplessness of Jesus and his disciples. It could be reassurance to the disciples not to be discouraged by their own small numbers and lack of resources. In Ezekiel's story, God had taken a single branch and caused an enormous tree to grow from it. There every nation of the earth can find a home. Such parables are to make us think out the meaning of the Kingdom.

Sunday 12 B

Job 38:1, 8–11
Psalm 106:23–26, 28–31
2 Corinthians 5:14–17
Mark 4:35–41

The Calming of the Storm

The relationship between God and the sea in the scriptures is ambiguous. In the first book of the Bible, God does not so much create the sea as bring it to order (Genesis 1:2). In its last book, there is no room for the sea in the new creation (Revelation 21:1). This reflects ancient Near Eastern mythology, which identified the sea with the forces of evil. So does the description of the sea we find in **Job**; it is seen as an unruly beast, to be kept in check by mist and cloud, and confined behind a bolted gate like a wild animal. The people of Israel were reluctant sailors.

The **Psalm** is a hymn to the God who is always ready to come to the aid of his own in distress, especially seafarers in trouble. God rescues them and brings them to their destination. John would have had this Psalm in mind when he described how Jesus came to his disciples in crisis on the lake and brought them to harbour (John 6:21).

Paul in **2 Corinthians** continues to reflect on his life as an apostle. Its ultimate inspiration is the personal love of Christ, who loved him and gave himself for him (Galatians 2:20); his Christianity is not a religion of doctrine or a book, but one inspired by the love of this person. No longer does he live with the powers of unaided human nature—the flesh—but he is now 'in Christ', a 'new creation'. Before his conversion, Paul looked forward to the new age in the future. His conversion taught him that this new age had already come through the death and resurrection of Christ (Galatians 1:4). The standards of the past no longer apply (Philippians 3:7).

We can understand the Gospel of **Mark** as a treatise for the beginner in Christianity. The reader is to grasp that Jesus is the Christ, the Son of God (1:1), and to learn what it means to be a follower of Jesus. Fellow pupils in this school are the Twelve, called at the lakeside (1:16–20) and on the mountain (3:13). They have already witnessed Jesus' authority: over disease and over demons during the day at Capernaum (1:21–39), in controversy in his encounters with opponents (2:1–3:6), and in teaching by his parables to the crowds (4:1–34).

Mark follows all of this up with four extraordinary examples of Jesus' authority. The first concerns the dominion of Jesus over nature in his calming of a storm, an activity that belonged to God alone (Psalm 107:29). He then exorcises a man possessed by a legion of demons (5:1–20), heals, by touch alone, a woman sick for twelve years and, finally, raises a twelve-year-old child from death (5:21–43). But then all this power exercised by Jesus is called into question because he cannot perform miracles in his home town (6:5). All these incidents contribute to the education of his disciples and of those who hear this Gospel.

Without warning Jesus orders his disciples to go across the lake. They take Jesus into a boat and set off, but run into a storm. Soon, whether exhausted by his ministry or at peace in the hands of his Father (Psalm 4:8), Jesus falls asleep on a cushion. The disciples might have been expected to turn to him for help in faith and trust; instead, they panic, calling out to him in a somewhat insolent tone, as if he were indifferent to their plight. At once, Jesus calms the storm, and bluntly challenges them, 'How is it that you have no faith? They make no reply; they can only discuss among themselves: 'Who can this be?' Even the wind and the sea obey him.' The lesson has failed; they have not recognised Jesus as the one with the power of God himself (Psalm 107) and have not behaved like true disciples in a time of stress.

Sunday 13 B

Wisdom 1:13–15; 2:23–24
Psalm 29:2, 4–6, 11–13
2 Corinthians 8:7, 9, 13–15
Mark 5:21–43

Disease and Death Overcome

Writing less than a century before Christ, the author of **Wisdom** looks back over the history of Israel and reflects how God's wisdom has been active in it from the start. He reaffirms the teaching of Genesis, that humanity did not come into being by chance, but was created through God's design in his own image (Genesis 1:27). As for death, this was not in God's plan, but it came about as result of the devil's scheming (Genesis 3:19). He goes beyond the teaching of Genesis in declaring how God's human creation is imperishable and immortal.

The **Psalm** is a song of thanksgiving for recovery from sickness. The psalmist will always be grateful. We note a contrast with Wisdom. God can rescue from sickness but this psalmist gives no hope beyond death. He is in the situation of Jairus before he met Jesus.

The Jerusalem apostles told Paul to remember the poor when they met with him (Galatians 2:10). He does so in **2 Corinthians** by encouraging his readers to imitate his other Churches in sending financial help to the poor of the Church in Jerusalem. His converts have a special responsibility because this is the mother Church. In a briefer version of the hymn of Philippians (2:6–11), he argues from the example of Christ. He was rich in possessing life with the Father (John 17:5); his impoverishment was his sharing of the human condition and acceptance of death on the cross. Paul does not ask for impoverishment, but a fair sharing of resources. He draws authority from scripture by recalling the experience of the ancestors in the desert, who all received a fair share of the manna that God sent from heaven (Exodus 16:18).

In our readings from **Mark**, we omit the Gerasene demoniac (5:1–20) and move to the third and fourth of Jesus' spectacular series of miracles: the woman with a haemorrhage and Jairus' daughter. We learn about the mighty power of this Jesus. In a moment, he cures a woman whom twelve years' treatment by expensive doctors have failed to help. With a word, he raises to life a twelve-year-old girl whom many had witnessed to be dead. These incidents, like the calming of the storm we heard last week, are part of the education of the disciples in the school of Jesus. Their response is unimpressive. In the first story they reply somewhat insolently to Jesus when he asks, 'Who touched my clothes?' In the second, the three who are allowed to remain with Jesus take no part. Do they join in the mocking laughter at Jesus when he says that the dead girl is not dead but only asleep?

It is the behaviour and example of the sick woman herself in the first account, and of Jairus in the second, that edify us. We may admire the initial faith of the woman, who believes that if only she could touch Jesus she would be cured. Her statement proves correct only for physical healing, since her condition afterwards is still one of fear and trembling. Only when she has told Jesus the whole truth, and has established an open personal relationship with him, is she told, 'your faith has restored you to health'.

As for Jairus, the father of the girl who has died, his faith initially extends only to the power of Jesus to heal the sick. Once she is dead, he is ready to listen to his friends and go home. But because Jesus tells him, 'Do not be afraid; only have faith', he remains. His trust in Jesus is repaid and he receives far more than he had believed possible. Both of these characters are presented by Mark as models for imitation. There are different levels of faith in Jesus. Persecuted by the emperor Nero, Mark's community needed the quality of faith shown by these two figures, who appear briefly on the stage of the gospel story and disappear (Mark 14:9).

Sunday 14 B

Ezekiel 2:2–5
Psalm 122
2 Corinthians 12:7–10
Mark 6:1–6

Rejection at Home

The book of **Ezekiel** begins with a vision of God, arguably the most awesome in all the prophets. This God speaks to Ezekiel and gives him his commission. God makes Ezekiel his messenger and gives him his Spirit, but does not promise success. Ezekiel's mission is to a defiant people who will ignore a message from God. The sin and corruption that have brought about the loss of land and Temple will hold Israel back from listening to a prophet sent to it by God himself.

The **Psalm** is a hymn of lamentation, a prayer to God for mercy in a time of trouble, made in a spirit of confidence and trust. The picture before us is that of an unfaithful slave looking for forgiveness from his master.

Titus returned from Corinth with bad news. Paul's enemies have won control over the **Corinthians** (12:18). They have convinced them that Paul is not an apostle and has taught a false gospel. Paul's reply is in the language of a fool (11:1). He boasts about his origins and the hardships the gospel had brought him (11:21–29). This is the only defence he can use against the 'arch-apostles' (12:11) who think themselves so superior because of their successes and gifts, but who refuse to find a place for the cross of Christ. Yes, he was privileged with revelations from the Lord, but these have not made him proud. They have made him more conscious of his weaknesses: 'I was given a thorn in the flesh'. The Lord has refused his repeated prayer for deliverance. For Paul, the apostle is one who gives his all in the service of the gospel. The grace of God in weakness is sufficient reward.

In **Mark**'s story of Jesus, his first successes in healing and in controversy (1:21–3:6) ended with Jesus' anger at the hard-heartedness of the religious authorities and the plot of the Pharisees and Herodians to destroy him (3:1–6). Similarly, his mighty miracles overcoming nature (4:35–41), the forces of hell (5:1–20), sickness and death (5:21–43) conclude with a story of rejection, this time by the people of his home town of Nazareth.

Jesus had left Nazareth to go to John the Baptist (1:9); now he returns. His disciples are following him. We ask how he will be received. What part will his disciples play? On the Sabbath, he teaches in the synagogue, but this time he wins no admiration, as he had in Capernaum (1:22). His audience are curious: they ask where he got his wisdom and power. His wisdom has shown itself in his teaching (4:1–34) and his power in miracles, such as the cure of Simon's mother-in-law (1:29–31) and the raising of Jairus' daughter (5:35–43). But he is simply their carpenter and his family live in the town. Repentance and belief in the gospel (1:15), the objects of his mission, have no chance. We heard in his parable of the sower how some fall away because of persecution or affliction (4:17). The people of Nazareth fall because of over-familiarity. Jesus' powers are paralyzed. Mark reports bluntly that he 'could work no miracle there', a statement too strong for Matthew, who modified the 'could not' to a 'did not' (Matthew 13:58). Now it is Jesus' turn to be amazed (5:20).

We are told nothing about his disciples. Theirs was surely a painful experience. Mark will soon relate how John the Baptist was rejected and executed by Herod (6:14–29). The fate of the Baptist and the ordeal of Jesus at Nazareth anticipate Calvary and prepare the disciples for possible rejection on their own mission (6:11) and for the announcement of the cross (8:34).

Sunday 15 B

Amos 7:12–15
Psalm 84:9–14
Ephesians 1:3–14
Mark 6:7–13

The Mission of the Twelve

The first of the great writing prophets of Israel, **Amos** lived in a time of material prosperity, but he knew that this prosperity was for the few at the expense of the many (8:4–7). Though he belongs to no prophetic guild, he is conscious of divine vocation. He was tolerated as long as he denounced the sins of the nations around Israel (1:1–2:5), but once he challenges the corruption of Israel itself (2:6–16), he is attacked as an interfering foreigner. Amaziah, priest of Bethel, tries to silence Amos. He cannot see his own responsibility for the corruption of the royal court.

A temple official contemplates the prosperity of the nation after the gift of rain in the **Psalm**. He gives thanks where it is due. He extols the qualities of the God of the Exodus, his mercy and kindness (Exodus 34:6–7), and attributes material blessings to the fear of the Lord and a respect for his justice.

Ephesians may be a circular letter addressed to Pauline Churches. It begins with the Jewish prayer form of a blessing (2 Corinthians 1:3–7). We bless God because of the love and wisdom shown in creation and in Christ. Christ gives creation its meaning. We bless God because he chose us from the beginning and though, because of sin, we were captives, we were given freedom through the blood of Christ and became God's children. This is the good news that we heard and believed. It has been sealed by the Spirit in baptism. We respond with holy lives. Thus Ephesians begins with a noble proclamation of Christian belief in the Trinitarian God and in human dignity.

So far in **Mark**'s story, we have heard of the call of the Four by the lake (1:16–20) and of the Twelve on the mountain (3:13–15), but we have been told nothing about independent activity or initiative on the part of the disciples. Now that they have seen Jesus enjoying the extremes of success (4:33–5:43) and failure (6:1–6), it is time for them go out on their mission. Jesus gives instructions. Like him, they are to cast out demons (1:26), to heal the sick (1:34) and to call for repentance (1:15). Their mission foreshadows that of travelling missionaries in every age of Christianity.

Jesus' first order to them concerns their equipment. It is a list of what they are not to take with them. They are to be like Jesus in carrying almost nothing apart from a staff for the road and a pair of sandals. Heading the list of forbidden baggage is bread. The section of Mark that we are beginning is often known as the 'bread section' because of the number of times the word is mentioned (6:7–8:21). Mark may be hinting at the Eucharist, a doctrine easily misunderstood by outsiders (14:22). Missionaries of Mark's own time would reflect that, though they often lacked material resources, they had the Eucharistic presence of their Lord with them.

Jesus' next orders concern procedures in the event of acceptance or rejection. Like himself, they will at times receive a good welcome, as he had in the house of Simon (1:29). But, at other times, they will share in his Nazareth experience of rejection (6:1–6). Some will even share the fate of John the Baptist, whose tragic death at the hands of Herod fills the gap in Mark between the departure of the disciples and their return (6:14–29). They are not to react violently to a lack of welcome, but simply depart, shaking the dust from their feet, as Paul and Barnabas did at Antioch in Pisidia (Acts 13:51). In the event, their mission proves successful. Their anointing of the sick with oil is continued in the Church to this day in the Sacrament of the Sick.

Sunday 16 B

Jeremiah 23:1–6
Psalm 22
Ephesians 2:13–18
Mark 6:30–34

Sheep without a Shepherd

Jeremiah lived in the days of the corrupt last kings of Judah. Nathan's prophecy to David seems to have come to nothing (2 Samuel 7:4–17). Kings, who should have been shepherds of their people, have made way for foreign tyrants. The prophet knows that God will not abandon his own, even if only a remnant survive. In a messianic text, he foresees an ideal future king who will embody in himself the very qualities of God. His name, Yahweh-our-integrity, reads in Hebrew very like Zedekiah, the last king of Judah. The one who fulfilled this prophecy of the Good Shepherd was Jesus himself.

The **Psalm** describes God as ideal ruler and shepherd. With such a shepherd the people survive bad times when they pass through the valley of darkness and appreciate good times when, as their host, God feeds them at a banquet.

According to **Ephesians**, God brings everything together in Christ (1:10). Division between Jew and Gentile belongs to the past, thanks to the blood of Christ. His death brought about the reconciliation of humanity and the whole world to God (Romans 5:1; 2 Corinthians 5:19), and ended separation between human groups. The wall in the Jerusalem Temple, set up to keep Jews and Gentiles apart, had been pulled down in principle by Christ long before it was physically destroyed by the Romans in AD 70. For those in Christ there are no divisions, wrote Paul (Galatians 3:28). According to John, the Good Shepherd, Christ, died to bring into one the scattered people of God (John 10:16; 11:52).

After describing the death of John the Baptist, showing him as the forerunner of Jesus not only in his life (1:7) but in his death (6:14–29), **Mark** reports the conclusion of the mission of the Twelve. Only here, apart from at their call (3:14), does he call them apostles, because they have been the representatives of Jesus. They tell Jesus all that they have done and taught; sadly, we are given no details of their report.

Mark alone at this point includes Jesus' invitation to his apostles to rest awhile. Like the shepherd in the Psalm, Jesus gives repose. Matthew tells us how, on another occasion, Jesus invited his disciples to rest because his yoke is easy and his burden light (Matthew 11:29–30). Elsewhere in the New Testament, it is rest to which the Christian looks forward as a final reward (Hebrews 3:11; Revelation 14:13), a rest corresponding to that for which Israel longed after its desert wanderings (Deuteronomy 12:10).

After his activities in Capernaum (1:21–34), Jesus withdrew to a desert place to pray (1:35). He was soon interrupted by Simon and those with him (1:36). The apostles, too, are deprived of their peace by the crowds that have seen their departure. Just as Jesus attracted crowds from every corner of the Holy Land (3:7–8), now crowds run to the apostles from every city. We are not told about their reaction, because Jesus takes control. In Matthew, he took pity on the crowds and healed their sick (14:14). Mark adds a motive for his pity: they are like sheep without a shepherd. He sees in Jesus the true shepherd of whom Jeremiah wrote (Jeremiah 23:4). The first task of this shepherd is to teach them many things, although Mark is silent about the content of his teaching (1:22). We have already learnt from the parables of Jesus (4:1–34) how such teaching can produce a hundredfold (4:8) and provide shelter for all nations, represented by all the birds of the sky (4:32). After he taught them, this shepherd gave physical food by multiplying the loaves and the fishes.

Sunday 17 B

2 Kings 4:42–44
Psalm 144:10–11, 15–18
Ephesians 4:1–6
John 6:1–15

The Feeding of the Five Thousand

Elijah and Elisha are the first prophets of Israel about whom we have solid information. They lived a hundred years before Amos, the first of the writing prophets. Their memory is passed on chiefly in the form of traditions about their amazing deeds. **2 Kings** gives us no fewer than ten legends about Elisha (4:1–8:15). Today, we read how he fed one hundred men with twenty barley loaves. His own confident authority is contrasted with the bewilderment of his servant. Jesus in John fed five thousand with five barley loaves, to the surprise of his disciples.

The **Psalm** is a call to praise God, because of the care he exercises for his creation in providing it with food. In Jewish tradition it has been used as a prayer several times a day; for Christians it is a traditional grace before meals.

The exhortation section of **Ephesians** begins with an appeal to the authority of Paul in prison. The Christian is to exercise the virtues in which Christ excelled, such as the humility hymned in Philippians (2:3, 8) and the gentleness proclaimed in Matthew (11:29). Above all, they are called to unity, a major theme in John (17:21). The unity achieved between Jew and Gentile (2:14) is to mark all Christian life. For Christians, unlike the polytheistic unbelievers around them, there is one God, who is Father of all things. There is one Lord, the Christ to whom the Father has given his own name (Philippians 2:9), and a single Spirit (1 Corinthians 12:4). The Church is one body (1 Corinthians 12:12), with a single faith and a single baptism. This is a key passage in ecumenical discussions and a goad to divided Christians to lament their disunity.

Each Gospel describes how Jesus fed a crowd with a few loaves and fish (Mark 6:30–44; 8:1–10; Matthew 14:13–21; 15:32–39; Luke 9:10–17). For the next five weeks, we read **John**'s account of the event and its sequel. This is the fourth of Jesus' signs in John (2:11; 4:54; 5:9). The discourse that follows takes the form of an encounter, not with an individual such as Nicodemus (3:1–21) or the Samaritan woman (4:7–42), but with a hostile crowd. Jesus is in Galilee, followed by crowds who, like Nicodemus, are impressed by his signs (3:2), though we are not told that they believe his teaching.

He goes up a mountain, and sits with his disciples. For some he is a new Moses on another Sinai, or a rabbi giving instruction (Matthew 5:1). It is Passover, the festival recalling Israel's liberation from Egyptian slavery (2:13; 13:1). Jesus raises his eyes and sees crowds approaching (4:35). He knows what he will do. Jesus in John knows about people and events (1:47; 13:3). He tests Philip by speaking about loaves. This Philip announced to Nathanael that he had found the one written of in the prophets (1:45), so he should know that Jesus has other ways of feeding the crowd than by spending 200 denarii on bread. Andrew had proclaimed Jesus as the messiah to Peter (1:41), but he can only wonder how a boy with five barley loaves could feed such a crowd. Both disciples have a long way to go before they will recognise Jesus himself as the Bread of Life who can feed the people without money and loaves (6:35).

Jesus feeds the crowd. The feeding is described in Eucharistic terms (Mark 14:22–23). The meal over, the crowd greet Jesus as the prophet who is to come into the world, echoing the words of Moses when he speaks of a prophet like himself (Deuteronomy 18:15). We know that Jesus was greater than Moses (1:17). The crowd want to make him king. He is indeed a king, but only in the sense he will explain to Pilate at his trial, the king of those who listen to the truth (18:37), a king who would reign from the cross (19:19). Jesus flees back up the mountain.

Sunday 18 B

Exodus 16:2–4, 12–15
Psalm 77:3–4, 23–25, 54
Ephesians 4:17, 20–24
John 6:24–35

Encounter with the Crowd

The God of **Exodus** was an active God. He made sure his people escaped from Egyptian bondage by inflicting ten plagues on the Egyptians (Exodus 7–11). He made his people into a strong nation by testing them (1 Peter 1:7). The first test was about water: the people complained of the bitterness of the water of Marah. God heard their cry and enabled Moses to sweeten it (Exodus 15:22–27). The second test, here, concerns food: they miss the food they enjoyed in Egypt (Numbers 11:5). Again God hears them and gives them manna from heaven.

The **Psalm** celebrates the part played by God in the history of his people. He has never allowed their stubbornness and disobedience to cancel out his own fidelity. The manna—the bread from heaven, the food of angels—is one example of his mercy.

Many of those addressed in **Ephesians** came from pagan backgrounds, whose standard of moral behaviour was bleak (Romans 1:29; 1 Peter 4:3; Ephesians 4:18–19). The author appeals to them to make all this a thing of the past: the way of life of the 'old self'. The Christian way is different; it is life according to the person of Christ. They have learnt Christ; they have heard him. They have put on his body in baptism; when they put on the new baptismal garment, they put on the 'new self'. This means a new way of life, which is to be characterized by the truth, goodness and holiness of Christ. Humanity before Christ was marked by the sin of Adam (Romans 5:12); after Christ, it cultivates the qualities of Christ, the new man, the new Adam (1 Corinthians 15:45–48).

In **John**, we read of Jesus' encounters with individuals whom he leads, step by step, to a deeper understanding of himself and his mission. His meeting with the Samaritan woman is an example. Gradually he brought her to an understanding of the living water that he offered (4:1–42). We approach his encounter with the crowd to whom he offers the bread of life in a similar way.

On the day after the feeding of the five thousand, the crowd find Jesus again. They address him as Rabbi (1:38) and ask when he arrived. Have they forgotten how they proclaimed him a prophet and king the day before? They show no interest in those events and their meaning. Jesus replies with an Amen saying—these are sayings that challenge the hearer with a hitherto unknown truth. He tells them not to look for the sort of food that perishes (like yesterday's food [6:27]), but to work for food that endures for eternal life. Ignoring this new sort of food, the crowd take up his word 'work': what are they to do, to be doing the works of God? 'Believe in the one he has sent', Jesus replies. Some see here a combination of Paul's doctrine of faith (Romans 5:1) and the teaching of James on works (James 2:14).

The crowd refuse to believe that Jesus is 'the one he has sent' unless they see a sign. Jewish tradition expected prophets to give proof of their call. Moses had given the sign of the manna, 'He gave them bread from heaven to eat' (Exodus 16:15). With another Amen saying, Jesus challenges them to recast this text. They are not to say that Moses gave, but rather that the Father gives. It is not manna that God gives but the true bread that has come down from heaven and gives life to the world. When Jesus told the Samaritan woman about the water that welled up to eternal life, she had asked Jesus to give it her (4:14). The crowd ask Jesus for this bread of life. He announces to them that he himself is that bread. He can now lead them to the next stage of understanding of himself and his mission.

Sunday 19 B

1 Kings 19:4–8
Psalm 33:2–9
Ephesians 4:30–5:2
John 6:41–51

The Murmuring of the Crowd

After his defeat of the prophets of Baal on Mount Carmel (1 Kings 18), we read in **1 Kings** how Elijah feels drained. He is overcome by a sense of inadequacy. He wants to die, and withdraws into the desert. But God has not forgotten him, and sends an angel to feed him. Legends tell how angels fed Adam in paradise. God gave his people manna, the food of angels, in the wilderness (Psalms 78:25). Angels ministered to Jesus in the desert (Mark 1:13). And thanks to this food, Elijah walks for forty days and forty nights to the mountain of Horeb, where Moses had met God (Exodus 19). Elijah completes his pilgrimage.

The **Psalm** thanks God for deliverance from trouble. Traditionally, it is connected with an incident in the life of David (1 Samuel 21:11–16). We can also apply it to our Elijah story. The reference to seeing and tasting prepares us for the Bread of Life in John.

The letter to the **Ephesians** is, above all, concerned with the Church. Elsewhere Paul calls each believer a temple of the Holy Spirit (1 Corinthians 6:19). In Ephesians, the whole Church is a temple of the Holy Spirit. An offence against the Church is an offence against the Spirit. Behaviour that appears merely anti-social, such as loss of temper and name-calling, is a sin against heaven (Luke 15:21). We forgive one another because God forgives us (Luke 11:4). Although Christian morality may not differ in content from the best of secular morality, it is different in its motivation. Christians know that they are children of God (Romans 8:15), delivered from the power of sin by Christ 'who loved me and who sacrificed himself for my sake' (Galatians 2:20). They live their lives 'in Christ' (2 Corinthians 5:17).

For the first time in **John**'s account of the sequel to the feeding of the five thousand, the crowd turns hostile. The evangelist calls them 'the Jews', his term for Jesus' enemies. They murmur against him, as the Israelites had murmured against Moses in the desert (Exodus 16:2; 1 Corinthians 10:10). They no longer look for food that perishes, true; they seek the bread that offers them eternal life (6:34), but they refuse to accept Jesus himself as this bread. How could he have come down from heaven when they know his parents? They argue like those in Jesus' home town whose lack of faith had astonished Jesus and prevented him from performing any miracle there (Mark 6:1–6).

Bluntly, Jesus tells them to cease their murmuring. When they demanded a sign from him to authenticate his claim, they quoted from Exodus (16:15). Now he quotes the prophet Isaiah (54:13): 'They will all be taught by God'. They can only come to him if the Father draws them to him, and Jesus himself is the sole means for the Father to do so. This Gospel witnesses to Jesus as the great revealer of the Father. He is God's word (1:1), the Father's means of communication (14:9). Jesus bears witness to what he has seen and heard above (3:32). He offers God's revelation as living water (4:10), and speaks openly to the world (19:20). He makes known to his disciples all he has heard from the Father (15:15). The word he speaks is food for eternal life just as earthly bread is food for temporal life. When we think of the Jesus as the Bread of Life, we are to think of his Word as well as his Flesh in the Eucharist.

Finally, he refers to the manna that Moses gave (Exodus 16:15). His audience claim Moses as their hero (9:28). But both Moses and their ancestors, whom he had fed, are dead. The bread that Jesus gives, which is identical with him, brings with it eternal life. Through its means, believers will have life and have it more abundantly in this earthly life (10:10), and at the last day, he will raise them from physical death.

Sunday 20 B

Proverbs 9:1–6
Psalm 33:2–3, 10–15
Ephesians 5:15–20
John 6:51–58

Real Food and Drink

Besides the loaves multiplied by Elisha (2 Kings 4:42–44), the manna provided for rebellious Israel by Moses (Exodus 16:2–4) and the bread given to Elijah by the angel (1 Kings 19:4–8), any discussion of food in the Old Testament must include Wisdom's banquet in **Proverbs**. The house that she has built is the school where she passes on her learning. Its seven pillars it identify it with the world that God built on pillars (1 Samuel 2:8). The meat and wine she offers symbolize the richness of her instruction; her invitation, offered to the whole city, symbolizes its universal application.

The **Psalm** is a continuation of last week's song of thanksgiving. Wisdom now addresses her children and, in a very simple theology, identifies prosperity with piety. Strong lions may starve to death, but the one who listens to Wisdom need want nothing.

Ephesians continues its exhortation to Christian living. Following Jewish wisdom tradition, the author urges his readers to attend to the needs of the times and to discern in them the will of God. Theirs is to be a community full of life, but life that comes from the Holy Spirit rather than from excess of wine (Acts 2:15). Their worship is to involve the exercise of the talents of each, particularly in music and song (1 Corinthians 14:26). This is to be a worship that never ceases, continuing in the silence of their hearts. The whole of their lives is to be adoration and sacrifice to God (Romans 12:1). They are to live out their conviction that God is above all and through all and in all (4:6), one who brings all things together in Christ (1:10).

Last week, the Jews (which in **John** means those hostile to Jesus), murmured because of his teaching; now they fight among themselves. They fight because Jesus claims to be the Bread of Life, not only in the sense of being God's revelation, but also because his own physical flesh is that bread. Here we find the explicit Eucharistic teaching of the discourse, very relevant to John's readers and ourselves because only in the Eucharist can we now see the Son (6:40). John reports nothing about the Eucharist in his account of the Last Supper, where he substitutes the washing of the feet (13:1–20).

Words for 'eat' and 'life' dominate our passage. Jesus uses two words for *eat*, both repeated four times. One of them, *trogo*, leaves no doubt that physical eating is in mind. The Eucharist is more than a symbol or a sign to be adored. The body and blood of Christ are to be eaten and drunk. The effects of the Eucharist are described in terms of *life*. There is life for the world. There is life for the individual, described as eternal life. There is the life that comes from abiding in Jesus. In brief, the giving of life summarises the whole ministry of Jesus in John. Through the work of the Son, God wants to share with us his most precious possession, his own life.

As elsewhere in John, Jesus insists that a relationship with himself means a relationship with the Father (14:9). By sharing in the life of the Son, the believer shares the life that the Father gives the Son. The Son and the Father will make their home in the believer who loves him and keeps his word (14:23). The Eucharist implies a response of love and obedience together with a permanent indwelling of the Son. The discourse has come to its end; we now know that food for the crowds that came to Jesus was not to be bought with 200 denarii, as Philip thought (6:7), nor was it to be found in the basket of the little boy discovered by Andrew (6:9), but in the Word and Sacrament brought by Jesus, who continues to give himself as the Bread of Life.

Sunday 21 B

Joshua 24:1–2, 15–18
Psalm 33:2–3, 16–23
Ephesians 5:21–32
John 6:60–69

The Confession of Peter

Shechem is one of the ancient holy places of Palestine. Situated between two mountains, Gerizim and Ebal, it is close to Samaria, the place where Jesus met the woman at the well (John 4). **Joshua** reports the old tradition that, once the conquest of the Land was complete, the whole of Israel, even those, such as the family of Rahab (Joshua 6:25), who had not shared the desert experience, as well as other inhabitants of the land, assembled at the shrine and committed themselves to the God who had brought the tribes out of Egypt. At Shechem, Israel rejects the many gods of their ancestors and the many gods of the nations around, and becomes a single people committed to one God.

Our **Psalm** guarantees the protection of God to the just, such as those who committed themselves to him at Shechem. It is quoted in the letter of Peter as encouragement to his readers to lead a good life (1 Peter 3:12) and by John in his Gospel when he wrote that not a bone of Jesus was broken (John 19:36).

Ephesians includes what is called a household code. Such codes give advice to guide the behaviour of different members of a household. Christian authors use them to prove that Christianity is not an enemy of social order. Social structures can glorify God (Colossians 3:16–4:1; 1 Peter 2:18–3:7). Thus marriage is not a merely human institution but a relationship patterned on the love that Christ has for his Church. The prophets had taught that God was the husband of his people (Isaiah 54:6). Ephesians tells us that Christ is married to his Church, and that it is in this marriage that the text of Genesis (2:24) finds true fulfilment.

The crowds disappear, but the disciples remain, many of them only to complain. They find this word hard. Do they mean the teaching of the discourse as a whole? Or just its climax in which Jesus identified his flesh with the Bread of Life in the Eucharist? Jesus makes no compromise, but warns them that they are also to see the Son of Man going to where he was before, a reference to his future, when he will be lifted up, both on the cross and in the Ascension (3:14; 12:32). They will not understand him unless they open themselves to the grace of the Father, which alone can draw them to belief (6:44). Like all who will see the Kingdom of God, they have to be reborn through the Spirit (3:5).

In the Synoptic Gospels, Peter had spoken up for the other disciples at Caesarea Philippi when he confessed Jesus to be the messiah (Mark 8:29). In **John**, Peter had already come to this belief at the Jordan river, on the word of his brother Andrew, when he first met Jesus (1:41). The confession that Peter makes here is one of a series in this Gospel. The Samaritans recognised Jesus as Saviour of the world (4:42). The man born blind believed in him as the Son of Man (9:38). Martha called Jesus the Christ, the Son of God (11:27). Peter acknowledges Jesus as the one who has the words of eternal life; he is the great revealer, the Holy One of God. John wants his readers to make these confessions their own (20:31).

There had been departures from the community for which John wrote (1 John 2:19). It is probably to these that we owe the emphasis in the narrative on lack of belief and the mention of Judas (6:71). Apostasies may well have come about because of a failure to accept doctrines such as this about the Eucharist. Jesus not only brought them living water that symbolized both his teaching and the Spirit (4:14; 19:34); he was the true bread on which they were to feed in order to come to eternal life with the Father (14:2).

Sunday 22 B

Deuteronomy 4:1–2, 6–8
Psalm 14:2–5
James 1:17–18, 21–22, 27
Mark 7:1–8, 14–15, 21–25

Pure Religion

Six hundred years before Christ, the book of **Deuteronomy** took its final shape. Much of its content is a list of the laws that Israel should observe. Law in itself can be dry and uninspiring. The understanding of law found in Deuteronomy is life-giving and humane. The observance of this Law helped the nation survive centuries of foreign domination. Good law has qualities that identify it with wisdom and discernment. Other nations are to envy Israel's Law as well as Israel's God.

The **Psalm** lists the qualities required of those who wish to worship in the Temple in Jerusalem. In word and deed, they are to imitate the justice and truth of God (Exodus 34:6). Those who love and respect their neighbour will be comfortable before God.

The letter of **James** enjoys the authority of the brother of the Lord (Mark 6:3), the leader of the Jerusalem Church (Galatians 2:9). In our passage, he answers three questions. Who is God? God is the father of lights. He created the stars (Genesis 1:15). Their movements in the heavens contrast them with God, who is unmoving and solid, ever reliable. Who are we? We are the children of God through his word of truth (Romans 8:14). This word may be the gospel that has been preached (Colossians 1:5) or his Son (John 1:1, 12). How do we worship this God? Through the practice of true religion. In this letter, with its stress on deeds, this means care for the orphan and the widow. James echoes language familiar to his Jewish-Christian readers from the humane provisions of their Law which we have heard in Deuteronomy and in the Psalm of today (Deuteronomy 10:18; Exodus 22:21).

From the Gospel of **Mark**, which we rejoin after five weeks, we learn how, by the time of Jesus, the noble ideal of Law described in Deuteronomy had degenerated. The Pharisees, who objected to the healing of the man with the withered hand on the Sabbath (3:1–6), reappear. With them are the scribes from Jerusalem, who accused Jesus of being in league with Beelzebul (3:22). They criticize Jesus for allowing his disciples to eat bread with unwashed hands (2:23). Mark interrupts his narrative to explain the washing customs of the Pharisees. Did his Gentile readers need this explanation, or is he quietly urging the Jewish Christians in Rome to see something of the absurdity of these oral additions to the original Law (Romans 14:21)?

In his reply, Jesus makes a counter-accusation. He calls his critics hypocrites, because, in their attention to its detail, they have misunderstood the original intention of the Law. (Matthew develops this charge of hypocrisy much further [Matthew 23].) In previous controversies, Jesus has concluded the discussion with a saying of his own (2:17, 27). Here, he appeals to prophetic tradition by quoting Isaiah, who lived in a time of material prosperity that depended on exploitation of the weak. True religion comes from the heart, not from the lips (Isaiah 29:13; 1:10–20). This text is also quoted in Colossians, to protect Pauline converts from being burdened with ascetic practices of purely human origin (Colossians 2:22). Jesus also cites their custom of *korban*, which deprived needy parents of financial support in the name of religion (7:9–13).

The second half of our reading telescopes two sayings of Jesus. In the first, a parable spoken to the crowds, he teaches that it is only those things that come out of a person that make the person unclean. As in his parable chapter (4:1–34), he explains privately to his disciples that he is speaking about the evil that comes out of the heart. He defines this evil in a list of twelve vices that remind us of Paul's works of the flesh catalogued in Galatians (5:19–21).

Sunday 23 B

Isaiah 35:4–7
Psalm 147:7–10
James 2:1–5
Mark 7:31–37

The Deaf Hear and the Dumb Speak

Besides promises of comfort and salvation, we find in **Isaiah** warnings and predictions of terrible events to come. At his call, the prophet was warned that he was being sent to a people who would not use their ears to hear or their eyes to see (6:10). But this is not God's last word; his final message is one of comfort and encouragement (40:1). He will bring his people salvation; deaf ears will hear and dumb mouths will speak. In the desert streams of water will appear. God will bring victory out of defeat. Israel looked for the realisation of these hopes when the messiah came.

The **Psalm** praises God, not just because he created the world (147:6), but because he looks after the oppressed and the helpless. A king is judged by his care for the weak and poor. God is hailed as king because he keeps faith forever with those in need.

We learnt from **James** last week that our religion is to be one of action, not words (1:22). In theory, we know that the God of our faith does not make distinctions between people; Peter learnt this when he welcomed the Gentile Cornelius into the Christian community (Deuteronomy 10:17; Acts 10:34; 1 Peter 1:17). But in our practical lives, we know what happens when two strangers enter our assembly, one rich and the other poor. We welcome the first into the best place (Luke 11:43; 20:46) and let the poor man sit on the floor. We forget God's concern for the poor recorded in the Old Testament (Psalm 146:7; Psalm 35:10; Isaiah 61:1) and the teaching of Jesus in the Gospels, where the Kingdom is promised to the poor (Matthew 5:3; 11:5; Luke 4:18). God does not look out for class distinctions but for those who love him (Exodus 20:6).

With Jesus' dispute with the scribes and Pharisees about the traditions of the elders concluded, **Mark** describes his move into Gentile country, where he meets a Syro-Phoenician woman, a Greek, who gives an example of lively and courageous faith which all can admire and imitate (7:24–30). Jesus then travels in a great circle to the sea of Galilee, so as to pass through the Decapolis region, also Gentile. There, meeting one who suffers from deafness and defective speech, he takes him aside, puts his fingers into his ears, touches his tongue, looks up to heaven and prays, 'Be opened'. The cure is successful. The man's ears and tongue do what God intended them to do.

Readers of Jewish background would recognise in Jesus' activities how Isaiah's prophecy was being fulfilled (35:4–7). Here was proof that the Kingdom of God, the subject of Jesus' preaching (1:15), was dawning. His miracles were part of his messianic work (Matthew 12:28; Luke 11:20). A Gentile reader would rejoice because the cures that so far in Mark's story had benefited only Jews (1:21–39), were now being offered to Gentiles.

But we are to think beyond physical healing. In the 'parable chapter', Jesus had called on those with ears to hear, to hear (4:9–23). But many failed to listen (4:13–20; 8:18). Pharisees plotted to destroy him (3:6); his family thought him mad (3:21); scribes thought him in league with Beelzebul (3:22). Many suffered from speech defects such that they did not respond to his summons to repent and believe (1:14–15) and lacked a tongue to confess his identity (8:27). Their lips, not their hearts, gave him honour (7:6). After the miracle, the crowds disobey Jesus' command to keep quiet about it. With defective speech, they proclaim Jesus as a miracle worker, not as the Christ, the Son of God (1:1).

Mark's readers could identify with the man who was cured. Like him, they lived in Gentile territory and in their baptism they had received enlightenment, hearing the word *Ephphatha*—'Be opened'.

Sunday 24 B

Isaiah 50:5–9
Psalm 114:1–6, 8–9
James 2:14–18
Mark 8:27–35

Passion Prediction

The third Servant Song of **Isaiah** presents us with a picture of the ideal disciple. Such a disciple has an ear alert to hear what God has to say. Neither verbal insults nor physical abuse will turn him aside from his path. He knows that he is not alone and that God is at his side (Psalm 139). Like Christ preparing for his passion, he can say, 'I am not alone because the Father is with me' (John 16:32). Like Paul, he understands that God acts as his defence lawyer (Romans 8:31). Peter's reaction in the Gospel suggests that he has not meditated on this song.

The **Psalm** is the song of someone recovered from illness or other distress. Suffering is past. The Lord has given a ready ear to the cry of trouble. The way is open for a future life spent in God's presence.

The attack in **James** on those who rely on faith alone has been taken as a criticism of Paul and his doctrine of salvation by faith (Romans 3:28; Philippians 3:9), as if Paul did not insist that faith works through love (Galatians 5:6). Faith, for James, is the ready acceptance of God's word (1:18) and works are the response of those who know that to hear the word and not to put it into practice, is to deceive oneself (1:22). To hear the word, is to welcome the poor stranger (2:2) and not to turn away the hungry brother or sister. James is faithful to his Jewish heritage with its concern for the poor (Deuteronomy 15:7) and to other New Testament teaching which declared that God's love could find no place in the one who saw a brother or sister in need and closed his heart (1 John 3:17). James's practical Christianity finds Christ in the needy, as Jesus himself describes so elegantly in his description of the final judgment (Matthew 25:31–46).

We omit in **Mark**'s story the feeding of the four thousand (8:1–10), the demand of the Pharisees for a sign (8:11–13), Jesus' lament over his disciples' blindness and deafness (8:14–21) and the cure of the blind man of Bethsaida (8:22–26). We now find Jesus questioning his disciples about his identity. Previously, after the calming of the storm, they had asked the question themselves but could not answer (4:41). This time, Peter, speaking for himself, replies that Jesus is the Christ, the anointed one.

Jesus offers no word of congratulation but orders silence. Peter is correct in applying the title to Jesus (1:1), but he fails to use it correctly. He may understand it as referring to an anointed king, a David sent by God to liberate Israel from the foreigner (2 Samuel 7). He may be thinking of an anointed prophet; Jesus had called himself such a messiah in Nazareth according to Luke (4:18).

The Christian understanding of Christ must include the ideas of suffering, death and resurrection (Romans 1:4). Jesus, for the first time in this Gospel, announces that the Son of Man must suffer and die. This is open teaching, as opposed to teaching in parables. The Son of Man was a glorious, triumphant figure (Daniel 7:13); who ever heard of a suffering Son of Man? Peter is scandalized (4:17) and rebukes Jesus, in words Jesus himself used when casting out a demon (1:25). Jesus rebukes Peter in turn, giving him the name of Satan (Job 1:1), the tempter (1:13). He is thinking human thoughts, not the thoughts of God. So serious is Peter's misunderstanding that Jesus solemnly calls all the disciples to him, with the crowds, and announces a new requirement for all those who would come after him. They are not only to follow him (1:17) and be with him (3:14); they have to deny themselves and take up the cross after him. They may lose their lives for his sake and that of the gospel. These are words of great relevance to the Marcan community in Rome, whose very existence was threatened by the persecution of Nero.

Sunday 25 B

Wisdom 2:12, 17–20
Psalm 53:3–6, 8
James 3:16–4:3
Mark 9:30–37

True Greatness

The book of **Wisdom**, written shortly before the time of Christ, was probably a product of Jewish exiles in Egypt. In this speech, attributed to an enemy, we have an example of the verbal persecution such communities would have endured. The speaker attacks the virtuous man, who, belonging to Israel, would have shared the self-understanding of his people as being God's sons (Hosea 11:1). Matthew would have the passage in mind when he described how the chief priests taunted Jesus as he was dying on the cross (Matthew 27:43). Church fathers regarded these lines as a prophecy of the passion of Christ.

In the **Psalm**, the just and persecuted man replies to those intriguing against him. His opponents live only for this life and deny God. He lives confident in the help of the living God who, in his goodness, will deliver him.

Our passage from **James** falls into two parts. The first is the conclusion of a discussion about what constitutes true wisdom (3:13–18), written in the tradition of Old Testament wisdom teachers. His words echo Paul and the Gospels. The vices he condemns are also condemned by Paul (2 Corinthians 12:20); the peaceful qualities he seeks are those taught by Jesus, particularly in the Beatitudes (Matthew 5:1–11). In the second part, he seeks the root causes of quarrels that are destroying the peace of the community. People are using wrong methods to get their way, the violent means of the wicked, as described in our first reading, instead of the peaceful weapon of prayer employed by the Psalmist. Those who know how to pray properly will ask for what is appropriate and will find their prayer answered (Matthew 6:33; 1 John 5:14).

The heart of **Mark**'s Gospel is his account of Jesus' journey from Galilee to Jerusalem (8:27–10:52). In this section, the crowds are out of sight and Jesus directs his teaching primarily to his disciples. Mark is making clear to actual and potential members of his community what the way of Christianity (Acts 9:2) might imply. Together with Peter and the disciples, they had to learn the full meaning of the word 'Christ' (8:29) and to discover the true path of authentic discipleship (8:34).

Now, for the second time, Jesus warns his disciples that the Christ is the Son of Man who will be betrayed and put to death. These things had also been said of John the Baptist, the forerunner of Jesus (1:14; 6:19). Jesus will also rise again; the disciples had glimpsed resurrection glory at the transfiguration (9:3). But far from understanding, they become more afraid (4:41).

In Capernaum again (1:21; 2:1), they enter a house. Before, when alone with Jesus, his disciples have questioned him about what they do not understand (4:10; 7:17). Now he questions them: what have they been discussing on the road? They admit that their topic was status and power. They have not been listening to Jesus (9:7).

His response is solemn. He sits down, adopting the teaching position of a rabbi, and formally summons the Twelve. First he speaks and then he acts. His teaching is that it is the one who is last of all and servant of all who is the first in the sight of God. His action is to pick up a child. In human eyes, a child is an example of powerlessness, dependence and vulnerability. In God's eyes, a child is a symbol of greatness in a Christian community. Total dependence on God is the starting point of true discipleship. A saint relies totally on God and allows full scope to his grace. To welcome a saint is to welcome Jesus and the Father who sent him. The Christian God is the one who brings the dead to life (Romans 4:17) and whose grace is perfected in weakness (2 Corinthians 12:9).

Sunday 26 B

Numbers 11:25–29
Psalm 18:8, 10, 12–14
James 5:1–6
Mark 9:38–43, 45, 47–48

Not One of Us

In **Numbers**, Moses shared with God responsibility for Israel during their desert journey. The strain on Moses proved too great and God gave him seventy assistants, communicating with them through the Spirit. These seventy were predecessors of the later ecstatic prophets (1 Samuel 10: 10). They were appointed outside the camp at the Tent of Meeting. When two others, Eldad and Medad, who have stayed in the camp, suddenly prophesy too, Joshua objects. Moses rejects his intolerance. He upholds God's freedom to communicate outside his own structures. He wants everyone to share the prophetic gift. Like Paul in Corinth, he wants all to be prophets (1 Corinthians 14: 5). The true prophet upholds God and his Law.

The **Psalm** meditates on the qualities of this Law, which reflect the characteristics of God himself. This is a model prayer for the prophet; it helps to safeguard his ministry from conscious and unconscious sin.

In **James**, we read an attack, not so much on riches as on the methods used to acquire them. His teaching has its roots in the Old Testament and in the Gospels. The Law in Leviticus condemned those who deprived labourers of their wages (Leviticus 19: 13). Amos prophesied against those who crushed the needy (Amos 8: 5). In the Gospels, Jesus warned against the acquisition of treasures which moth and woodworm destroy (Matthew 6: 19) and, in the story of the poor Lazarus and the wealthy Dives, spoke of the reversal that would come at Judgment (Luke 17: 19–31). The same God who had heard the cry of his oppressed people in Egypt (Exodus 3:7) is alert to the pleas of workers who go unpaid in our day.

Sayings of Jesus on topics about Christian discipleship are incorporated into **Mark**'s account of Jesus' journey to Jerusalem. They owe their present position to key phrases that are easy to remember. The first is the expression 'in my name'. The disciple John speaks for the first time. He objects to the activity of a stranger who is casting out demons in Jesus' name, yet does not belong to their group. Were John and his friends jealous because, though the Twelve were given power at their call to cast out demons (3: 15), they had failed to do so in the incident with the epileptic boy (9: 28)?

Jesus bluntly condemns John. Like Peter, he is still thinking the thoughts of men (8: 33). Whoever uses the name of Jesus cannot be his enemy. His real enemies are the hardhearted Pharisees (3: 5) and the scribes who sinned against the Holy Spirit (3: 29). The incident is remarkably like that between Moses, Joshua and the unknown prophets, Eldad and Meldad (Numbers 11). The promise that follows, of a reward to anyone who gives a cup of water to Jesus' disciples, also depends on the name of Jesus. The disciples are those who 'belong to Christ'. The sayings in the second half of our passage are bound together by the Greek word **σκανδαλίζω**, 'scandalize'. If the first in the Kingdom have become like children, the 'little ones' (9: 36), then no penalty can be too severe for the one who causes them to stumble in their faith (14: 21). The uses of this word that follow concern either the individual believer or the community as a whole, since the community was often compared to a body (1 Corinthians 12: 12). To speak of losing a hand, a foot or an eye is hyperbolic, but even Paul used strong language to remind himself that salvation was not guaranteed. Like an athlete, he had to discipline his body (1 Corinthians 9: 27). The alternative to salvation is called Gehenna, a valley in Jerusalem, once used for child sacrifice (Leviticus 18: 21), which became the symbol of the corruption and death that awaited those who rebelled against God (Isaiah 66: 24).

Sunday 27 B

Genesis 2:18–24
Psalm 127
Hebrews 2:9–11
Mark 10:2–16

Marriage and Divorce

The climax of the creation story in **Genesis** is the creation of the woman from the man. God's first remedy for the loneliness of the man was the introduction of the animals, which he was invited to name—a sign of his superiority to them and of the respect he was to afford them. But they could not be his equal. For this, the man needed a woman, made from himself, to be his helpmate. This word does not imply subordination, since elsewhere God himself is described as being one's help (Exodus 18:4; Deuteronomy 33:7). Thus the author teaches us that God's plan of monogamous marriage is as old as the creation of the world.

The **Psalm** reflects a simple theology of earthly blessings in return for fidelity to God (Leviticus 26). A large, prosperous family is included among them. Arriving at the Temple on pilgrimage, such a family is blessed by the temple priests.

Nobody knows who wrote the Letter to the **Hebrews**. Its special contribution is its teaching on the priesthood of Christ, combined with a deep insight into his true humanity. Our extract shows how the theology of today's Psalm is an over-simplified one. Although Jesus was most faithful and obedient to God's law, he entered into glory through suffering. His career of humiliation and exaltation (Philippians 2:6–11) had been foretold in another Psalm (Hebrews 2:6; Psalm 8:4). These sufferings ended the need for the ancient cult of the Jerusalem Temple and opened salvation to all. Because he was no angelic being and belonged to the human family, we are all his brothers and sisters, and share in the sanctification that his sacrifice has won.

When **Mark** describes Jesus' journey to Jerusalem, he imagines him accompanied not just by his original disciples but by all future hearers of the Gospel. With the disciples, they are to learn about the way of Christianity and to be challenged by the newness of Jesus' teaching. Having arrived on the far side of the Jordan River, Jesus finds himself in a double conflict. The first is with the Pharisees. Once more, they test him. Previously, they had asked for a sign from heaven (8:11); later, they will demand to know whether taxes should be paid to Caesar or not (12:15).

Now they question him about divorce. According to Deuteronomy, divorce was permitted (Deuteronomy 24:1–4), though interpreters differed about the grounds required. Teachers such as Shimmel were very strict, while others, such as Hillel, were astonishingly lax. In his reply, Jesus sides with neither. He prohibits divorce altogether, arguing not from Mosaic legislation but from the original plan of God, when God created woman from man and made her his helpmate (Genesis 2:18–24). Here Jesus defends women who, according to the laws of the time, had no rights. He forbids his critics to play fast and loose with an institution that belongs to God's original creation. Such teaching was risky for Jesus as he travelled through the territories of the much-divorced King Herod. Matthew, in his Gospel, was to allow divorce on the grounds of unchastity (5:32; 19:9). Paul permitted a believer to separate from an unbeliever (1 Corinthians 7:15). Neither allowed divorce for the hardness of heart that Jesus condemned.

His second conflict is with his own disciples, who want to send away children who have been brought to him. Like women of the time, children had no legal rights. We know that to receive a child in Jesus' name is to receive Jesus himself. Their powerlessness, vulnerability and dependence are a symbol of greatness in the Kingdom (9:36–37). Mark challenges the Roman world to respect women and children as Jesus did.

Sunday 28 B

Wisdom 7:7–11
Psalm 89:12–17
Hebrews 4:12–13
Mark 10:17–30

A Rich Man Comes to Jesus

Solomon was traditionally the wisest man in all Israel. His reputation was that of a man who had prayed for the right things and had not been misled by worldly vanities (2 Kings 3:6–9). The book of **Wisdom** appeals to the memory of the young Solomon as a man who valued wisdom more than sceptres, thrones, riches, possessions, precious stones, gold and silver or health and beauty. Its readers are not to think that God has abandoned them because they are not enjoying worldly prosperity; those who have wisdom are in possession of the greatest of God's gifts. Christians would identify this wisdom with Christ (Luke 7:35).

The **Psalm** is a meditation on the shortness of life, possibly by someone doomed to an early death. The prayer is for wisdom, which brings with it love and joy, qualities which Paul would later describe as fruits of the Holy Spirit (Galatians 5:22).

The author of **Hebrews** alternates between doctrine and exhortation. He warns his readers to take seriously the Psalmist's plea, 'If only you would listen to him today, "Do not harden your hearts"' (Psalm 95:7–8; Hebrews 4:7). The word of God is not to be taken lightly. By his word, God created the world (Psalm 33:6); God's word, once spoken, does not return to him empty (Isaiah 55:11). According to John, that Word became flesh in Christ (John 1:14). We are all destined to be judged in God's presence (1 Corinthians 3:13). For this writer, the word is a 'two-edged sword'. By attending to his word here and now, we make sure that judgment will mean acquittal. In the words of Jesus, it will have borne rich fruit (Luke 8:15).

Having included Jesus' instructions about marriage in his journey narrative, **Mark** now introduces teaching about riches. In the Rome of the day, his readers would have had little prospect of worldly wealth, thanks to the terrible persecution inflicted by Nero. They had to understand that there was more to life than plentiful possessions.

As Jesus resumes his journey, a man runs to him and throws himself down before him. He asks for eternal life, much as Solomon had looked for wisdom. But, unlike Solomon, he is unwilling to pay the price. He will keep the Decalogue but, because he has not grasped that its commandments are the key to a personal covenantal relationship with God, he becomes the only person in the Gospel to refuse Jesus' call to follow him. He goes away sad, rejecting the love that Jesus has for him. He does not know that the love of Jesus is worth more than all the worldly riches he possesses.

Jesus turns to his watching disciples to declare the incompatibility of riches and the Kingdom of God. This shocks them so much that he has to repeat the teaching, adding the saying about a camel going through the eye of a needle. He still does not convince them; they know the biblical tradition that associates worldly success with the blessings of God (Deuteronomy 28:1–14). His reply to their further objection is one of the most enigmatic of gospel sayings, 'For men ... it is impossible, but not for God: because everything is possible for God'. We are to recall this when reading about Jesus' prayer in Gethsemane (14:36).

Finally, Peter asks what reward he and his friends will get for having followed Jesus and left everything (1:16–20). He is promised the eternal life for which the rich man was searching. This young man had not waited to be told that sacrifice for the sake of God is rewarded, even in this life, a hundredfold, though there will also be persecution (8:34). The one who surrenders to God and does his will becomes a member of a new family (3:34).

Sunday 29 B

Isaiah 53:10–11
Psalm 32:4–5, 18–20, 22
Hebrews 4:14–16
Mark 10:35–45

False Ambition

The obvious human means of Israel's deliverance from exile was the activity of Cyrus, the king of Persia (Isaiah 45:1). A less obvious means was the willing acceptance of suffering by God's Servant, whether we understand by this figure the faithful remnant of Israel or the prophet himself. By such suffering, and not by traditional sacrifices, the whole people are saved from the effects of sin. This fourth Servant Song of **Isaiah** was fulfilled, according to the words of Philip to the Ethiopian (Acts 8:35) and the teaching of Peter (1 Peter 2:24), in the death and resurrection of Christ.

The **Psalm** is a hymn to God, who created the world and continues to care for it. The only worthy human response is reverence, trust and the practice of the justice and mercy that God loves (Hosea 6:6; Matthew 9:13).

Last week, the author of **Hebrews** gave a warning. This week, he offers encouragement. He derives it from his understanding of Christ as High Priest. Like the Jewish High Priest, Jesus had privileged access to the Holy of Holies, but unlike him, he entered the real Holy of Holies in heaven (Revelation 4). He has passed through the heavens (Acts 2:33) and ministers next to the throne of God himself. There he intercedes for us (Romans 8:34), so that we may have access to God. Because he has lived a truly human life, he knows the sort of weaknesses that we meet in life. In one of the boldest statements in the New Testament, he is said to have been tempted in every way that we are ourselves but, in contrast to us, he did not sin. The Gospels offer us a narrative that specifies the form these temptations might have taken (Matthew 4:1–11).

Mark's account of the journey to Jerusalem is punctuated by Jesus' three predictions of his future sufferings. Each time, the disciples resist this teaching (8:32; 9:34). After the third prophecy, which we hear today, two disciples, James and John, disgrace themselves. They not only ignore Jesus' warnings, but also betray their misunderstanding of the Kingdom that he has been preaching, in word and action, since their call by the lake (1:16–20). They presume that in his Kingdom high worldly offices on his right and on his left will be available to them as his courtiers. The only people to occupy these positions in the Gospel are the two thieves on the right and left of Jesus on the cross (15:27).

Jesus speaks mysteriously in his response about a cup and a baptism. In scripture, a cup is a symbol of a person's fate (Jeremiah 49:12). At times, it is associated with God's righteous anger against sin (Isaiah 51:17). Jesus will speak of it again in Gethsemane (14:36). In its original meaning, baptism implies letting go, a self-abandonment to whatever destiny God has in store. Both here refer to the future passion of Jesus and confirm that a disciple must be ready to carry the cross behind Jesus (8:34). James and John declare their readiness to share both cup and baptism but, at Gethsemane, they fall asleep (14:40).

The other ten disciples, far from rebuking their fellows' false ambition, show that they share it. Jesus has to elaborate the instruction he gave about greatness in the Kingdom, in word and action, after his previous prediction of the passion (9:35). Their ideas about authority should not be those of secular society. They are to remember Isaiah's Servant Song, and how the Servant gave his life as a ransom, or atonement, for many (Isaiah 53:10). This text, together with Jesus' words over the cup at the Last Supper (14:24), are the only direct indications in Mark of the salvific purpose of the death of Jesus. They point the way to a positive doctrine of suffering.

Sunday 30 B

Jeremiah 31:7–9
Psalm 125
Hebrews 5:1–6
Mark 10:46–52

Bartimaeus Follows Jesus

The greatest intervention of God on behalf of Israel was the Exodus from Egypt. When the people found itself again in exile from its home, **Jeremiah** and Isaiah looked forward to a new Exodus. Jeremiah addresses those banished in 721 BC in a poem of restoration. He promises that God will bring them back, even the blind and their lame among them. This chapter also speaks of Rachel weeping for her children (Matthew 2:13) and gives us the prophecy of the new covenant referred to in the institution of the Eucharist at the Last Supper (Luke 22:20).

The **Psalm** is a pilgrim song sung in Jerusalem at the feast of Tabernacles. It reminds God of his goodness in past days in bringing his people back from a distant land, and asks him to show that goodness once more by providing rain for a good harvest.

The special contribution of **Hebrews** is to portray the priesthood of Jesus (2:17; 3:14). This priesthood is at once similar to, and distinct from, the priesthood of the Jewish Temple. It is similar in that Christ also had to offer sacrifice for sin, but different in that he himself was without sin (4:15; 7:27). It is similar in that Christ was chosen by God as other priests were, but different in that ordinary priests belonged to the priestly family of Aaron and he did not. As God's Son, he was chosen directly by God. We have learnt this earlier in the letter from the teaching of a Psalm (Psalm 2:7; Hebrews 1:5). Another Psalm tells us (110:4) that he was a different sort of priest, a priest according to the order of Melchizedek, the priest of the Most High who had brought out bread and wine and blessed Abraham (Genesis 14:18–19).

Jesus' journey to Jerusalem in **Mark** begins and ends with accounts of the healing of blind men. The first, at Bethsaida, is performed in two stages. The man initially sees men like trees walking (8:22–26). He is a symbol of Peter, who was prepared to accept Jesus as a triumphant Christ but not as the suffering Son of Man (8:33). The second, the healing of Bartimaeus, is also to be understood in a wider symbolic sense. We not only learn about the ability of Jesus to heal the blind but are also instructed how a true disciple is to behave.

James and John had asked Jesus for places at his right and his left in his glory (10:37); Bartimaeus prays for what he really needs: his sight. His prayer is one that the disciples, who had eyes that did not see and ears that did not hear (8:18), should have prayed themselves but never did. Initially, Jesus ignores the petition of Bartimaeus. His cry of 'Son of David' proves that his understanding of Jesus is limited. The ever-fickle crowd tells him to keep quiet. But Bartimaeus perseveres. When Jesus gives orders for him to be called, the crowd cries, 'Courage ... get up; he is calling you'. Like the lame man in Isaiah (35:6), he leaps up to go to Jesus. He throws aside his cloak—his means of livelihood by day and of warmth at night. (The Law forbade anyone to take a man's cloak from him overnight [Exodus 22:26].) Because Jesus is calling, he casts aside his most valuable possession. When he repeats his petition for the third time, Jesus gives him what he wants.

Bartimaeus is the perfect disciple. He puts his limited faith to good use and earns the praise of Jesus. Not for him the other disciples' reluctant and fearful following (10:32), but a willing and enthusiastic joining of Jesus on the way, wherever that way might lead. His prayer has been keenly imitated through many generations. Like the converts to whom Peter wrote, he is brought into a 'wonderful light' (1 Peter 2:9).

Sunday 31 B

Deuteronomy 6:2–6
Psalm 17:2–4, 47
Hebrews 7:23–28
Mark 12:28–34

The Good Scribe

In the days of the kings of Israel, when the nation suffered much from internal and external strife, many looked back to the time in the desert when God had given them his Law (Hosea 11:1). Recalling God's love and care for them, they became even more conscious of their own infidelity and sinfulness. **Deuteronomy** dates from this time; it summons Israel to return to an uncompromising and wholehearted dedication to their one God, in words that Israel treasured as a wonderful digest of its faith, put into the mouth of Moses.

The **Psalm** recounts how a faithful Israelite puts Deuteronomy and its commands into practice. Conscious of how God has proved a deliverer from dangers, the psalmist determines to rely on God alone, while giving him many titles to deepen this devotion.

In **Hebrews**, our author continues to contrast the priesthood of Christ with that of the Temple priests. Because they were human and mortal, they were many, whereas Christ remains the single priest because he lives for ever. Those priests sinned and needed to offer many sacrifices. Christ made a single sacrifice and this was himself. He is now exalted in heaven, but the effects of his sacrifice go on in the continuing intercession he makes on our behalf (Romans 8:34). His appointment as priest did not come about through the prescriptions of the Law, but through an oath that God himself swore, as is confirmed by the verse of a Psalm (110:4). He is a priest of a different order from the rest, a priest of the order of Melchizedek, the mysterious figure who blessed Abraham and to whom Abraham gave tribute (Genesis 14:18).

Mark reports how, during his brief ministry in Jerusalem, Jesus moved in an atmosphere of confrontation. His mission there began with the cleansing of the Temple (11:15–18). Interrogated by the authorities, Jesus responded with the parable of the vineyard and the tenants, which they realised was directed at them. He escaped arrest because of his popularity (12:1–12). A series of controversies with the various religious parties followed, which balance the critical encounters in Galilee at the beginning of his public mission (2:1–3:6).

But today we read the one exception to these conflicts. A scribe comes to Jesus enquiring which is the first commandment of all. Our previous knowledge of scribes from Jerusalem puts us on our guard. It was they who had accused Jesus of casting out demons through Beelzebul (3:22), and they had been warned of the danger of committing the sin that cannot be forgiven (3:29). Jesus answers this scribe with two texts from scripture: we must love God with all our powers (Deuteronomy 6:5), and we must love our neighbour as ourselves (Leviticus 19:18). This, the most positive teaching of Jesus about the Law that we find in Mark, illuminates his previous criticisms of its practice (7:13; 10:5). Law must be informed by love (Galatians 5:14). In reply, the scribe not only compliments Jesus but, like a good rabbinical student, repeats his teaching. Jesus in turn praises the scribe as being 'not far from the Kingdom of God'. Like Bartimaeus, he appears on the gospel stage only to disappear immediately. He also resembles the woman of Bethany, in that we are to respect his memory and imitate his attitude (14:9). This scribe's way of thinking makes him good soil for the values of the Kingdom (4:8). In including Jesus' praise for this intellectual leader of Judaism, Mark reminds his Roman readers, especially those of Gentile background, of the debt that Christianity owes to the older religion. They were not to despise the roots from which Christianity sprang or the Jewish Christians in their community (Romans 1:16).

Sunday 32 B

1 Kings 17:10–16
Psalm 145:7–10
Hebrews 9:24–28
Mark 12:38–44

The Widow in the Temple

Among the stories told about Elijah in **1 Kings** is one about a widow who lived in Zarephath, a place situated outside the borders of Israel. She is at the end of her resources. She can foresee only death for herself and her son. Yet when Elijah demands from her all that she has to live on, she gives it to him. In return, God causes a miraculous multiplication of her tiny stock of oil and flour. Jesus recalls this story at the beginning of his ministry in Luke (Luke 4:26).

The **Psalm** belongs to the final group in the whole collection, all of which praise God. He is king in Zion and, like a good king, counts among his responsibilities the care of the widow and the orphan (Jeremiah 22:3).

In **Hebrews**, the author continues to contrast the priesthood of Christ with that of the Temple priests. The Temple that Christ entered is the true dwelling place of God in heaven, not some temple made with human hands (Mark 14:58). Because he is permanently at home in this true Temple, he has no need to go into it again and again, like the priests in Jerusalem who exercised their ministry year by year in the Holy of Holies. The blood that he offers is not that of animals slaughtered in sacrifice but his own, shed on Calvary. The Day of Atonement observed each year in Israel is always being celebrated in heaven (Leviticus 16). All this happens on our behalf. Like the Isaian Servant, Jesus took on himself the sins of all (Isaiah 53:12). It is the fate of humans to die and then be judged, but faithful believers look forward to Christ emerging from his sanctuary in heaven to take them to himself at his second coming (1 Thessalonians 4:16).

According to **Mark**, Jesus' first action in Jerusalem was to cleanse the Temple; to justify this action, he quoted words spoken by prophets long before (11:17; Isaiah 56:7; Jeremiah 7:14). His final action in the Temple is to warn the people about the scribes and the example they give. Again, he quotes the prophets to justify his charges. Now, as then, the scribes are consuming the property of widows (Isaiah 10:2; Zechariah 7:10). Severe though his indictment is, it is mild compared with the sevenfold condemnation of the scribes and the Pharisees reported by Matthew, who probably had in mind the faults of the authorities among the rival Jewish groups of his own day in Antioch (23:13–32).

The word 'widow' serves as a theme to introduce the only direct teaching of Jesus addressed to his disciples so far in Jerusalem. He has seen a widow putting all she has into the temple collection box. Commentators are divided on whether Jesus is lamenting or praising her action. Previously, he had condemned the tradition of the elders because it caused children to neglect their parents in the name of religion (7:12–13). Surely this widow's first responsibility is to ensure that she has enough to live on. By giving it all up, is she not tempting God (Matthew 4:7)?

Others follow the more traditional interpretation in praising the widow because, anticipating Jesus in his coming passion, she offers all that she possesses to God. Like the woman who anointed Jesus' head, preparing his body for burial, she has given everything (14:8). Her commitment to God and trust in him are total. Unlike James and John, asking for seats with Jesus in his glory (10:37), or the scribes, looking for places of honour at banquets, she wants nothing for herself. She joins the ranks of Bartimaeus (10:46–52) and the good scribe (12:28–34) in putting before the reader attitudes well worth imitating by those longing for the realisation of God's Kingdom. On this note the public ministry of Jesus ends and Mark is ready to tell the story of his last days.

Sunday 33 B

Daniel 12:1–3
Psalm 15:5, 8–11
Hebrews 10:11–14, 18
Mark 13:24–32

The Coming of the Son of Man

The world of apocalyptic literature, with its visions and fantastic imagery, is alien and bewildering to our modern world. There are four apocalypses in the book of **Daniel**; our passage concludes the last of them. The author writes to encourage his readers, in crisis because of Antiochus Epiphanes (175–164 BC), the Greek king who tried to crush the Jewish religion. References to names written in a book and to times of terrible distress are familiar in such writings (Revelation 20:12; 8:6–12), but new in this passage is the hope of resurrection. This is the first Old Testament witness to the hope that if God's faithful must pay for their fidelity with their lives, they will be given new life hereafter. Daniel's words are echoed in Matthew's parables (13:43) and in John (5:29).

The **Psalm** is a prayer of supreme confidence in God, in which a sick person prays to be saved from the grave. It was later understood as a prayer for deliverance from the corruption of death. Peter, in his pentecost sermon, finds it fulfilled in the resurrection of Christ (Acts 2:27).

We leave the letter to the **Hebrews** with a final contrast between Christ and the priests of the Old Testament. They carried out their duties day by day, repeating sacrifices that were incapable of dealing with sin. Christ, on the other hand, the true fulfilment of the future anticipated in the ancient royal Psalm, is sitting at God's right hand in heaven as he makes intercession for us (Psalm 110:1). His sacrifice of himself is valid for ever. All that remains is his final triumph, which will come about at the parousia when he comes to claim his people for his own (1 Corinthians 15:24).

Jesus' longest uninterrupted speech in **Mark** takes place at the end of his ministry in Jerusalem, before the story of his passion begins. Jesus sits on the Mount of Olives, from where the whole city and temple are visible. He speaks of future tribulation for the city and its Temple, and of the eventual coming of the Son of Man. He is preparing his disciples for this future. At the same time, Mark is reassuring his readers that God knows all about the troubles that they are having to endure from Nero, the emperor of their time. We may compare this speech with the farewell speeches we read in the Old Testament, such as those of Jacob to his sons (Genesis 49) and of David to Solomon (1 Kings 2). Its apocalyptic language puts it in the tradition of books such as Daniel which arose out of crisis.

The times of persecution and false messiahs, the subject of the first part of the discourse, are distinguished from the coming of the Son of Man with his angels (8:38). This will be heralded by the cosmic chaos foreseen by the prophets (Isaiah 13:10; Ezekiel 32:10), which is described in poetic, apocalyptic terms—the only language available to portray what human discourse cannot directly describe. This Son of Man (Daniel 7:13) will come to gather in the elect, to bring them home. Such events are intended to encourage and not to terrify the reader. Paul comforted his converts in Thessalonica with similar words (1 Thessalonians 4:18).

The parable of the fig tree is designed to bring the hearers back to earth. They are to watch out for the signs of the times and behave accordingly. As to when all this is to happen, the Gospel gives contrary indications. It will be in the time of this generation (9:1), yet not even the Son knows the day or the hour. In that generation, the death and resurrection of Jesus takes place, and this brings about the end of the old heaven and the old earth (2 Corinthians 5:17). If the time of the end is unknown even to the Son, it is not for human beings to speculate about it. It is more important to remember the words of Jesus which will endure for ever.

Christ the King B

Daniel 7:13–14
Psalm 92:1–2, 5
Revelation 1:5–8
John 18:33–37

Jesus before Pilate

The four beasts from the sea in **Daniel** are universally identified with empires that had oppressed Israel in the past (7: 1–12). There is less agreement about the identity of the Son of Man who comes from heaven. Some identify him with the Saints of the Most High, Israelites who resisted Antiochus Epiphanes (7: 27); other ancient books, such as the book of Enoch, make him a heavenly figure who comes in judgment at the end. At the close of Matthew's Gospel, the Risen Lord claims the authority of this Son of Man for himself (Matthew 28: 18).

The **Psalm** traditionally presents God ascending his throne after he has created the world. It is one of a group that reminds Israel that God himself is their true king. It is the reality of his reign that Jesus came to proclaim (Mark 1: 15).

Like Daniel, **Revelation** was written to help the faithful in crisis. One reading suggests that its author expected that the emperor Domitian would soon insist on everyone in his empire worshipping him as a god, an impossible demand for Christians. To prepare them for this test, the author gives Christ three memorable titles. First, he is a 'faithful witness', an example for those soon to witness for their faith. Second, he is the 'Firstborn from the dead', a reminder that those who give their lives will follow him in sharing in the resurrection. Third, he is 'Ruler of the kings of the earth'. Powerful though earthly tyrants might seem, he himself is their real ruler (John 18: 37). Like the Son of Man, he will come on the clouds (Daniel 7: 13) when he will find those who share his priesthood and kingship (Exodus 19: 5) awaiting him.

Each Gospel tells us that Jesus was officially condemned as king of the Jews (Mark 15: 26). Pilate, the Roman governor, would not have been interested in any purely religious charge. We owe to the Gospel of **John** some explanation of the real nature of Jesus' kingship. The theme first emerges at the feeding of the five thousand. At its conclusion, John tells us that Jesus fled alone up the mountain because the crowd wanted to make him king (6: 15). Obviously, they had the wrong idea of his kingship. As a nation under foreign rule, they were looking for a liberator to deliver them, much as David long ago had freed their ancestors from the Philistines. Again, crowds tried to make him king as he entered Jerusalem; this time he sat on a donkey to demonstrate the lowly nature of his kingship (12: 13).

On trial before Pilate, Jesus is asked whether he is king of the Jews. He replies with a question for Pilate: why is he asking about his kingship? The reader knows that, for this evangelist, it is Pilate who is on trial before Jesus. The blunt Roman answers with a practical question, 'What have you done?' The reply shows that he and Jesus live on different planes. Jesus does not deny that he has a kingdom, but his is a kingdom with no home in this world. If it had, he would, like earthly rulers, have subjects or servants, but we know from the Last Supper that his disciples were no longer servants but friends (15: 15; Mark 10: 45).

But Pilate wants an answer. So Jesus admits that he is a king, and offers a definition of his kingship in terms of his mission. This is to witness to the truth, to reveal the Father to the world (18: 20–21). Those who belong to his Kingdom are the ones who listen to his voice and his revelation, like the sheep who recognise the voice of the Good Shepherd (10: 16). Pilate can demonstrate whether he belongs to that number. But, having asked, 'What is truth?', he does not wait for an answer and leaves the presence of Jesus. He does not belong to the kingdom of truth (14: 6).

Year C
The Year of Luke

LUKE REVISED MARK for a Gentile rather than a Jewish Christian audience. His is a Gospel of 'salvation for all flesh' (Luke 3:6). His 1,149 verses divide into 24 chapters and they begin with a preface (Luke 1:1–4). In this, he makes a special claim for 'order'. This is reflected by his solemn introduction of Jesus preaching in the synagogue of Nazareth and announcing his mission of 'good news for the poor'. His Jesus is one who is constantly at prayer (Luke 3:21) and who gives an example of perseverance (Luke 9:51). Jesus is constantly on the move and encountering people, most of them in need and lacking status in society. The Jesus of Luke is a saviour for the whole of humanity. He is a visitor to our world, who has come to direct our feet into the way of peace (Luke 1:79). His disciples recognise their weakness. They ask Jesus to teach them to pray (Luke 11:1) and to increase their faith (Luke 17:5). Jesus reassured them in their weakness (Luke 5:1–11), prays for them before he goes to his suffering (Luke 21:31–32) and sets out in pursuit of them when they are lost and bewildered (Luke 24:13–35). If those outside the boundaries of Christianity know anything about the gospel story, it is usually Lucan material that they know. The stories of the good Samaritan (Luke 10:29–37) and the penitent thief (Luke 23:39–43) belong to the culture of the world.*

* Edmonds, *Rediscover Jesus*, 26.

Year C
The Year of Luke

THE SUNDAYS OF ADVENT*

*The **First Readings**, taken from the Old Testament, are described as 'prophecies about the messiah and the messianic age, especially from Isaiah'. They have therefore an importance of their own apart from the gospel reading.*

*The **Second Readings** 'from an apostle serve as exhortations and proclamations in keeping with the various themes of Advent'. In this Year C, we have three readings from Paul and one from the letter to the Hebrews.*

*The **Responsorial Psalms** are designed to help with the understanding of the First Reading, to deepen some significant theme, to clarify its message.*

*In the **Gospel Readings** we reflect on the three comings of Christ: at the end of time, in his public ministry, in his birth. The evangelist selected is the one whom we will hear for the remainder of the year.*

THE CHRISTMAS SEASON

The readings for Christmas and Epiphany are taken 'from the Roman tradition'. On other days, we learn by means of the readings about Jesus' childhood, the virtues of family life, the mystery of the Incarnation, the Virgin Mother of God, and the mystery of the baptism of Jesus.

* Quotations from 'General Introduction', *Roman Missal*, nn. 92, 95.

Advent I C

Jeremiah 33:14–16
Psalm 24:4–5, 8–9, 10, 14
1 Thessalonians 3:12–4:2
Luke 21:25–28, 34–36

Hope for the Future

To the people of Jerusalem, besieged in 588 BC by the Babylonian armies, **Jeremiah** offers a message of restoration. He looks forward to a renewed Davidic dynasty (2 Samuel 7:13), a flourishing people of Judah and a capital city of Jerusalem whose new name, 'Yahweh-our-integrity', would reflect the justice and righteousness of God himself. Christians believe that such prophecies found fulfilment in Christ.

The **Psalm** combines a consciousness of the faithfulness and love of God, as revealed in the covenant at Sinai (Exodus 34:6–7), with a realisation that without the wisdom that comes from God a truly human life is impossible.

Paul's first letter to the **Thessalonians** is the earliest of the New Testament writings. The Christian community at Thessalonica was young in the faith. Paul knows that, though they have begun their Christian life well (1:3–10), they need to improve its quality, particularly in their love for one another and in their personal holiness. As a good pastor, he gives no orders, but first prays for them and then appeals to them in the person of Christ. He prays for an increase in their love; Paul knew the depths of the love of God (Romans 8:39) and wanted his communities to mirror it (4:9–10). He prays for an increase in their holiness, a quality of God (Leviticus 19:2) they needed in order to resist the loose sexual morality of the day (4:3–8). As so often in his letters, Paul does not tire of repeating the name of the Lord Jesus Christ. Paul never forgot that he was Jesus' apostle and servant (Romans 1:1). Paul's prayer for his converts can be the prayer of every pastor at the beginning of Advent.

By the time **Luke** wrote his Gospel, the expectation of an early second coming of Christ had receded and, although persecution was a reality for the young Church, it took the form of a general hostility to a strange religion rather than an attempt to exterminate it. This background is reflected in Luke's account of Jesus' own words about his second coming, which we heard two weeks ago in Mark's version.

The events of the End are described in the same strong apocalyptic language that we found in Mark, a language that stresses the sovereignty of God over the whole of his creation. Luke, however, abbreviates the Old Testament references to the sun, the moon and the stars, and concentrates on events on this earth and the human beings spread all over it. This is consistent with the universal nature of this Gospel, which is to be preached to the ends of the earth (Acts 1:8).

In Mark, this teaching was addressed to Peter and James, John and Andrew, the four disciples called first (Mark 13:3; 1:16–20). In Luke, it is public and for all (21:6). Like the Beatitudes, it is personal (6:20), addressed both to the original audience and to the reader. Believers are not to be afraid but to welcome the End and the coming of the Son of Man as their deliverance (Romans 8:23). Though this second coming may be far off in the future, it is not to be forgotten. The Word that they have heard is not, like the seed in the parable, to be choked by the cares of life (8:14), nor overwhelmed, like the steward in another parable, by the debauchery and drunkenness so prevalent in those days (12:45). Because the day will come without warning, their preparation for it is to be a life of watchfulness and prayer. They have only to look at the teaching and example of Jesus himself. He has taught about the need to pray always (18:1) and, like the first disciples and Mary before the coming of the Spirit (Acts 1:14), gave an example of watchful perseverance (22:43).

Advent 2 C

Baruch 5:1–9
Psalm 125
Philippians 1:3–6, 8–11
Luke 3:1–6

The Word Comes to John

Israel's return from Babylonian exile in 538 BC fell short of prophetic expectations. Later, **Baruch** revived these hopes. Jerusalem will be a priestly city, wearing on her head the mitre of Aaron, the High Priest (Exodus 28:36–38). She will rejoice in the new name that Jeremiah had promised (33:16). Her exiled children will return, in another Exodus, on a straight road through the mountains, and enjoy shade in the desert, because God will level the hills and give rain to make the trees sprout (Isaiah 40:3; 41:18).

The **Psalm** belongs to the group sung by pilgrims travelling to Jerusalem. They remember the joy of deliverance from exile. They pray God's goodness to give them good rains and plentiful harvests.

Paul begins **Philippians** with a prayer of thanksgiving. We learn about Paul himself: about his joy and his optimism, despite the mortal danger threatened by his imprisonment. We learn about the Philippians. Paul loves them as Christ loves them. They are partners in Paul's work. Possibly they have financed it; certainly he can rely on their support at his coming trial. We learn about God and Christ. God is a living and true God (1 Thessalonians 1:9), active in history, who will complete what he has begun. Christ is the inspiration of all Paul's efforts, and he prepares his converts for the Day of Christ which, for Christians, has replaced the prophetic Day of the Lord described by the prophets of old (Amos 5:18). Paul's words continue to challenge and inspire all Christians in the season of Advent. Here we find a prayer that can provide a model for our own.

Last week, we heard about events leading to the second coming of Christ. This week, we learn about his first public manifestation through the words of John the Baptist. Because **Luke** is convinced that Christianity belongs to the wide world and has a message for all of it (Acts 26:26), he writes first of the rulers of the world into which Christ came. Some of these will play a part in the gospel story; the reader already knows that, between them, Pilate, Herod Antipas and the Jewish High Priests were responsible for Jesus' death. This sole mention of Tiberius Caesar, the Roman emperor, reminds us how his successors were in a position to hinder or assist the spread of Christianity in its early years and in the time of Luke (Acts 16:37–39; 18:15). But the word of God came to none of these dignitaries, rather to John the Baptist.

Luke gives us the longest account in the Gospels of the activity of John the Baptist, which prepares for the ministry of Jesus. John's mission is relevant for the reader, because it anticipates that of the early Church. Like Peter in Jerusalem on Pentecost Day, he preaches a baptism of repentance for the forgiveness of sins (Acts 2:38). We have already learnt about this John in Luke's infancy story. His task, according to the angel Gabriel addressing his father Zechariah, was to prepare a people fit for the Lord (1:13–17); according to Zechariah himself, it was to give his people knowledge of salvation (1:76–79).

Mark had introduced the Baptist with a quotation from scripture attributed to Isaiah (Mark 1:2–3). Luke expands Mark's text (Isaiah 40:3–4). The filling in of the valleys and laying low of the hills echoes both the words of Mary in her Magnificat about the powerful being brought low from their thrones and the lowly being lifted up (1:52) and Jesus' teaching in the Beatitudes about the poor possessing the Kingdom of God (6:20). The pronouncement that 'all flesh shall see the salvation of God' anticipates the preaching of the gospel to both Jew and Greek in the Acts (1:8; 26:29).

Advent 3 C

Zephaniah 3:14–18
Isaiah 12:2–6
Philippians 4:4–7
Luke 3:10–18

The Preaching of the Baptist

When Josiah was king (639–609 BC) and **Zephaniah** was writing, Israel enjoyed material prosperity and was free from foreign oppression. But these positives went with the negatives of religious infidelity and moral corruption, which prompt the prophet to warn of coming judgment. He gives us a picture of God which shows how things might be. God does not want to be remote and severe. He would like to be among his people as a judge who acquits, a warrior who fights its battles, a reveller taking part in the jubilation and dancing of its festivals. He is a God of joy.

A song from **Isaiah** takes the place of the Psalm. The opening sections of Isaiah are preoccupied with the wickedness of the nation and God's displeasure at it. He prefers to bring comfort (Isaiah 40:1) and wants his people to drink in joy at the well of salvation.

Paul began **Philippians** by writing of his joy (1:4). As he approaches the end of the letter, he returns to this theme. He wants his converts, his 'joy and crown' (4:1), to share his feelings. Their joy is to be deep-rooted; they know that the Lord is near (Matthew 1:23). Such knowledge helped Paul to endure his imprisonment (1:7) and enabled his converts in Philippi to survive in the hostile society around them. In their imprisonment there, Paul and Silas sang hymns to God (Acts 16:25). They were not alone; they shared their lives with the Lord, thankful for past benefits, asking him in prayer for what they needed in future. Their protection was the peace of God, given them through Christ (Romans 5:1). Now they were in Christ Jesus, part of his body as a new creation (2 Corinthians 5:17).

Every Gospel speaks of the public preaching of John the Baptist, but only **Luke** tells us how it was received. The religious authorities, who were to prove so hostile to Jesus, ignored John and his message (20:5–6). The type of person who will listen to Jesus also listens to John. Among those who now ask, 'What must we do?' are the tax collectors, the soldiers and the crowds. These same crowds will later hang on the words of Jesus (19:48) and go home 'beating their breasts' after the crucifixion (23:48), while tax collectors and sinners will all come close to Jesus to hear him (15:1). John does not demand improved sacrificial worship in the Temple, but asks for a proper sharing of resources and an end to extortion and intimidation. He is already preaching 'the good news to the poor' (4:18). The baptism of repentance he preaches is to be ratified by human behaviour that recognises its responsibilities for others.

So receptive are the people to John's preaching that they think he may be the Christ. His preaching is even more successful than that of Jesus himself! In Jesus' ministry, it was only Peter, speaking up on behalf of his fellow disciples, who would recognise Jesus as the Christ (9:20). John rejects the title of Christ, and goes on to announce the one to come in the language of the prophets who had spoken of the Day of the Lord (Amos 5:18; Malachi 3:23). His prophecy will be fulfilled in a way he did not expect in the more gentle events of the fire and Holy Spirit of pentecost, rather than in some fiery judgment (Acts 2:1–4). Then again the crowds would ask Peter, 'What must we do ...?' (Acts 2:37).

All this activity Luke describes as announcing the good news. For him, the Baptist was not only the predecessor of Jesus, but of the evangelizers of the early Church. Their preaching of the good news of Jesus the Christ (Acts 5:42) was a continuation of what John had begun, and it prepared the people for the coming of the Holy Spirit in baptism (Acts 2:38).

Advent 4 C

Micah 5:1–4
Psalm 79:2–3, 15–16, 18–19
Hebrews 10:5–10
Luke 1:39–44

The Visitation

While Assyrian armies were threatening Jerusalem eight centuries before Christ, **Micah** spoke out oracles detailing how God will rescue his people. Among these is a prophecy about a true shepherd who will rule on God's behalf. He will be born in Bethlehem (the house of bread), David's family home (1 Samuel 16:1). Here Jesus was born, and Matthew quotes this prophecy in his account of the visit of the magi (Matthew 2:6).

The **Psalm** reflects a time when Israel was threatened by foreign armies. God is invoked as shepherd and as a king enthroned on the cherubim who travelled with them as they journeyed with the Ark of the Covenant (1 Samuel 4:4). If God will but smile on his people, all will be well.

The letter to the **Hebrews** is a work of doctrine and exhortation. Its author speaks of the sufferings of Christ on behalf of humanity (2:9), of the obedience that he learnt through these sufferings (5:8), and of his exaltation into heaven where he now sits at the right hand of God and makes intercession on our behalf (9:24). We have confidence in him because, apart from sin, he has been tested exactly as ourselves (4:15); he has called us his brothers (2:12). Today we hear of his entry into this world, his birth story told in the language of Psalm 40. The words of the psalmist become the words of Jesus as he takes on himself the human condition (John 1:14). He leaves his life in glory with the Father (John 1:1; 17:5) for a new life on earth, a life of obedience. His food is now to do the will of him who sent him (John 4:32) and he teaches his disciples to do the will of the Father (Matthew 7:21). To his obedient offering, we owe our salvation and sanctification.

On recent Sundays we have heard about the second coming of Christ (Advent 1) and about the preparations made by John the Baptist for his public manifestation to Israel (Advent 2 and 3). Today, we learn from **Luke**'s infancy account how God prepared for the birth of Jesus (chapters 1–2). Luke tells us about two sets of parents and two children. Zechariah and Elizabeth, the parents of John the Baptist, belong to the Old Testament. Like Abraham and Sarah, they were promised by God a child in their old age (1:13; Genesis 17:17). Their child is to mark the end of the age of the Law and the Prophets (Luke 16:16). He is to turn many of the sons of Israel to the Lord their God (1:16). Zechariah was struck dumb by the angel because he did not believe; he had forgotten how God gave the child Isaac to Abraham and Sarah, despite their advanced years (1:20). Mary, the mother of Jesus, has been informed by Gabriel how, in a more wonderful intervention of God, she will become a mother without the cooperation of a human father. Her child will be the Son of the Most High (1:32). Mary believed; she said, 'let what you have said be done to me' (1:38).

Today, the two mothers meet. The Baptist, still in the womb, leaps for joy, anticipating his joy in the good news he would proclaim in his life (3:3). His joy contrasts with the struggles in the womb of the twins of Rebecca (Genesis 25:22). Elizabeth, his mother, filled with the Holy Spirit like an ancient prophet, pronounces a double blessing on Mary. The first reflects her role as mother of her Lord. By bringing to birth the true Davidic king (1:32), she is doing more for Israel than the blessed women of the past, such as Jael, who had overcome Sisera (Judges 5:24), and Judith, who had defeated Holofernes (Judith 13:18). Elizabeth blesses Mary a second time because she has believed. Her words anticipate those spoken by Jesus during his ministry, that his mother was one of those 'who hear the word of God and put it into practice' (8:21).

Holy Family C

1 Samuel 1:20–22, 24–28
Psalm 83:2–3, 5–6, 9–10
1 John 3:1–2, 21–24
Luke 2:41–52

The Finding in the Temple

In 1 **Samuel**, Hannah, the aged mother of Samuel, reminds the reader of other women in biblical history who gave birth to sons in their old age, such as Sarah, the mother of Isaac (Genesis 21:2), and Elizabeth, the mother of John the Baptist (Luke 1:7). So grateful is Hannah that 'Yahweh was mindful of her' (1 Samuel 1:19) that she presents her child to Eli, the priest of the temple at Shiloh, so that he can serve the Lord for ever. He will become the successor of Eli and the means that God uses to introduce the monarchy of Saul and his successors to Israel.

The **Psalm** is one of those that pilgrims to Jerusalem would sing to glorify the Temple. The desire for God and the dedication to the Temple—his dwelling place—expressed in it conveniently link the story of Samuel and the gospel narrative about the child Jesus.

John's Gospel reminds us that those who accepted the Word made flesh received power to become 'children of God' (John 1:11). **1 John** defines what this means. Such a privilege does not signify that we have already achieved the peak of our Christian calling; he cannot define the glorious future that God has in store for us, when we shall see him as he is. And, as a privilege, it does not guarantee our salvation. We are expected to 'believe in the name of ... Jesus' and 'love one another'. This is a unique New Testament description of the demands of the Christian life. We may compare it with the double command of love of God and neighbour found in Mark (12:29–31), and Paul's description of Christian existence in Galatians as 'faith that makes its power felt through love' (Galatians 5:6).

The final incident of **Luke**'s infancy narrative takes place in the Temple of Jerusalem. This is where his Gospel began and where it will end (24:53). It is the only gospel story about the childhood of Jesus. It is significant for its own sake and for its relationship to the rest of Luke's work.

Since Simeon spoke his prophecy over the child and its mother (2:34–35), twelve years have passed. We know that in those years Jesus grew to maturity, was filled with wisdom and enjoyed God's favour (2:40). Each year, as was expected of a devout family, they would travel to Jerusalem for the Passover (Deuteronomy 16:16). But now he is twelve years old, the age when a Jewish boy was obliged to observe the Law, he does not return with his parents. After three days—for the reader a hint of the future resurrection—he is found in the Temple, already displaying the wisdom that he would personify during his ministry (11:31).

His mother, in tones of anguish, asks him why he had done this to them. The reader recognises how the sword of which Simeon spoke has cut Jesus off from his earthly family and pierced the heart of Mary (2:35). Jesus' answer is a single sentence, his first recorded words. He explains that 'I must be busy with my Father's affairs'. This statement helps us to understand the rest of the Gospel, in which a divine necessity is at work (24:26) and in which Jesus lives in close union with his Father until the end (10:21; 23:46), but at this stage his mother cannot understand these truths. Although in Luke's account she had been informed about the identity of her Son as the 'Son of God' (1:35) and about his mission, which would bring about the 'the falling and ... the rising of many' (2:34), she has to share with other believers a path of non-understanding. Meanwhile, Jesus returns with his parents to Nazareth, where he lives a life of obedience to them. Luke tells us no more until he pictures for us Jesus at prayer, eighteen years later, after receiving the baptism of John (3:21).

Baptism of the Lord C (Sunday I C)

Isaiah 40:1–5, 9–11
Psalm 103:1–4, 24–25, 27–30
Titus 2:11–14; 3:4–7
Luke 3:15–16, 21–22

Jesus is Baptized

Ancient custom insisted that candidates for baptism be familiar with the major stages in the history of our salvation. They were to know about God's promise to Abraham (Genesis 12:1–3), his covenant at Sinai with Moses (Exodus 19:5), as well as his words of comfort to Israel in exile with which Deutero-**Isaiah** begins. John the Baptist applied these words of Isaiah to his own ministry (Luke 3:4). The concluding description of God as the shepherd of his people prepares us for Jesus' identification of himself as the Good Shepherd (John 10:11). Jesus had compassion on the people because they were like sheep without a shepherd (Mark 6:34).

The **Psalm** is a meditation on the glories of God in creation. God may have his dwelling in glory, but he still looks after all that he has made. The Spirit that he sends out is an agent of rebirth and renewal. This is the same Spirit that came down on Jesus at his baptism.

We hear again two passages from the letter to **Titus** which are read at Christmas. They are rich in truths of our faith. They identify Christ with God's loving favour and grace, and indeed with God. They recall his sacrificial death as the price of our salvation. They mention God's gift to us of the cleansing waters of rebirth and the renewing action of the Spirit. Through these, we belong to the people that is God's own. Vatican II stressed how the Church is the People of God. We look forward to the second coming of Christ, and to the fulfilment of the promise to us of eternal life. The second part of our reading may well have been a hymn of an early Christian community.

Luke's account of the baptism of Jesus falls into two parts. In the first, the people wonder whether John the Baptist is the Christ. He denies it and assures them that a stronger one than he is coming, who will baptize with the Holy Spirit and with fire. He expects an Elijah-type figure (Malachi 3:23), who will call down fire from heaven to destroy God's enemies (2 Kings 1:10, 12, 14; Luke 9:54). Later, the Holy Spirit will indeed come in the tongues of fire that appear at pentecost (Acts 2:3)

In the second part, the people meet Jesus for the first time. He is among those who have come for baptism, and is at prayer after his own baptism. The Jesus of Luke is a model of prayer for future Christians. Of fire there is no sign but, instead, Jesus sees the Holy Spirit in the shape of a dove, the bird that brought the olive leaf to Noah after the flood to signify a new era between God and his creation (Genesis 8:12). At the same time, he hears his mission from the mouth of God himself. God does not speak to Jesus by means of an angel, as he had spoken to Zechariah (1:12) or Mary (1:26). Jesus hears words traditionally addressed to Israelite kings at their coronation (Psalm 2:7). As God's Son, he is the true successor of David (2 Samuel 7). As the one with whom God is well pleased, he is the Servant foreseen by Isaiah (42:1). Like the Isaian Servant, he will be as one who serves (22:27) among his disciples and his blood will be poured out for them (22:20).

The baptism of Jesus at the Jordan is to be supplemented by a second baptism of suffering and death. It is then that fire will be poured out on the earth and it is a baptism for which he longs (12:49–50). The baptism and mission of the Christian cannot be understood in terms of the Jordan to the neglect of Calvary (Romans 6:3). We are not told when the apostles were baptized, but Jesus did tell James and John that they were to be baptized with the baptism with which he was baptized (Mark 10:38).

Year C
The Year of Luke

THE SUNDAYS OF LENT*

*The **First Readings** take us through the 'history of salvation':*

Sunday 1	*Confessing God's goodness*	*Deuteronomy 26:4–10*
Sunday 2	*Covenant with Abraham*	*Genesis 15:5–12, 17–18*
Sunday 3	*The burning bush*	*Exodus 3:1–8, 13–15*
Sunday 4	*Entry into the land*	*Joshua 5:9–12*
Sunday 5	*Isaiah promises restoration*	*Isaiah 43:16–21*
Passion Sunday	*The Suffering Servant of Isaiah*	*Isaiah 50:4–7*

Second Readings: *'The reading from the letters of the apostles have been selected to fit the gospel and the Old Testament readings, and, to the extent possible, to provide a connection between them.'*

Sunday 1	*Confess Jesus is Lord*	*Romans 10:8–13*
Sunday 2	*He will transfigure our bodies*	*Philippians 3:17–4:1*
Sunday 3	*Lessons for us*	*1 Corinthians 10:1–6, 10–12*
Sunday 4	*New creation*	*2 Corinthians 5:17–21*
Sunday 5	*I want to know Christ*	*Philippians 3:18–14*
Passion Sunday	*Jesus humbled and exalted*	*Philippians 2:6–11*

*The **Responsorial Psalms** are designed to help with the understanding of the First Reading, to deepen some significant theme, to clarify its message.*

*The **Gospel Readings** of **Sundays 1 and 2** are always about the temptations and transfiguration of Jesus, this year according to Luke. **Sundays 3 to 5** are texts from Luke—about the need for repentance (Luke 13), the parable of the Father and his sons (Luke 15)—plus John's woman caught in adultery (John 8). On Passion Sunday (**Sunday 6**), the passion story according to Luke is read.*

[On Sundays 3–5, the Gospels of Year A may be repeated: the Samaritan Woman (John 4), the Man Born Blind (John 9) and the Raising of Lazarus (John 11). If not, they should be read during the week.]

* Quotations from 'General Introduction', *Roman Missal*, nn. 97, 100.

EASTER AND THE SUNDAYS AFTER EASTER

*The **First Readings** are always from the Acts of the Apostles, about 'the life, witness and growth of the primitive Church'. Every year, we hear on Easter Sunday the preaching of Peter to Cornelius, on Ascension Day the story of the ascension and on Pentecost Day about the descent of the Holy Spirit. We learn about the life of the early Christians in Jerusalem. In this Year C, we learn about the missionary activities of Paul and Barnabas, about the Churches they evangelized and about the proceeding of the so-called Council of Jerusalem. We also hear the story of the death of Stephen.*

*The **Second Readings** form a semi-continuous reading of the Book of **Revelation.** This book, the last in the Bible, finds its appropriate place in this final stage of the three-year lectionary. Its conclusion celebrates 'the joyous faith and sure hope proper to this season'.*

*The **Responsorial Psalms** are designed to help with the understanding of the First Reading, to deepen some significant theme, to clarify its message.*

*The **Gospel** is always the same on **Sundays 1 and 2**: it is taken from John and tells of the three persons at the tomb on Easter Day and the story of Thomas on the second Sunday. On **Sunday 3** we learn from John about the appearance of the Risen Lord in Galilee and about his commissioning of Peter. **Sunday 4** always provides a passage from John 10, the shepherd chapter. **Sundays 5, 6 and 7** provide extracts from the Last Supper discourse in John—its beginning, about the dwelling place of Father and Son and about peace, with an extract from the final prayer of Jesus for those who will believe because of his disciples.*

[Ascension Day and Body and Blood of Christ are often celebrated on the Sunday following rather than the traditional Thursday; hence they are included here.]

Lent I C

Deuteronomy 26:4–10
Psalm 90:1–2, 10–15
Romans 10:8–13
Luke 4:1–13

Temptations in the Desert

Lent is a time when our first readings on Sundays summarise for us the history of God's saving care for his people. The solemn confession of the people recorded in **Deuteronomy** provides a convenient outline of their understanding of how their story began. This book probably dates from the religious, social and political crisis that Israel experienced during the time of her exile from her land and Temple. It summons Israel to reform and renewal. Our passage quotes a solemn confession of the people as they offered the first fruits of the crops; they recall their wanderings with the patriarchs and the oppression in Egypt from which God delivered them through Moses. God has heard their cry and given them their present fertile land. Hearts conscious of God's past benefits stay loyal to him in the present.

The **Psalm**, an expression of confidence in God, describes a group of pilgrims at prayer day and night in the Temple. The priests set them on their way. Whatever difficulties lie before them, they pray to God to bring them safely through.

Paul in **Romans** reflects on words from Deuteronomy (30:14), understanding them not as commandments brought by Moses, but the salvation won by Christ. This salvation is no private affair but a matter for public confession, 'Jesus is Lord' (1 Corinthians 12:3). Neither is it to be merely a form of words; it is to be a belief rooted in the heart. In the past, only Israel called upon Yahweh. Now all nations can call upon Christ, and will be kept safe in time of testing and temptation.

Having been baptized, according to **Luke**, among all the people (3:21), and being full of the Holy Spirit (Acts 6:5), Jesus makes his way to the desert and is there tempted, tested by the devil. According to Hebrews, Jesus was tempted 'in every way that we are, though he is without sin' (Hebrews 4:15). By himself experiencing temptation, Jesus, the model Christian, points the way to all believers who have to pray, 'Do not put us to the test' (11:4; 22:40, 46).

The devil first urges Jesus, hungry after forty days without food, to turn a stone into a loaf. But Jesus will never use his powers to satisfy his own needs. He will feed five thousand with five loaves (9:14) and give his body as food (22:19), but he will not force God to give him manna, as God had given Israel in the desert (Exodus 16:31); his food is to do the will of the Father (John 4:34). He resists this temptation, like the others, by an appeal to the Word of God found in Deuteronomy (8:3). Believers appeal to this Word in time of temptation. They know they will not be tempted beyond their strength (1 Corinthians 10:13).

Luke began his account of Jesus' ministry with a list of the political authorities of the day (3:1–2). The devil now claims that all these belong to him. Jesus knows from the baptismal Psalm that, as Son of God, all the nations are 'his heritage' (3:22; Psalm 2:8). Again, he replies to the devil with a quotation from Deuteronomy (6:15). But the devil too can quote scripture (Psalms 91:11–12), disguising himself 'as an angel of light' (2 Corinthians 11:14). Should not Jesus make a dramatic gesture to win support, as Judas the Galilean had done a few years before (Acts 5:37)? But now, as later in his ministry, Jesus refuses to provide signs from heaven (Deuteronomy 6:16; Luke 11:16). To do so is to tempt God, to follow one's own will and not the will of God (22:42). Jesus taught his hearers to listen to the Word of God and put it into practice (8:21). He does the same.

Lent 2 C

Genesis 15:5–12, 17–18
Psalm 26:1, 7–9, 13–14
Philippians 3:17–4:1
Luke 9:28–36

Transfiguration on a Mountain

Abraham is always the topic of the first reading on this Sunday of Lent. Paul calls him 'our father in the eyes of God' (Romans 4:17), because Abraham believes God's promises of descendants and land, as related in **Genesis**. God made these promises to Abraham because of his faith and not, says Paul, because of anything he had done (Romans 4:3; Galatians 3:6); his faith foreshadows our faith in Christ. Abraham ratifies this relationship with God by ceremonies like those used by kings of the time when binding themselves by treaty. Typical of these is to cut certain animals in half. The performance of such a gesture symbolizes the fate of a covenant partner who proves unfaithful (Jeremiah 34:18).

The expressions of trust found in the **Psalm** would be at home on the lips of Abraham. The poet's searching for God's face anticipates the transfigured Christ as the three disciples saw him on the mountain. His invitation to stand firm is fitting encouragement for the disciples as they made their way with Jesus to Jerusalem (Joshua 1:6).

Paul uses various images to describe the effects of the work of Christ in his dying and rising from the dead on our behalf. In **Philippians**, he employs that of transformation or transfiguration. There were many popular stories around in those days about gods and goddesses who adopted human forms and about humans taking the shape of animals. Paul uses such imagery to describe the future of his Christians in Philippi who, he was sure, were being transformed into the copies of the glorious body of Christ (2 Corinthians 3:18).

Luke tells the transfiguration story in his own way. As in the other Gospels, the scene follows Jesus' first prediction of his future passion, with his promise that some of those present will see the Kingdom of God (9:27). Straight afterwards, Jesus goes up the mountain with three disciples to pray. The prayer of Jesus is a continuing theme in Luke. Jesus prayed at his baptism (3:21) and spent a whole night in prayer on a mountain before he chose the Twelve (6:12).

On this occasion, his outward aspect changes; he wears the appearance of glory, the state that is to be his final destiny after his resurrection (24:26; 9:22). His disciples are privileged to see this glory, a feature of the fullness of the Kingdom. Luke alone tells us that the conversation between Jesus, Moses and Elijah is about the *exodus* that he will complete in Jerusalem. This recalls the exodus that Israel had experienced long ago through the desert; the life of Jesus gives these ancient events their full meaning (24:44). Jesus had his own journey to complete which would lead him first to Jerusalem (9:51) and finally to paradise (23:43; Acts 1:11).

When Jesus is alone, Peter makes his suggestion about the three tents, as if they are present at some heavenly feast of Tabernacles and there is nothing left for them on earth (Acts 2:11). The voice from heaven, that had once spoken to Jesus at his baptism, now speaks again (3:22). It again proclaims the identity of Jesus, but now it adds, 'Listen to him'. These words from Deuteronomy (18:15) tell Peter that Jesus, not Moses or Elijah or anyone else, is the teacher he must hear, even when he speaks a new teaching about passion and resurrection. So Luke ends his account of this mystery. There is no conversation about Elijah as they descend. With the glimpse of Jesus' glory that they have experienced, the disciples are prepared for whatever future awaits them (Romans 8:18; 2 Peter 1:18).

Lent 3 C

Exodus 3:1–8, 13–15
Psalm 102:1–4, 6–8, 11
1 Corinthians 10:1–6, 10–12
Luke 13:1–9

Call for Repentance

Moses dominates **Exodus** as the leader of his people and the friend and instrument of God. Like Jesus, he is given an infancy narrative (Exodus 2:1–10). After years in which nothing seemed to happen, he meets God at the burning bush in the mountain wilderness of Horeb. Here God reveals himself as the one who is to deliver Israel from slavery and bring them to their own land. Here, too, Moses learns that the God of the patriarchs is his God as well, a God with a special name, 'I Am who I Am', pointing to his freedom, majesty and mystery.

The description in the **Psalm** of the kindness and mercy of God, quoting Exodus (34:6–7), reminds us that God did indeed fulfil his promise to Moses to deliver his people from oppression, and encourages us to make a positive response to the appeal for repentance that we hear in the Gospel.

Paul presumed that his readers in Gentile **Corinth** knew about Moses and traditions of salvation history such as the Exodus and desert journey of Israel. Paul explains their relevance to his own converts, because such things were written for their instruction (Romans 15:4). Their ancestors, too, had been baptized, but into Moses rather than Christ (Romans 6:3). Paul identifies the rock in the desert from which they had drawn water with Christ (Numbers 20:11). Yet, despite all these signs of the mercy and fidelity of God, the Israelites have failed to enter into the land promised them. Their lack of response is a warning to Christians not to ignore calls for repentance.

A turning away from sin and a turning to the Lord were always part of the message of Israel's prophets (Hosea 6:1). In **Luke** today, we hear of three ways in which Jesus reinforces this prophetic appeal to repentance. John the Baptist had preached repentance (3:3) and Jesus defined his own mission as one of bringing sinners to repentance (5:32). Long ago, Nineveh had repented at the preaching of Jonah (11:32), but the cities of Chorazin and Bethsaida refused to respond to Jesus (10:13). Peter continued this message of repentance on Pentecost Day (Acts 2:38). Jesus would use vivid parables to illustrate how great joy in heaven results from repentance on earth (15:7, 10).

First he appeals to a recent tragedy. When informed of the Galileans killed by Pilate in Jerusalem, Jesus the Galilean does not threaten retribution. He denies that these people died because they were sinners. Neither they nor their parents have sinned (John 9:3). Their fate is a symbol of the risk run by those who reject the mercy of God that Jesus is extending in his proclamation of the Kingdom (4:43).

Secondly, Jesus reminds his hearers of those in Jerusalem who perished when a tower collapsed. Their fate of death through accident causes Jesus again to call for repentance before it is too late. Jesus is using the drastic language of the prophets who went before him.

Jesus' third appeal is by way of the parable of the fig tree. Here is a tree that is useless to its owner. Like the vineyard in Isaiah (5:1–7), to which God compared his fruitless people, it never produces fruit. Such a tree resembles a person who does nothing with life, like the attendant asleep when the master comes (12:37) or the unproductive servant (12:45) who spends his time in debauchery and drunkenness (21:34). The owner of the tree is merciful; he will allow it a year of grace and permit his gardener to help its growth with manure. Jesus uses these three stories to bring the sinner to repentance.

Lent 4 C

Joshua 5:9–12
Psalm 33:2–7
2 Corinthians 5:17–21
Luke 15:1–3, 11–32

The Father and His Sons

Joshua was the successor of Moses; he brought Israel into the land promised to Abraham. Once more they celebrate the feast of Passover, which began their liberation (Exodus 12). The manna, which God had provided in response to their complaints (Exodus 16), now ceases. The name Jesus is a version of Joshua. It was at a Passover that he died (John 13:1), and he gave us to eat, not manna, but his own body (John 6:31–34). He has gone ahead of us to prepare the place of perfect rest (Hebrews 3–4).

The **Psalm** of thanksgiving is associated with David, when he pretended to be mad at the court of the Philistine king (1 Samuel 21:11), but it suits anyone conscious of divine deliverance, whether the Israelites saved from the desert, or a younger son reconciled to his father as in the gospel story.

The key word used by Paul here in **2 Corinthians** is 'reconciliation'. This is another image that Paul employs to explain what has happened as a result of Christ's salvific work. Before Christ, the world was in a state of enmity with God; his only response could be one of anger at the sin that held all in its tyranny (Romans 1:18; 3:9). But, somehow, the sinless one was made into sin, and its power was destroyed. Hence reconciliation came about between God and humanity, and between members of God's family. Paul sees himself as a minister of this reconciliation; his task as an apostle is to take this two-fold reconciliation further. Luke makes the same point through his account of how the younger son began his life again in his father's house.

Jesus was criticized for welcoming sinners and eating with them. **Luke** tells us how he replied to his critics with a parable about a man who has two sons. The younger son nullifies three aspects of his life by abandoning his family, his nation and his religion. He leaves home to live among foreigners, making no attempt to seek help in his troubles from his many fellow exiles. He works among pigs—unclean animals—a fact which shows that the religion for which his ancestors had suffered so much means nothing to him. But God has not abandoned him; he comes to himself and is able to admit his sin and its effects. He is prepared to live as a slave; he will make no claim to seek for himself his former status.

The father's concern for his son is such that he puts aside normal ways of behaving for a man of his culture. Instead of disinheriting his son, he watches out for him. Seeing him far away, he runs out to greet him. He does not even allow his son to finish his speech of repentance. While the son is still speaking, his father invests him with greater authority than before, symbolized by robe, ring and sandals. Forbidden to be a servant, he is awarded a higher status than ever in his family.

The elder son has not been wasting time looking out for his brother. He is hard at work. His questions to the servants show that they know more about his family than he does. His father comes out to plead with him. He neither addresses his father as 'father' nor speaks of his brother as 'brother'. He understands the slaughter of the calf in terms of reward, not as a gift or a token of joy. He will not accept his place in the family, preferring to live as a servant. His father does not rebuke him; he just speaks of the good news of the return of his other son. Does the elder son go in to the feast? Do the Pharisees who were criticizing Jesus recognise themselves in the elder son? Do we?

Lent 5 C

Isaiah 43:16–21
Psalm 125
Philippians 3:8–14
John 8:1–11

The Woman Caught in Adultery

Last week, we celebrated with Joshua the entry of the people into the land that God had promised Abraham (Joshua 5). But, because of their sinfulness and infidelity, the people are expelled from this promised land and driven into exile (2 Chronicles 36:14). The consoling message of Deutero-**Isaiah** is that God's fidelity and mercy are greater that his justice. For those who repent, forgiveness awaits. In former days, God saw the distress of his people in Egypt and rescued them through the Exodus (Exodus 3:7). Now he promises a new Exodus to bring them back from Babylonian exile. He will provide ways that are smooth and water to satisfy their thirst in the desert heat.

In a prayer for rain and a good harvest, the **Psalm** celebrates the deliverance from exile that God achieved on behalf of his people. God's mercies in the past give grounds for hope in present distress.

Writing to the **Philippians**, Paul gives us a rare glimpse into his personal feelings and attitudes. On the road to Damascus (Acts 9) he had been intending to capture Christians. Instead, he was captured by Christ, a name repeated five times in our reading. This experience taught him that all his previous zeal and achievements, as one utterly committed to his religion, counted for nothing towards personal salvation. He owes everything to the fact that Christ has loved him and given himself for him (Galatians 2:20). But he cannot be complacent. Using an image from athletics, he compares himself to a runner racing towards the winning post. He knows that he could still stumble before the final prize is his (Galatians 5:5; 1 Corinthians 9:25).

We have learnt from Luke's account of Pilate's massacre of the Galileans (13:1–9) that Jesus does not condone sin; we have discovered from the parable of the two sons how, like the father of those sons, God waits and longs to forgive sin (Luke 15:13–32). Both of these attitudes are illustrated in the story of the adulterous woman found in **John**. Because this story is omitted from many manuscripts of John's Gospel, it is often treated as a tradition deriving from the Jerusalem ministry of Jesus in Luke (21:38), the Gospel that gives so many examples of Jesus' mercy towards sinners, expressed in personal encounters with individuals such as the woman who anointed him (Luke 7:50) and the penitent thief who died with him (Luke 23:43).

The scribes and the Pharisees know all about the demands of the Law (Deuteronomy 22:23), but they have much to learn about its application (Luke 11:42). Their interest in this case is in the embarrassment they see that they can cause Jesus, not in the welfare of the woman. They are suspicious of his attitude to the Law. They want him to support an act of defiance against the Roman authorities, who would not allow them to put anyone to death (John 19:16). They are using this woman's life as, on another occasion, they used a Roman coin to test Jesus' loyalty to Caesar (Luke 20:20–26; 23:2).

The message of John is that God sent his Son to save the world, not to condemn it (3:17); if some are condemned, it is because they themselves choose to reject Jesus. Jesus does not judge anyone (8:15). It is no sentence of condemnation that he writes on the ground. This writing recalls a verse of Jeremiah: 'All who abandon you will be put to shame, those who turn from you will be uprooted from the land, since they have abandoned the fountain of living water' (Jeremiah 17:13). Jesus is the source of living water. He promised it to the woman of Samaria; it will flow from his side after his death on the cross (4:10; 19:34).

Passion Sunday C

Isaiah 50:4–7
Psalm 21:8–9, 17–20, 23–24
Philippians 2:6–11
Luke 22:14–23:56

The Passion of Jesus

One of the so-called Servant Songs from **Isaiah** prepares us for our reading of the passion of Jesus. Originally this Servant might have been intended as a description of the prophet himself, or it could have been a portrait of the people of Israel as a whole, forced to endure the privations of exile and loss. But early Christians identified the Servant with Christ, as Philip explained in Acts to the Ethiopian eunuch who was reading a Servant Song as he returned from his Jerusalem pilgrimage (Acts 8:26–40).

In the **Psalm** we hear the voice of the innocent man who suffers. His enemies toss their heads and they divide his garments as the enemies of Christ would do as he endured the cross (Mark 15:24; Luke 23:34). Like the Servant, the Psalmist does not allow suffering to extinguish his faith. Paradoxically, it deepens it and the Psalm concludes with an appeal to all to praise God.

The **Philippians** were Paul's favourite Church, but they had their faults. They were selfish and too full of themselves (2:2–3). Paul's remedy is to put before them the story of the career of Christ as a mirror in which they can view themselves. Perhaps quoting a familiar Christian hymn that recalled Christ's humiliation and exaltation because of his willing obedience, Paul may be contrasting the glory that Christ enjoyed as pre-existent Son with his earthly suffering (John 17:5). According to others, he is portraying Jesus as the new Adam, who chose to obey, unlike the old Adam, who disobeyed the command of God (Romans 5:12). Paul's own life followed the same pattern; 'because of Christ, I have come to consider all these advantages that I had as disadvantages' (3:7).

We approach the passion story of **Luke** by concentrating on a single part of it. The arrest scene (22:47–53) sets the tone for the remainder. It falls neatly into three parts. In the first, Jesus meets Judas and Judas approaches Jesus to kiss him. The actual kiss is omitted. This evangelist passes over the more revolting and harrowing details of the passion. Jesus speaks first, addressing Judas by name. Even now, he continues his ministry of calling sinners to repentance (5:32). This is the first of several personal encounters of Jesus in Luke's story, which climax in his conversation with the good thief (23:43).

In the second part, Jesus encounters his disciples, whose flight Luke does not mention (Mark 14:50). When they see Jesus in trouble, they crowd round to protect him, and they only desist in obedience to his instructions. They are the ones who stand by him in his trials (22:49). He refuses their help because the passion is a necessity he must accept (24:46). He heals the slave of the high priest who is the victim of his disciples' enthusiasm. His ministry of doing good and healing continues even at this stage (Acts 10:38).

In the third part, Jesus speaks to his enemies. The reader sees the irony of the situation. He whose birth was greeted with a song of peace by angels from heaven (2:11), and who has taught his followers to love their enemies (6:35), is now threatened with swords and clubs. The only explanation is the power of darkness, but we know that he overcame this in his desert conflict with Satan (4:1–13). So Jesus goes to his death, with his innocence acknowledged even by Pilate and Herod (23:14–15). His body is given and his blood poured out 'for you' (22:19–20), so that repentance and the forgiveness of sins can be proclaimed to all the nations (24:47). Luke tells a familiar story in his own particular way that will encourage and console all who hear it (1:1–4). As elsewhere in this Gospel, Jesus provides a pattern and example for Christian behaviour.

Easter 2 C

Acts 5:12–16
Psalm 117:2–4, 22-27
Revelation 1:9–13, 17–19
John 20:19–31

Believing without Seeing

According to the Gospels, Jesus worked many miracles, sometimes by mere touch (Mark 6:56). Outside the Gospels, Paul does mention his own ability to perform wonders, but does not stress it (Romans 15:19). **Acts** is an exception. There we read how signs and wonders are a feature of Christian life in Jerusalem (2:43). We are offered examples in the healing of the lame man in the Temple (3:1–10) and of the awesome fate of Ananias and Sapphira, who deceived the apostles (5:1–11). For Luke, this ability to perform miracles proves that the disciple is to be like the master. If Jesus worked miracles by touch (Luke 8:44), Peter does so by his shadow and Paul by his handkerchief (Acts 19:12).

The **Psalm** of last week (*see Easter Sunday Year A*) is repeated and continued. For the Christian, the 'day of the Lord' is now the day of resurrection and the blessing on 'him who comes' (Mark 11:9), is not addressed to the devout pilgrim entering the Temple, but for Christ coming to his bereaved disciples after Easter.

The Churches of Asia were under threat. Rumour had it that the Roman authorities were soon to insist on full observance of emperor worship; all would have to cry, 'Caesar is Lord'. John, the leader of these Churches, is already in exile because of his activities on behalf of the gospel. He reflects on how to prepare his people for their coming ordeal. Like the authors of Daniel, strengthening the people in the time of the wicked king Antiochus Epiphanes two hundred years before, he writes an **Apocalypse**. For us, this is a strange type of literature, but, properly understood, it can encourage our confidence in the final victory of Christ.

Last week we heard **John**'s account of the events of the morning of the first Easter Day. This week we learn what happened in the evening of the same day, and of events that followed a week later. On both occasions, Jesus appears to his disciples despite the locked doors of the room where they are meeting. His first gift to them is the peace that he had promised them during the final meal he took with them (14:27; 16:33). Their response is one of joy (16:22).

The final words of Jesus before his death were 'it is accomplished' (19:30). This is true of the work of Jesus himself, but it is not true for the disciples. Their task is just beginning. The witness that Jesus gave to the world is theirs to continue. Just as the Father had sent Jesus into the world, Jesus is now sending them. But they will not be left to their own resources. They will have with them the Holy Spirit; this is how Jesus will continue his presence with them. He had prepared them for this in his teaching about the paraclete during the Last Supper (14:16–17, 26; 15:26; 16:7–15).

A week later, the disciples are able to say to Thomas, who was absent from that first meeting, 'We have seen the Lord'. Just as these disciples failed to take in similar words addressed to them earlier by Mary Magdalene (20:18), so Thomas refuses to accept their testimony. Jesus has shown them his wounded hands and side; Thomas demands that he should not only see them but be able to touch them too. Continuing in his role of shepherd looking out for lost sheep (10:11), Jesus challenges Thomas to pass from unbelief to belief. Thomas responds with the most profound confession of Jesus' identity in the whole Gospel. Jesus for him is more than 'Lord'; he is 'My Lord and my God', a truth which was proclaimed right at the opening of the Gospel (1:1). It is the confession that the author of this Gospel wants us all to make, because if we make it, we are on the way to true life. Jesus is that way, and the truth and the life (14:6).

Easter 3 C

Acts 5:27–32, 40–41
Psalm 29:2, 4–6, 11–13
Revelation 5:11–14
John 21:1–19

Jesus and Peter

When Jesus warned his disciples that they would be brought before the Jewish courts, he promised them the assistance of the Holy Spirit (Luke 12:11). In the **Acts**, the Peter who, while Jesus was confessing his identity before the Jewish authorities, had three times denied that he ever even knew his Lord (Luke 22:54–63), finds himself transformed when face to face with the Jerusalem Sanhedrin. The disciple is now like his Lord; he speaks up with boldness and confidence. God is now for him the first reality. He will obey his God whatever the cost; he knows that the God who raised Jesus from the dead will protect him too. To suffer humiliation for such a God is a source of pride and honour. Like Paul, he can rejoice in his sufferings because they make him more like Christ (Colossians 1:24).

The **Psalm** was originally a song of thanksgiving by one who had recovered from serious sickness. It is easily applied to Christ praising the Father after his resurrection or to Peter expressing gratitude for deliverance from his persecutors.

Like some ancient prophet, John finds himself transported to God's throne room. There he witnesses the worship that goes on day and night (Isaiah 6:1; 1 Kings 22:19). Now Christ, as the Lamb who has suffered, has taken his place with his Father (John 1:29). Our reading introduces us to one of the many hymns of praise found in **Revelation**, which combines traditional biblical language with expressions at home in the worship of the Roman emperor. Such heavenly worship is to be a model for our own earthly liturgies.

The places and disciples mentioned at the start of **John's** last chapter remind the reader of previous events in this Gospel. The Sea of Tiberias recalls for us the feeding of the five thousand (6:1–15), and Cana recalls the transformation of water into wine and the restoration to life of the royal official's servant (2:1–11; 4:46–52). The presence of Simon Peter and Thomas brings to mind their vivid confessions of commitment and faith (6:69; 20:28). So we are not surprised to read of the abundance of fish caught by the disciples or of Peter's threefold declaration of his love for Jesus.

Both incidents point to the future. The evangelist carefully numbers the fish: there are 153 of them. They could be a symbol of all the nations of the world to whom the gospel is to be preached. According to the teachers of the time, there existed 153 species of living creatures. The net is not broken. This could be a pointer to the unity that Jesus desires for his followers. When he spoke to the Jews during his ministry, they were often split and divided (7:43; 9:16). His Church is to treasure its unity, like that of the garment without seam for which the solders cast lots (19:25). Jesus gives Peter his commission only after he has declared his love. He has to do this to atone for his denials (18:17, 25, 27), and to give an example for those who will follow him in exercising responsibility for the Church of Christ. Peter's task is given him in the language of sheep and lambs. He is to be the shepherd of the flock of Jesus. The best commentary on this expression is to be found in Jesus' own description of himself as the Good Shepherd, which we hear next Sunday (John 10:11–18). Peter, like Jesus, is to know his sheep by name and be a means of their salvation. As Jesus knows the Father, Peter is to know Jesus (14:9). He is to be a principle of unity for the divided and bring to unity those who have strayed (1 John 2:19). He is to be ready to lay down his life for them, as indeed he eventually does.

Easter 4 C

Acts 13:14, 43–52
Psalm 99:1–3, 5
Revelation 7:9, 14–17
John 10:27–30

The Good Shepherd

The missionary in **Acts** who proved an outstanding witness of the Risen Lord 'to the ends of the earth' (1:8; Isaiah 49:6), was Paul. His adventure in Pisidian Antioch on his first 'missionary journey' resembles that of Jesus in Nazareth (Luke 4:16–30). The initial enthusiasm of Paul's own people turns to hostility, but Gentiles welcome his message, just as the people in Capernaum had accepted Jesus (Luke 4:32). Following Jesus' instruction when he sent out his disciples on mission, Paul and companions shake the dust off their feet (Luke 9:5). Their feelings of joy and experience of the Holy Spirit guarantee that their action is correct. The gospel is to be preached first to the Jew and then to the Gentile (Romans 1:16).

Our **Psalm** concludes a series that celebrates the kingship of God. He is a king who has won a people for himself (Exodus 19:6), which calls itself God's own flock. As its shepherd, God exercises the qualities he revealed at Sinai (Exodus 34:6; Isaiah 40:11).

Last week we heard in **Revelation** of the worship that marks the life of heaven. Now we find ourselves in the interlude between the opening of the sixth and seventh seals by the Lamb. At the start of this section we were informed that there were 144,000 saved in heaven (7:4). To reassure us that this number is symbolic rather than literal, we learn that this represents a vast number, impossible to count. God does not abandon his own. The blood of Christ won them salvation (John 19:34; 1 John 5:6). They are safe from physical danger and psychological distress. They live in God's own tent (Psalm 15:1; Revelation 21:3) under the protection of Christ, the good shepherd (Isaiah 40:11; John 10:14).

Each year on this Sunday, we read from the 'Shepherd' chapter of **John**. The texts we read in previous years were set at the time of the Feast of Tabernacles when Jesus proclaimed himself the 'light of the world' (8:12) and illustrated this by his cure of the man born blind (9:1–41). Today the background is the Feast of Dedication, which commemorated the people's liberation from the oppression of the pagan king Antiochus Epiphanes. Jesus continues to speak of himself in terms recalling the great liberator of Israel, King David, who was called from being a shepherd of sheep to become shepherd of his people (2 Samuel 5:2). He challenges his audience to make up their minds about his identity and significance.

Jesus appeals to two truths. The first concerns those who accept his message and person, such as the man born blind. Those who hear this gospel will readily identify with such people. They are the sheep for whom Jesus laid down his life (10:11). They are the recipients of eternal life; they can possess the abundance of life that Jesus had from the Father (10:10). The second concerns the Father, whose name Jesus has come to make known to the world (17:6). The thief has to steal the sheep that belong to Jesus not just from the hand of Jesus but from the hand of the Father too. (The word 'hand' is omitted in our translation.)

Our reading concludes with one of the great christological texts of this Gospel, 'the Father and I are one'. This is to repeat what was said at the opening of the Gospel, 'the Word was God' (1:1), and anticipates the confession of Thomas at its conclusion, when he acknowledges Jesus as 'My Lord and my God' (20:28). If, later in the Gospel, Jesus tells his disciples that the Father is greater than he is (14:28), this says no more than that during his earthly life Jesus experienced limitations which would no longer affect him when he was restored to the glory that he shared with the Father 'before the foundation of the world' (17:24).

Easter 5 C

Acts 14:21–27
Psalm 144:8–13
Revelation 21:1–5
John 13:31–35

Farewell Discourse

In **Acts** the faith, patience, endurance, love, persecution and sufferings that characterized Paul's first 'missionary journey' (2 Timothy 3:10–11) are summed up as the 'many hardships' we have to endure 'before we enter the kingdom of God'. Thus Paul relives the passion of Jesus, who has to 'suffer and so enter into his glory' (Luke 24:26), and does what he can 'to make up all that has still to be undergone by Christ' (Colossians 1:24). The Churches that he has evangelized pray and fast so that they may appoint elders, just as the Church of Antioch had set apart Paul and Barnabas for the work of God (13:3), confident that God will use them as he has worked through Paul.

The **Psalm**, recited three times daily in Jewish prayer, reflects the importance of thanksgiving and praise in worship. God's 'mighty deeds' for his people now include his achievements in bringing the gospel to Gentiles through Paul and Barnabas.

Revelation ends with a vision of the heavenly Jerusalem coming to earth. Such hopes express confidence that God will not abandon his faithful. The language echoes that of the final verses of Isaiah (65:17; 66:22). God announces a new creation. Traditionally expected at the end of time, this has already happened through the death and resurrection of Christ (2 Corinthians 5:17). As second Adam, he has repaired the damage done by the first (Romans 5:19). He continues to challenge his Church to respond to God's initiatives by his cry, 'Now I am making the whole of creation new'. Paul, too, refers to a 'new creature' (Galatians 6:15). The 'new creation' in the final pages of the Bible contrasts with the first creation at its opening (Genesis 1:1–2:3).

The key to understanding the passion in **John** is the farewell discourse that precedes his passion account (John 13–17). Today, we hear its opening. Jesus has washed the feet of his disciples, and Judas has gone out into the night (13:30). Now Jesus is alone with those whom he will call his friends because he has revealed to them all that he has heard from his Father (15:15). He speaks to them as Jacob spoke to his sons, preparing them for the future (Genesis 49).

This beginning is dominated by two words. The first is *glory*. In the Old Testament, human beings could not see God, but they could glimpse his glory. The people saw it in the desert (Numbers 16:19); Ezekiel saw it in his visions (Ezekiel 10:4). The Johannine community see it in Christ (1:14). Paradoxically, its clearest manifestation for John occurred in the passion; this was the time when the prayer of Jesus, 'glorify your Son', was answered (17:1). The reader is to understand the passion as the climax of the revelation of God's glory in Christ (2:11).

The second word is *love*. If the first half of the Gospel is about the life brought by the good shepherd so that we may have it more abundantly (10:10), the second half is about the love of God (3:16). He loved his own to the end (13:1) and this end was accomplished with his death on the cross (19:30). A commandment, the only such in John, goes with this love. The disciples are not commanded to love Jesus, but to love one another (15:17). Jesus began the passion by washing their feet (13:5) to symbolize his coming death on their behalf. They were to wash each other's feet (13:14) as a symbol of their mutual love, a love whose only limit is death. There can be no greater love than to lay down one's life for one's friends (15:13). This commandment is the subject of a beatitude: 'Now that you know this, happiness will be yours if you behave accordingly' (13:17). And Jesus is not only addressing his disciples; he addresses all who are 'children of God' because they believe in his name (1:12).

Easter 6 C

Acts 15:1–2, 22–29
Psalm 66:2–3, 5–6, 8
Revelation 21:10–14, 22–23
John 14:23–29

Orphans No Longer

The first Christians had their moments of tension. The events that conclude Paul's first journey in **Acts** are an example. Christians of Jewish background know that it is through full observance of the Law given to Moses on Sinai that God's people have survived loss of land, city and Temple. Paul has admitted Gentiles from Antioch, Derbe and Lystra without insisting on full observance of this Law. James, the leader of the Jerusalem Church, urges a compromise: Gentiles are to meet the traditional demands made on strangers living in Jewish communities (Leviticus 17:8–16). This meeting in Jerusalem is often known as the first Church Council. Luke would see the procedure adopted as a model for solving other problems in Christian life and mission.

Our **Psalm** is either a thanksgiving or a prayer for a successful harvest. God's care for Israel is seen as part of his care for all peoples. Such concern brought about Paul's missionary successes and was the motive for James's readiness to compromise in the demands he and the 'Jerusalem Council' made on foreigners.

Revelation, like other apocalyptic literature, concludes with a vision of God's final triumph. This is described in traditional terms supplemented by the truths of the gospel. The vision of the restored Jerusalem enjoyed by Ezekiel (48:31–35) now includes the names of the twelve apostles. Unlike the earthly Jerusalem, it contains no Temple, since Christ is its Temple (John 2:21) and the glory of God is not confined to the Holy of Holies in the interior of the Temple (Ezekiel 10:18), but illuminates the whole city.

The difference between Jesus and other historical figures for the Christian believer is the confidence that Jesus still lives and dwells within the individual and the community. Jesus explains various ways in which this is true in the Last Supper discourse reported by **John**. Two disciples asked Jesus when they first met him, 'Where do you live?', and he replied, 'Come and see' (1:38–39). Jesus now gives a more complete answer. Not only he, but also the Father, have a dwelling, and this is within the person who loves him and keeps his word. So we learn that it is not only the mystic who enjoys divine indwelling, but this is a privilege available to all faithful Christians.

Earlier in the Gospel, when Jesus cleansed the Temple, he spoke of the 'sanctuary that was his body' (2:21). Later, after his resurrection, the disciples remembered this (2:22). Similarly, after his glorification, when his disciples recalled his entry into Jerusalem mounted on a donkey (12:16), they realised that in it Jesus had fulfilled words spoken long before in prophecy by Zechariah (9:9). They could remember and understand these things through the gift of the paraclete. This is another way in which Jesus continued his spiritual presence with his disciples when the days of his physical presence with them were ended.

Another gift that Jesus promised his disciples at the supper was his peace. Twice when he appeared to them as their Risen Lord after the resurrection his first words were his greeting of peace (20:19, 21). This peace is not the ordinary sort of peace that the world gives, but the peace that Jesus himself enjoys in his union with his Father. It is not the result of negotiation or contract, as in human relationships; it is the peace that comes across in the words of Jesus in this discourse, showing his acceptance of the death that loomed before him (17:1). Paul speaks of peace as a fruit of the Holy Spirit, together with love and joy (Galatians 5:22).

The Ascension C

Acts 1:1–11
Psalm 46:2–3, 6–7, 8–9
Hebrews 9:24–28; 10:19–23
Luke 24:46–53

Raised to Heaven

The opening of **Acts** solemnly describes the start of the third stage of world history for Luke. The time of Israel and the time of the earthly Jesus are past, and the time of the Church begins. Moses was prepared for his mission by a forty-day stay on the mountain (Exodus 24:18). Elijah (1 Kings 19:8) and Jesus spent forty days in the desert (Matthew 4:2). At the end of a similar period, the disciples were promised the same Holy Spirit that had anointed Jesus as he began his mission (Luke 3:22) and they were appointed his witnesses to the ends of the earth. This mission was symbolically completed by the arrival of Paul in Rome but meanwhile the disciples are to cease gazing upward into heaven and devote themselves to the continuation of Jesus' ministry in this world.

The **Psalm** was probably first sung after some great military victory. The Ark of the Covenant was solemnly carried through Jerusalem to the Temple, where God was greeted as the Lord Most High (Genesis 14:18) and as Great King. On Ascension Day we apply it to Christ, now exalted in heaven as the Lord of all creation.

The author of **Hebrews** pictures the arrival of the exalted Christ in heaven. He imagines heaven as the true Temple and Christ as its High Priest. Christ is no ordinary priest, because the sacrifice he offered was himself and need never be repeated. Because we have such a priest, we will not be excluded from this heavenly sanctuary by some temple veil (Mark 15:38), but can be confident that the faith that was sealed by baptism will be crowned by our own entry into heaven.

The final verses of **Luke**'s Gospel explain what it means to be a witness of the Risen Lord (Acts 1:8). We learn the content of the message to be preached: that Christ suffered and rose from the dead, and that this was according to the scriptures (1 Corinthians 15:3). We will hear Peter (Acts 2:14–36), Paul (Acts 13:16–41) and others (Acts 8:35) proclaiming this in the Acts. The response to this message should be repentance leading to the forgiveness of sins. Peter demanded this of the crowds in Jerusalem for pentecost when they said to him, 'What are we to do?' (Acts 2:37).

The message is for all nations. Simeon had prophesied how the child Jesus would be a light to the Gentiles (2:32); the Church is to continue his mission of turning the Gentiles from darkness to light (Acts 22:18). The journeys of Paul in Acts, which ended in Rome, the 'ends of the earth' (Acts 13:47), show us how this happened in practice. The mission owed its effectiveness to the Holy Spirit. The same Spirit which had anointed Jesus at his baptism (3:22), would anoint the Church at pentecost (Acts 2:4) and take initiatives in directing its mission (Acts 13:2; 14:6–10).

The Gospel closes with a blessing. It began with crowds waiting outside the Temple for Zechariah to bless them. He was struck dumb, and their wait was in vain (1:21). The Risen Lord now gives this much-delayed blessing. The disciples find themselves full of joy despite his physical absence—the joy that arises from cooperating with the divine plan (Acts 13:52). They praise God, like so many in Luke's Gospel who receive God's favour (1:46; 17:15); they imitate the angels who sang at Jesus' birth (2:13). The Gospel ends in the Temple, where it began (1:8), however it is not Zechariah but the apostles who will proclaim God's salvation and sing his Benedictus (1:67). The Christian community in Jerusalem were the first of many who would treasure their teaching (Acts 2:42). With such great power the apostles gave their testimony to the resurrection (Acts 4:33).

Easter 7 C

Acts 7:55–60
Psalm 96:1–2, 6–7, 9
Revelation 22:12–14, 16–17, 20
John 17:20–26

Prayer for Unity

The ultimate expression of Christian witness is martyrdom. In **Acts**, Stephen, one of the seven on whom the apostles laid hands (6:6), a person of eloquence and learning (7:1–53), is the first to give his life for Christ. As he dies, 'full of the Holy Spirit' (Luke 12:12), he has a vision of Jesus as the ascended Son of Man standing at the right hand of God and interceding for him (Luke 9:23–26). Stephen dies as Jesus himself had died, with words of forgiveness for his enemies (Luke 23:34) and in union with his Lord (Luke 23:46; Psalms 31:5), a model Christian. He is a disciple who dies as his master died, and leaves an example of a Christian death.

In the **Psalm**, God is proclaimed King and worshipped by the whole of creation. Not just Stephen, but all peoples will see his glory. He is the God whose judgment will vindicate his faithful, in contrast to the unjust court that condemned Stephen.

Jesus himself is the main speaker in the final chapter of **Revelation**—and indeed of the whole Bible. He claims names for himself familiar from the opening of the book; he is the Alpha and the Omega (1:8), the First and the Last (1:17), the Root of David (5:5), the bright morning star (2:28). He offers the right to the tree of life, which puts us in mind of that other tree of life which had brought disaster to the first humans (Genesis 2:9). His final promise is that he will come soon, so that all may drink of the water of life promised to the Samaritan woman (John 4:11). John has witnessed to all these truths in his book. The final words of this very special book, and of the Bible, are words from liturgy and worship, 'Come Lord Jesus'.

The Last Supper discourse of **John** has by now become the 'prayer of the hour' (17:1), a priestly prayer for the sanctification of Jesus' disciples (17:17). In this final section, Jesus prays for those who will believe because of the disciples sent out after the resurrection (20:21). We remember how Simon came to Jesus because of the word of Andrew (1:42) and how Nathanael had come because of the word of Philip (1:45). His prayer for them is that they should be one. Their unity is to mirror that of Father and Son, a unity that respects their individuality but unifies their salvific plan. During his ministry, the words of Jesus provoked division in his hearers (10:19); sadly after his departure some left the community (1 John 2:19). Such disunity is not the wish of the Father or the Son. They want the unity of the Church to remain unbroken, like the seamless robe that Christ left behind (19:24) by the cross, like the unbroken net that contained the 153 fish after the resurrection (21:11).

We note two other significant words in this final paragraph of the prayer. The first is *love*. This word is rare in the first part of the Gospel: 'God loved the world so much that he gave his only Son' (3:16). But it is frequent in the second half from the beginning of the passion story, 'He had always loved those who were his in the world' (13:1). Jesus' love for his own reflects the mutual love of Father and Son. Believers are to love Jesus (14:28) and to love one another (13:34). Someone who does not love his brother, whom he can see, cannot love the God whom he cannot see (1 John 4:20).

The other word that is repeated is to *know*. Earlier in the prayer, eternal life has been defined as 'to know you, the only true God, and Jesus Christ whom you have sent' (17:3). The whole life of Jesus has been a life of making the Father known (1:18). We know the Father best when we realise with 1 John that 'God is love' (1 John 4:8, 16). The discourse is now complete. And the evangelist now tells how, in the passion, the prayer was answered.

Pentecost C

Acts 2:1–11
Psalm 103:1, 24, 29–31, 34
Romans 8:8–17
John 14:15–16, 23–26

The Holy Spirit

Pentecost, for the Christian, celebrates the gift of the Holy Spirit. In **Acts**, this Holy Spirit is the power responsible for the spread of the gospel to the 'ends of the earth' (1:8). The Spirit chooses (13:2) and inspires its agents (6:5), directs their progress (16:6), gives solutions to their problems (15:28). As a leading actor in the drama that is the Acts of the Apostles, its arrival is marked by wind and fire. Its first achievement is to fill timid disciples with courage; this Holy Spirit is the promise of the Father (Luke 24:37, 49). Their success in preaching to representatives of so many nations gathered in Jerusalem prepares the reader for the Church's universal mission.

In the **Psalm**, which offers us a meditation on the goodness of God who created the world and keeps it in good order, we celebrate the role of the Holy Spirit in creation (Genesis 1:2) and in its renewal. We remember Ezekiel's vision of the bones that came to life again as a result of the action of God's Spirit (Ezekiel 37:10).

According to Paul in **Romans**, before Christ, humanity suffered under the regime of Sin, Death and Law. The Law could indeed tell us what was wrong, but had no power of itself to help us to overcome evil (8:2). Thanks to Christ, we now live under a new regime dominated by the Holy Spirit. Thanks to this Spirit, we are able to resist sin and realise our dignity as children of God. Like Jesus himself, we can call God, 'Father' (Mark 14:36). We have Christ for our brother and are fellow heirs with him. This Christ promises his followers that his heavenly Father will give the Holy Spirit to those who ask him (Luke 11:13).

In **John**, the Holy Spirit first appears in the form of a dove to John the Baptist; the Spirit came down on Jesus and rested on him (1:32). Jesus spoke about this Spirit to Nicodemus, who came to him by night: a person had to be reborn by water and the Spirit in order to enter the Kingdom of God (3:5). To the Samaritan woman at the well, Jesus spoke about true worship as 'worship ... in spirit and truth' (4:23), that is, a worship inspired by the Holy Spirit and in accord with the revelation that Jesus brought.

But the Spirit could not be given until Jesus had 'been glorified' (7:39). This glorification took place in the events of Easter (17:1), and it is no accident that when John describes the death of Jesus, he tells us that Jesus 'gave up his Spirit' (19:30). The water that came from his side, pierced by the soldier's spear, symbolized this Spirit (19:34). Because of his death on the cross, it was possible for him formally to breathe the Holy Spirit over the apostles on Easter Day as he sent them out and commissioned them for their work in the world (20:22).

As he prepares them at the Last Supper for his passion and for their own future, Jesus instructs his disciples about the Holy Spirit. Today, we hear two of these statements. The Spirit will be with those who love Jesus and who observe his commandments—which, in John, are summed up in his command that they should love one another (13:34)—and those who love Jesus should keep his word, which means believing in him (5:38). This Spirit will be a gift of the Father, and as paraclete—which is a legal term—will be their defender and their comforter as they live without the physical presence of Jesus. It will be their teacher and help them to remember and understand all that Jesus has taught them (2:22). It will be for them all that Jesus had been for them while he was still with them physically (1 John 2:1). So John combines the understanding we find in Acts, of the Spirit as an external force, with that of Paul, who sees the same Spirit as a person who dwells within the believer.

Trinity C

Proverbs 8:22–31
Psalm 8:4–9
Romans 5:1–5
John 16:12–15

The Three Persons

According to **Proverbs**, God was not alone when he created the world. He was accompanied by the figure of Wisdom. Wisdom is the master craftsman who helped to design the world; Wisdom is like a small child who plays in God's presence to delight him and the people whom he is to bring to life. This figure of Wisdom is described elsewhere in more austere language as the Spirit that God breathed over the world at its creation (Genesis 1:2; Psalm 104:30). Wisdom reappears at the beginning of John's Gospel as the Word who was to become flesh in Christ (John 1:1, 14).

The **Psalm**, inspired by the opening of Genesis, takes up the theme of creation. Awesome and inspiring as the created universe is, God in his goodness and mercy has allowed humanity to feel at home in it and to take charge.

There are two trinities in our passage from **Romans**. The first consists of the persons whom later doctrine would call the persons of the Holy Trinity. There is God the Father, to whom our relationship is described as one of peace. Through Christ we are reconciled to him. There is Jesus, who is called Lord and Christ. Lord is the name given to God in the Old Testament; Christ is the word for the promised anointed one of God (2 Samuel 7:16). There is also the Spirit, who is said to pour the love of God into our hearts. Each of these persons has a role and function in our relationship with God. The second trinity mentioned is made up of what will later be called the cardinal virtues of faith, hope and love. We grow in each of these through the work of the three persons of the Holy Trinity.

All three members of the Trinity are mentioned in our reading from **John**. The Father is mentioned explicitly as the one who shares all that he has with the Son. Implicitly he is the one from whom the Spirit has learnt the complete truth. The Son is the one who is speaking. He is addressing his disciples at the Last Supper, but he admits that at this time it is impossible for him to say everything that he has to teach them. Here the one whom he calls the Spirit of truth steps in. This is the one we know as the third person of the Trinity, often called the paraclete in the Last Supper discourse.

In these final words of Jesus about the paraclete, we can distinguish several roles that belong to the Spirit. Previously in this discourse Jesus has described himself as 'the Way' (14:6). Now we learn that the Spirit is the one who is to be a guide on the way. Moses had prepared his people for entry into the promised land, but Joshua was the one who led them into it as their guide (Deuteronomy 34:9). This Spirit, like Jesus, does not teach truth on its own initiative but only what it has learnt from the Father. And just as Jesus has prepared his disciples for the future, so will the Spirit. It is to be the continuing presence of Jesus in the world when he is no longer with them physically.

During his lifetime, particularly in the events close to his death (17:1), it was the Father who would glorify Jesus. From now on, the Spirit will be the agent of this glorification, because it will pass on what belongs to Jesus. Thanks to this gospel passage, and the others in this discourse when Jesus speaks about the paraclete, the Holy Spirit (14:15–17, 26; 15:26–27; 16:7–11), we deepen our knowledge of the God whom we confess, not only as one in contrast to the multiplicity of gods that were acknowledged when the Gospels were first written, but also as a trinity of persons who continue to be alive and active in the world where we live.

Body and Blood of Christ C

Genesis 14:18–20
Psalm 109:1–4
1 Corinthians 11:23–26
Luke 9:11–17

Feeding the Crowds

Melchizedek, the king of Jerusalem who blesses Abraham, is one of the more mysterious figures in **Genesis**. He appears again in our psalm as the ideal priest-king (Psalm 110:4). The letter to the Hebrews sees him as a precursor of Christ (Hebrews 5:6). The bread and the wine that he brings to Abraham will be used in the sacrifice that goes with the blessing he offers. Christians later saw in this sacrifice a foreshadowing of the Eucharist.

The **Psalm** also mentions Melchizedek. It belongs to the group used originally in the coronation ritual of a new king. Although a king had priestly duties, he did not belong to the priestly tribe of Levi. Neither did Jesus, and so his priesthood was identified in Hebrews with that of Melchizedek (Hebrews 7).

Our passage from **1 Corinthians** is the earliest account we have of the institution of the Eucharist. Jesus' words over the bread inform us that his body is 'for you'. This language is both personal and sacrificial. Elsewhere Paul remarks how Christ 'loved me and ... sacrificed himself for my sake' (Galatians 2:20). He made the old sacrifices obsolete. The expression 'new covenant' is introduced in his words over the cup. Matthew and Mark refer to 'the covenant' (Matthew 26:28; Mark 14:24); Luke and Paul to the 'new covenant' (Luke 22:20). The background to the first is the action of Moses, sprinkling the blood of sacrificed animals over the people (Exodus 24:8). For the second, we have the prophecy of a new covenant in Jeremiah (31:31). The Eucharist transforms our relationship with God. Through it, in the words of Jeremiah, God plants his Law, writing it deep in our hearts (Jeremiah 31:33).

If Genesis and 1 Corinthians remind us that the Eucharist is a sacrifice, **Luke**'s account of the feeding of the crowds assures us that it is also a meal. His Gospel records many meals of Jesus. At these meals, Jesus enjoyed the company not only of his own but of those whom conventional society rejected (15:2). The climax of these meals was his Last Supper when, going among his disciples as 'one who serves' (22:27), he gave them his own body and blood. The final scene in Luke shows him eating fish with his disciples after his resurrection from the dead (24:42).

The most massive meal that Jesus provided in his lifetime was for five thousand in Galilee. We are given few details. The tradition wants us to grasp how his disciples think only of human resources for dealing with the situation. Jesus transforms what he finds and produces more than sufficient food from a few loaves and fishes. The people are not fed singly, but in groups of fifty, reminding us that we live in a community. The language used to describe the miracle stresses neither the extravagant nor the marvellous, but anticipates the words of Jesus in instituting the Eucharist at the Last Supper (22:17-20). The feeding is significant because it anticipates the Eucharist in the Church. This memory was so important for the early Church that we have five other gospel accounts (Matthew 14:13–21; 15:32–39; Mark 6:30–44; 14:13–21; John 6:1–13).

Jesus breaks the bread before he gives it to the people. He will break bread again on the Emmaus road. This was the moment when the two dispirited disciples recognised him (24:35). The first Jerusalem Christians broke bread together in their life of prayer and sharing (Acts 2:42). The Christian community at Troas broke bread with Paul (Acts 20:7), and Paul did the same when shipwrecked (Acts 27:35). Thus, the feeding of the five thousand continues in the Church which knows that it lives on resources that are more than human. The Lord Jesus continues to provide food for our pilgrim journey.

Year C
The Year of Luke

THE 34 SUNDAYS OF THE YEAR*

These Sundays are divided into two blocks, separated by the three months of the seasons of Lent and Easter. Some Sundays which occur between the two blocks are always omitted. The Feast of the Baptism of the Lord is reckoned as the first Sunday of the Year.

The ***First Readings****, from the Old Testament, are intended to throw light on the gospel reading of the day. Never during this period is there any continuous reading from the Old Testament. To concentrate on the Old Testament passage without reference to the Gospel therefore seems inappropriate.*

The ***Responsorial Psalms*** *are designed to help the understanding of the First Reading, to deepen some significant theme and to clarify its message. It also prepares for the Gospel since the First Reading is related to the Gospel.*

The ***Second Readings*** *are taken from a New Testament letter. The reading is semi-continuous, which gives a preacher the opportunity to take the congregation through the particular letter. Only coincidentally does it have any relationship to the First Reading or the Gospel. No letter is proclaimed in its entirety and sometimes the unit given is incomplete.*

- *The First Letter of Paul to the Corinthians (Part Three)*
- *The Letter of Paul to the Galatians*
- *The Letter of Paul to the Colossians*
- *The Letter to the Hebrews (Part Two)*
- *The Letter of Paul to Philemon*
- *The First Letter of Paul to Timothy*
- *The Second Letter of Paul to Timothy*
- *The Second Letter of Paul to the Thessalonians*

The ***Gospel Reading*** *is taken from Luke. This Gospel is read throughout the year, except for the Easter season when John is usually read. We may therefore speak of Luke as the evangelist of the year.*

* See 'General Introduction', *Roman Missal*, nn. 105–107.

Sunday 2 C

Isaiah 62:1–5
Psalm 95:1–3, 7–10
1 Corinthians 12:4–11
John 2:1–11

Marriage at Cana

In the final part of **Isaiah**, we are in a different world from that described in the earlier chapters. There we met laments for the sinfulness and infidelity of the people (1:16). Later chapters offer them hope and comfort in the prospect that soon they will return from exile (40:1). Today the prophet uses poetic language to describe such a future. They will enjoy vindication and experience reconciliation. They will be a crown and a diadem for God to display. Finally, God will rejoice in them as a bridegroom in his bride.

The **Psalm** consists of phrases from many biblical sources, all used today to praise God. He is greeted as a king who has real care for his people. This Psalm may have been used at the feast of Tabernacles, when the thousands of lights in Jerusalem made night like day, as Isaiah visualised.

Paul's converts in Corinth prided themselves on the gifts of the Spirit. They estimated the quality of their Christianity by the flamboyance of those gifts. We continue to hear Paul in **1 Corinthians** teaching about the gifts of the Holy Spirit. He congratulates his troublesome converts on their spiritual gifts, but he also tries to bring order to their enthusiasm. He insists that, since these gifts came from a common origin, the Spirit of God, they must be for a common purpose and not divide the community. They witness to the same God, described as Spirit, Lord and God. The most important gift is that of preaching wisdom, which means for Paul the word of the cross (1 Corinthians 1:20), and the least is that of speaking in tongues. It is important to get the order of these gifts right.

The Gospel of **John** is rarely heard on Sundays outside Lent and Easter, but today, the beginning of 'ordinary time', it is fitting to recall the wedding feast at Cana, the beginning of Jesus' signs. We know little about Jesus and his family, apart from Luke's account of the twelve-year-old Jesus in the Temple (Luke 2:41–52).

The situation is a wedding. Marriage in the Old Testament is an image of the relationship between God and his people. When God gave his people the Law at Mount Sinai, it was as if he gave himself to them in marriage (Jeremiah 2:2). When Israel proved an unfaithful wife, God promised to take her back to the desert where they would renew their marriage vows (Hosea 2:19). This would be a new covenant replacing the first, binding the partners to each other by stronger bonds than ever (Jeremiah 31:32). In the New Testament, we learn from Paul about the marriage of Christ to his Church (2 Corinthians 11:2). In the Gospels, Jesus refers to himself as the bridegroom. His disciples will not fast as long as he, the bridegroom, is with them, but the time will come when he will be taken away from them through death (Mark 2:20).

At Cana, Jesus is not identified with the bridegroom. The stress is on the quality and abundance of the wine that the head steward tastes. He expects to drink from the water stored in the jars for Jewish rites of purification. Water is wholesome and tastes good; it is useful for cleanliness and refreshment. So too were the rites and customs of the old religion. But Jesus has brought something new, symbolized by the wine that the steward drinks. Its characteristics reflect wine spoken of by the prophets. Amos foretold a time when the mountains would flow with streams of wine, not water (Amos 9:13). For those with faith, such as the mother of Jesus in this Gospel, this time has now arrived through the presence and ministry of God's Son. The real bridegroom is now present, ready to reclaim an unfaithful people for God.

Sunday 3 C

Nehemiah 8:2–6, 8–10
Psalm 18:8–10, 15
1 Corinthians 12:12–30
Luke 1:1–4; 4:14–21

Good News for the Poor

Among the factors that enabled Israel to survive as a people after the return from exile in Babylon was a fierce attachment to the Mosaic Law. The scribe Ezra did much to encourage this. We read from **Nehemiah** today how he proclaims this Law to the people in Jerusalem. Whether he reads out from books of the Pentateuch, or just Deuteronomy, is disputed. His hearers certainly find it difficult and demanding, but their leaders urge them to respond with joy rather than sadness to the words they hear.

An attitude to God's Law that Ezra would have appreciated is expressed in the **Psalm**, which has earlier praised God for the wonder of his creation. Here it gives him equal praise for having prepared such a Law for his people as for the gift of life.

It is clear from the very start of **1 Corinthians** that divisions threaten the unity of the community (1:11). Paul continues his discussion of the gifts of the Spirit, insisting that all, slave or free, Jew or Greek, constitute one body in Christ, thanks to the Spirit. But such unity does not exclude diversity and, to show how this is so, Paul uses an image found elsewhere in the ancient world as well as in Shakespeare's play *Coriolanus*: the parts of the human body. Such body language can be used to justify inequality, but this is not the case here. All the parts of the body he mentions have a vital role. We can enjoy his description and admire Paul's dramatic skill in having the foot converse with the ear, especially since in Greek the words are so similar: the *pous* speaks to the *ous*. The parables of Paul reflect a different world from those of Jesus.

Today, we read two beginnings from **Luke**. The first is the preface to his Gospel which he echoes at the start of the book of Acts (1:1). Luke is the only evangelist to include such an introduction to his work. We note three points. He depends on sources, one of which was Mark's Gospel, so we can compare the differing approaches of these evangelists. Secondly, he is concerned about order, which encourages us to notice where he places significant events in his narrative. Thirdly, he writes to provide assurance to Theophilus, as a foundation on which to build using the instructions he has received.

The second beginning is the start of the public teaching of Jesus, and here we can see how Luke applies the principles expressed in his preface. Mark has an account of Jesus' preaching in Nazareth (6:1–6). Luke expands it, and tells us what Jesus actually says. The words of Jesus are the first public words in this Gospel. Instead of speaking of the Kingdom of God, as in Mark (1:15), Jesus quotes the prophet Isaiah (61:1–2). By putting this incident at the start of his story of Jesus, Luke has imposed his own order. It is as if he is saying to his reader, *If you want to understand the ministry of Jesus, this is where you must begin.*

The programme he announces, of preaching the 'good news to the poor', prepares us for the mission of Jesus and of his witnesses in Acts. Jesus' programme goes beyond that of the Baptist (3:10–14). He himself gives an example to those who follow him of inviting to his banquet 'the poor, the crippled, the blind and the lame' (14:21). In the Beatitudes, he will call the poor blessed (6:20). Careful readers of the words quoted from Isaiah will notice that Jesus has missed out all reference to a 'day of vengeance for our God' (Isaiah 61:2) and inserted from elsewhere in Isaiah a verse about liberty for the oppressed (Isaiah 58:6). In this way, Luke provides his readers with assurance that the ministry of Jesus is a continuation and consolidation of the work of God's prophets.

Sunday 4 C

Jeremiah 1:4–5, 17–19
Psalm 70:1–6, 15, 17
1 Corinthians 12:31 – 13:13
Luke 4:21–30

Jesus the Prophet

Part of the traditional pattern of the call of a prophet was reassurance by God (Exodus 3:11). **Jeremiah**, like Isaiah's Servant and like Paul, knows that his call goes back to the time he was in the womb of his mother (Isaiah 49:1; Galatians 1:15). Despite his youth (1:6), he need not hesitate to speak God's word before the most powerful in the land. Though he will exercise the strength of iron and bronze, he is not guaranteed success. He is still God's envoy even if his word is ignored (26:12). God promises to be with him.

The **Psalm** is a lament of one who has spent a lifetime in God's service, even, like Jeremiah, from his mother's womb. God's constant fidelity enables the speaker to endure times of persecution and rejection.

The hymn to love in **1 Corinthians** is probably the best known and quoted of all Paul's writings. He contrasts love with the other gifts of the Holy Spirit which were eagerly sought in Corinth, and of which we have heard in previous weeks. Without love, these are all useless for the community. He picks out two qualities that mark love: its patience and kindness. He lists eight vices that are incompatible with it. Finally, he emphasizes its permanence. It is part of the fullness of Christianity. It will always exist. God will never be without it. John identifies God with love (1 John 4:8, 16). The passage is a barometer to test out the quality of any Christian life. Christ himself is its best personification. The qualities of love are again listed in Paul's catalogue of the fruit of the Holy Spirit in Galatians; love heads the list and eight of its characteristics follow (5:22).

The atmosphere in the second part of Jesus' speech in the Nazareth synagogue in **Luke** is hostile. The astonishment of his hearers does not lead to praising God (2:20) and still less to commitment to Jesus (5:11). They express their curiosity about the one they call 'Joseph's son'. They are too familiar with him to listen to him (Mark 6:3). Jesus can only repeat the proverb that a prophet is not accepted in his own country.

Jesus has announced his programme with words from the prophet Isaiah (Luke 4:18; Isaiah 58:6; 61:1). He introduces it further by calling attention to two other prophets of Israel, Elijah and Elisha. They had brought salvation to a widow (1 Kings 17:9) and healing to a leper (2 Kings 5:1). In his ministry, Jesus will do the same (7:12; 5:12). Both were agents of God's mercy to foreigners. If the activity of Jesus in his ministry rarely extends to foreigners (17:18), the story of Acts is the history of how the Christian witness extended to the ends of the earth (Acts 1:8), to the joy of the Gentiles (Acts 13:48). The reader already knows this from the canticle of Simeon (2:32).

The reaction of Jesus' hearers is one of anger, followed by an attempt on his life. By driving him outside the city, they anticipate his passion, when he suffered outside the city gate (Hebrews 13:12). He escapes from their midst, just as later he will defeat his enemies by rising from the dead. From Nazareth, he moves to Capernaum where, in contrast, the crowds try to prevent him from leaving them (4:43). The same pattern of rejection by his own people and welcome by foreigners will be repeated in the ministry of Paul at Antioch (Acts 13:46). Luke has begun his account of the ministry of Jesus with a mini-Gospel, a dramatic scene that sums up his story of the whole. He makes Jesus a successor of the great prophets of the past, 'a great prophet by the things he said and did' (24:19), whom his people rejected through ignorance (Acts 3:17).

Sunday 5 C

Isaiah 6:1–8
Psalm 137:1–5, 7–8
1 Corinthians 15:1–11
Luke 5:1–11

The Call of Peter

If a prophet wanted a hearing, he had to prove that his vocation was authenticated by God. **Isaiah**'s account of his call follows this Old Testament pattern of vocation, experienced by Moses, Gideon and Jeremiah (Exodus 3:7–12; Judges 6:11–18; Jeremiah 1:4–7). Isaiah has a vision of himself present in the divine throne room. In such surroundings, Isaiah can think only of his sinfulness, of his unclean lips. But God reassures him. He not only can but will use Isaiah as his messenger, and he promises that he will himself be Isaiah's support on the mission on which he is to be sent.

The **Psalm**, too, finds its author in the heavenly court. It is a hymn of confidence and thanksgiving, a fitting prayer for one conscious of divine vocation like Isaiah and Jeremiah in the Old Testament and Peter and Paul in the New Testament.

The final problem with which Paul has to deal in **1 Corinthians** concerns the resurrection of Jesus. Some of his converts are denying it. Paul's reply gives us our earliest text about the resurrection, long predating the accounts we find in the Gospels. Paul writes in the mid-50s; he recalls his preaching of 49 and the instruction he himself received after his conversion in the mid-30s. The resurrection was a fundamental of Christianity from the beginning. Thanks to these words of Paul, we learn more than the Gospels tell us about the appearances of the Risen Christ. He regards his own conversion experience as such an appearance and treats this fact as putting him on a level with others to whom the Risen Lord appeared. He, too, was an apostle called by Christ (Galatians 1:2).

Luke helps his readers come to a more profound understanding of the mission and person of Jesus by substituting the dramatic scene of the preaching and the rejection of Jesus in Nazareth (4:16–30) for the summary of his preaching of the Kingdom that is found in Mark (1:14–15). He likewise expands the story of the call of Peter (Mark 1:16–20) to emphasize his importance and instruct readers in the nature and demands of their own Christian discipleship.

The scene is the public preaching of Jesus by the Sea of Galilee, such as Mark described in his parable chapter (Mark 4). He preaches the Word of God, the task that the Twelve saw as their vocation (Acts 6:2). The miracle of the great catch of fish puts us in mind of the similar event found in John, which took place after the resurrection (John 21:1–14). Peter's call to discipleship follows the same pattern as the prophetic call of Isaiah and of other personalities who played great roles in salvation history (Isaiah 6:1–8). Peter does not see God by the lakeside, but he glimpses his power and presence in the great catch of fish and, like Isaiah and Jeremiah (1:6), he is reminded of his own sin and inadequacy. We can imagine Peter reacting like this when he saw the Risen Lord; he could not forget his sin of having denied three times that he ever knew him when Jesus was on trial for his life (22:60; 24:34).

Again like Isaiah, he is reassured; his success in catching fish anticipates the future catch of 3,000 converts on Pentecost Day (Acts 2:41) and his career as a pillar of the Church of Jerusalem (Galatians 2:9). We hear of James and John, his partners, for the first time. They joined him in leaving everything to follow Jesus as Levi would (5:28). The Jesus of Luke makes radical demands (9:57–62), but inspires generous responses. The elders of Luke's own day (Acts 14:23; 20:17) would remember this call of Peter, and find in it courage and inspiration to follow their Christian vocation as leaders of God's people.

Sunday 6 C

Jeremiah 17:5–8
Psalm 1:1–4, 6
1 Corinthians 15:12, 16–20
Luke 6:17, 20–26

Blessings and Woes

Blessing and cursing are familiar biblical themes. After the first sin, God cursed the serpent and the soil (Genesis 3:14, 17), but he promised his blessing to Abraham and the nations (Genesis 12:1–3). He put before Israel the choice of blessing or curse, life or death (Deuteronomy 30:19). **Jeremiah**, like other wise men of his day, both in Egypt and Israel (Psalm 117:8–9), proclaims God's blessings for all who trust in him.

The **Psalm,** the first in the Psalter, belongs to the group of so-called Wisdom Psalms. Its author, like Jeremiah, finds inspiration in the scenery of the desert outside the city. The wise man who trusts in God and contemplates his Law is like a flourishing green tree by a riverside compared with a dried up desert shrub.

Resurrection continues to be the key word in our readings from 1 **Corinthians.** At this stage of his dispute with those who say there is no resurrection, Paul appeals to logic. In common with the authors of most other New Testament books, he argues for the truth of the resurrection of Christ. And just as in his letter to the Romans he names Christ Jesus, the Son of God, as the firstborn among many brothers (Romans 8:29), so here he describes Jesus as 'the first-fruits of all who have fallen asleep' (15:20). Without him, those who have died have perished; those still alive remain subject to the tyranny of sin (Romans 8:2) and, with their hope in resurrection dashed, are now the object of pity. Paul reminds Christians of every generation that they are children of the resurrection as well as of the cross. The gospel proclamation includes both (1 Corinthians 15:3–4).

The programme of the Kingdom that Jesus preached has been hinted at in the canticles of **Luke**'s infancy narrative (1:46–56, 68–79), and solemnly announced in Jesus' first words in Nazareth (4:16–30). In the Sermon on the Plain, read for three Sundays, Jesus proclaims the Kingdom to Jewish crowds from Jerusalem and Judaea, and to foreigners from Tyre and Sidon. His words are addressed to all who hear the gospel, of every age and nation. It is helpful to compare this sermon with Matthew's Sermon on the Mount (Matthew 5–7).

Like Moses on Mount Sinai (Exodus 24), Jesus has spoken with God in prayer on a mountain (6:12); he now he descends to proclaim God's ways to all who are ready to listen (Exodus 32). He begins to describe the Kingdom with the traditional language of blessing and curse. It belongs to the poor, to those who hunger and weep, to those who will suffer exclusion and insult because of the Son of Man (Jesus' usual title for himself). Often in the scriptures God is described as the one who has heard the misery of his people in Egypt (Exodus 3:7), as one who upholds the widow and the orphan (Psalm 146:9). Jesus will have reflected on all this in his prayer on the mountain beforehand. He will have seen his task as a mission to raise the poor out of their misery (1:52), and to proclaim a year of the Lord's favour (4:18).

Only Luke reports the four woes pronounced by Jesus. He threatens those who put their trust in riches, who are comfortable in abundance and satisfied to glory in their good name. Why these woes? The rest of this Gospel helps us understand. We will hear of the rich and avaricious fool who wanted to build himself bigger barns (12:16–21), of the cruel Dives, who ignored Lazarus at his gate (16:19). We will admire the almsgiving of Zacchaeus, who gave half his wealth to the poor (19:8) and, in Acts, the generous hospitality of the wealthy Lydia in Philippi (Acts 16:15). God's Kingdom transforms the values of this world into his own values.

Sunday 7 C

1 Samuel 26:2, 7–9, 12–13, 22–23
Psalm 102:1–4, 8, 10, 12–13
1 Corinthians 15:45–49
Luke 6:27–38

Love of Enemies

David was the greatest of the kings of Israel. A common title for Jesus in the New Testament is Son of David (Mark 10:48; Romans 1:3). In 1 **Samuel** we read how David, before he himself became king, passes up the opportunity of harming King Saul, who had so often harmed him. He might appear to give an example of the love of enemies that Christ preached in his Sermon on the Plain. But here, as elsewhere, the Old Testament falls short of the standards of the New. David only spares Saul because of his fear of God's anger if he were to maltreat the king whom God has anointed.

Our **Psalm**, in origin probably a thanksgiving for a cure from sickness, was later used as a hymn of gratitude for the deliverance of the nation from exile and from its sufferings. Its description of the kindness and mercy of God quotes Exodus (34:6–7); it prepares us for Jesus' description of God in the gospel reading.

Paul liked to compare Christ with Adam, the first man. Adam's disobedience allowed sin to come into the world. The obedience of Christ provided the remedy for sin (Romans 5:12–14). But because the creation of man is related twice in Genesis, In 1 **Corinthians** Paul argues from this to a distinction between our earthly and heavenly bodies. The first man was created in the image of God (Genesis 1:27); the second from the dust of the earth (Genesis 2:7). Now, in this time of the new creation, Christ's earthly body has, through his resurrection, become a heavenly body. Because he is the firstborn of many brothers (Romans 8:29), we too will have a heavenly body.

Twice we read in this second section of the Sermon on the Plain in **Luke** how Jesus instructed his disciples to love their enemies, and put before them various demanding examples of how they were to express such love. Rightly they could respond that such behaviour, like the Beatitudes that we heard last week, is impossible in the world where they, and we, live. Such a response is correct in so far as the Kingdom that Christ came to establish has not yet arrived in its fullness. Jesus is preaching what is sometimes called the ethics of the Kingdom. His audience is now not just the recently called disciples (6:12–16), but 'you who hear', which makes this gospel preaching a personal appeal to all who hear it.

Yet a beginning is possible because, according to the teaching of Jesus, the Kingdom has already begun; as he is later to announce, 'the kingdom of God is among you' (17:21). When we pray in the Lord's prayer, 'Your kingdom come' (11:2), we pray that this Kingdom will continue its growth rather than it should begin from scratch. We are not to forget the parables of the mustard seed and the leaven, which taught about the Kingdom. The smallest of seeds, said Jesus, produced the largest of trees (13:18–19).

Jesus encourages his disciples with further arguments. We know how we want others to treat us; let us treat them in the same way. Further, if we do not begin to live as Jesus teaches, then we are no better than the sinners around us. The choice that we have made to follow Christ, with Peter (5:11) and the Twelve (6:13), means nothing. Above all, we are to take courage from the example of God. As a God of mercy (Exodus 34:6–7), he is kind to the ungrateful and the wicked. True followers of Christ find themselves following not only the example of Jesus, but also the example of the God whom Jesus is revealing to them. The mercy that he shows is to be the pattern the disciple is to follow.

Sunday 8 C

Sirach 27:4–7
Psalm 91:2–3, 13–16
1 Corinthians 15:54–58
Luke 6:39–45

Concluding Parables

Two centuries before Christ, Ben Sira wrote **Sirach**, the longest of the Wisdom books of the Bible. It contains much sound moral instruction designed to ensure success in life for the young Israelite. As a good teacher, this author uses many homely images. They may well have been familiar to Jesus, who today echoes one of the wise sayings in our passage. Just as the fruit of a tree tells us the quality of that tree, so a person's words reveal the worth of the person who speaks them.

The **Psalm** begins with a glimpse of faithful worshippers in the Temple, as day and night they celebrate the love and truth of God (Exodus 34:6). It concludes with a temple priest blessing such people. He compares them to the strong majestic cedars of Lebanon, such as the trees that Hiram sent Solomon for the building of the Jerusalem Temple (1 Kings 5:22–23).

After the resurrection, according to Paul in **1 Corinthians**, our bodies will share the immortality and imperishability of the risen body of Christ. So he concludes this chapter on the resurrection with a hymn of victory, quoting words familiar from the prophets Isaiah (25:8) and Hosea (13:14). He repeats again what he taught in his letter to the Romans. Victory has been won by Christ because he has deposed the tyrants sin and death, whom Adam allowed into the world (Romans 5:12), and the Law too which, though it was 'sacred, just and good' (Romans 7:12) and told us what was right, had no power to bring the good about (Romans 3:20). Now, because we live in the Lord, in unity with the Christ who has set us free (Galatians 5:1), our work, like our faith, is not in vain (15:14).

The Sermon on the Plain in **Luke** finishes with a series of parables, vivid pictures put before the hearer and designed to provoke thought. The first concerns two blind men. We do not allow a blind man to guide another blind man, or else both may fall into a pit. This could be a general warning that teachers in the community must base their teaching on the truth that Luke was writing to Theophilus (1:4), lest they become wolves misleading the flock. Paul warned of such when he spoke to the elders of the Church of Ephesus in Miletus (Acts 20:29). More likely, the blind man is the sort of Christian who ignores the teaching of Jesus in this Sermon which calls for love of enemies and the sharing of possessions (6:27–38).

More tragic is the situation of those in the second parable who do not know their own blindness. Sensitive to specks in the eyes of others, they are ignorant of planks in their own. This could be a caution about criticizing others while failing to recognise one's own faults, but it is more likely to be a warning not to regard the teaching of the Sermon as applying only to other people—to some elite—for admiration rather than for action.

The third parable concerns trees and their fruits. The tree or vine is a common biblical image for the wise individual (Jeremiah 17:8; Psalm 1:3) or for the people as a whole, as in the preaching of Isaiah (Isaiah 5:3) and of the Baptist (3:9). In Jesus' parable of the fig tree in Luke (13:6) and in his cursing of the tree in Mark (11:14) the tree symbolizes unfruitful Israel. Here we must apply it to the Sermon on the Plain as a whole. The fruit that the Christian disciple is expected to bear is the teaching of the Sermon put into practice. This is what a good man produces from the treasure of his heart, the hundredfold that comes from faithful listening to the Word (8:15). The words that the believer speaks well up out of a heart that is full to the brim with the teaching of Christ.

Sunday 9 C

1 Kings 8:41–43
Psalm 116:1–2
Galatians 1:1–2, 6–10
Luke 7:1–10

The Centurion's Servant

King David had wanted to build a temple for God but, through his prophet Nathan, God had promised a 'house' for him instead, consisting of his descendants (2 Samuel 7:1–29). It was David's son Solomon who built a magnificent Temple. We hear today from **1 Kings** words from Solomon's prayer at its dedication. This is one of the great prayers of the Old Testament. It celebrates God's presence, which 'the heavens and their own heavens' cannot contain, within this Temple (8:27). Nor is it for one nation only; Solomon includes a petition for the foreigners who would come to pray in the Temple, so that all people would know the God of Israel.

The **Psalm** is the shortest of them all. It is a call to praise God because of his steadfast love and faithfulness, the traditional covenant virtues (Exodus 34:6). It calls not just on Israel but on all the nations. Paul uses this text to celebrate the breadth of God's goodness and mercy (Romans 15:11).

Galatians may surprise us because of the fierceness of its language, but it tells us much about Paul's own story, about theology and about Christian behaviour. Troublemakers are urging Paul's converts to reject the gospel Paul preached. They insist on the full observance of the Jewish Law. Belief in Christ alone, they say, is insufficient. Paul appeals to his own appointment as an apostle by Christ and the Father. He addresses the Galatians not with thanks, as expected, but with astonishment. And his twice-repeated verdict on his critics who preach a different gospel is that they risk exclusion from God by being put under a curse. He speaks as one who is the property of Christ, his slave.

When the child Jesus was brought into the Temple, Simeon had proclaimed to God that the child would be 'a light to enlighten the pagans and the glory of your people Israel' (2:32). When Jesus spoke in the Nazareth synagogue, he recalled how Naaman, a foreign leper, was cured by the prophet Elisha (4:27). Elisha never met Naaman; he was cured at a distance by obeying the instructions that Elisha gave him (2 Kings 5:1–14).

These verses prepare us for **Luke**'s account of how, after the Sermon on the Plain, which celebrated the mercy of God, Jesus gives an example of this mercy in action by curing the slave of a Gentile centurion. He is carrying out his mission of preaching the good news to the poor (4:18). Like Elisha, he never meets the person cured. In this Gospel, Jesus meets few Gentiles. The Gentile mission is described in the Acts of the Apostles, in which Peter baptized Cornelius, another centurion who, like the one in this gospel story, was a devout man and sympathetic to the Jewish nation (Acts 10:2). The first spoken words recorded by Luke after the death of Jesus were those of a centurion, who praised God and declared Christ innocent (23:47). Paul would see his mission as primarily dedicated to the Gentiles who, in turn, 'were very happy to hear this, and they thanked the Lord for his message' (Acts 13:48).

The words of the centurion about not being worthy for Jesus to enter under his roof have been incorporated into our Eucharistic liturgy. The words of Jesus about not having found such faith, even in Israel, encourage us to look outside our own narrow circle and recognise how the grace of God has no boundaries. After his encounter with Cornelius, Peter had this to say: 'God does not have favourites, but ... anybody of any nationality who fears God and does what is right is acceptable to him' (Acts 10:34–35). Solomon had prepared for this centuries before, in his prayer in the Temple (1 Kings 8:41–43).

Sunday 10 C

1 Kings 17:17–24
Psalm 29:2, 4–6, 11–13
Galatians 1:11–19
Luke 7:11–17

The Widow of Nain

In 1 **Kings**, we read of conflicts between the prophet Elijah and the forces of the Baalim, the false gods whose allies included King Ahab. Beliefs of the time identified death with such supernatural powers. Forced to flee from Ahab, Elijah is given hospitality by a widow. But suddenly her son dies. Elijah twice prays to God and, by raising the widow's son from death back to life, proves that the God of Israel is the true Lord both of death and life (2 Kings 4:18–37). Elijah then gives the child to his mother, words that are repeated exactly in our reading from Luke.

The **Psalm** is a prayer of thanksgiving after serious sickness, which would sound appropriate from the lips of the young men raised to life in 1 Kings and in Luke. Sheol was the place of the dead. This psalm would be used at the rededication of the Temple in 164 BC; it was as if the whole nation had recovered from illness.

Because both he and his mission are under attack in **Galatians**, Paul responds by giving rare information about himself (Philippians 3:5–16). He recalled how, because of his zeal for his ancestral religion, he had persecuted God's Church. He felt forced to do this because Christians were claiming that one who had been 'hanged on a tree' was the messiah (Galatians 3:13; Deuteronomy 21:23). But then God called him, as he had called Jeremiah (1:4–5) and Isaiah (49:1). We find more dramatic accounts of Paul's life as a persecutor in Acts (8:3; 22:4; 26:9–11). After his conversion, God gave him a mission to the Gentiles which he began immediately. He saw no need for approval from other apostles. He was convinced that God had called him directly.

In his initial speech in Nazareth, Jesus referred to the prophet Elijah and how he was sent to a widow in Zarephath whose son he raised from death (Luke 4:26). Now **Luke** gives us an account of how Jesus did the same. He even uses similar language to point out the parallel: both Elijah and Jesus, after raising the son, 'gave him to his mother' (1 Kings 17:23). This is not the only gospel narrative about Jesus awakening the dead. His raising of Jairus' daughter is related in Mark (5:42), Matthew (9:25) and Luke (8:55). John devotes a whole chapter to the raising of Lazarus (John 11). When John the Baptist sent messengers to Jesus from his prison, Jesus included in the list of his activities how the dead were being raised to life (Matthew 11:5; Luke 7:22). Such traditions about Jesus would prepare the first readers of the Gospels for the story of Jesus' own resurrection, which differed from those he performed on others in that he did not come back to this life to die again.

The incident of the widow of Nain deserves special attention as containing no mention of the faith either of the woman or her son. Jesus performs this miracle out of sheer pity: the Greek word used is far stronger than any translation. It refers to an emotion which affects the whole of one's being. The same word is used to describe the pity the Samaritan had for the man lying robbed and stripped by the side of the road (10:33).

The reaction of the onlookers is special, too. They speak of a great prophet having arisen among them, which takes us back to Jesus' sermon in Nazareth (4:18–30) and anticipates the words of the despairing disciples on the Emmaus road who had hoped in Jesus as 'a great prophet by the things he said and did' (24:19–21). They also speak of God having visited his people, using the same language that Zechariah employed in his canticle after the birth of John the Baptist (1:68). This image of Jesus making a divine visitation is a helpful way into understanding this Gospel and encourages us to respond with suitable hospitality.

Sunday 11 C

2 Samuel 12:7–10, 13
Psalm 31:1–2, 5, 7, 11
Galatians 2:16, 19–21
Luke 7:36–8:3

A Woman Anoints Jesus

The best known personal sin in the Old Testament, apart from that of Adam and Eve, is the sin of David with Bathsheba and David's subsequent murder of Uriah, her husband. Besides its human consequences, sin affects relationships with God. In **2 Samuel**, the prophet Nathan reports God's reaction to David's sin. It is the anguished response of a loving covenant partner, who punishes only with reluctance. David is not rejected but, henceforth, he will have to live with the effects of his sin. David repents; he makes no conditions.

The **Psalm** is a penitential psalm, which begins with a blessing on those who have had their sins forgiven. Like David, the sinner has made public confession of guilt. This leads to a deeper appreciation of the goodness and fidelity of God.

Paul in **Galatians** has just recalled the painful incident at Antioch when he rebuked Peter publicly for refusing to eat with Gentile Christians (2:14). He saw that Peter's conduct was compromising a fundamental doctrine of Christianity, that salvation comes to us as a gift of God, to which we respond through faith in Christ, and not by our own efforts. Paul sees how personal our belief is as a result. Christ died for each of us personally out of love. Every one of us can make our own the words of Paul that Christ loved me and gave himself for me, whether previously we were Jew or Gentile. Through baptism we have been crucified with Christ (Romans 6:5). He rose from the dead with new life and we partake in that life (Romans 6:4). If we attempt to add other means of salvation to this one, then we make the death of Jesus as of no importance.

Each of the Gospels includes an account of a woman anointing Jesus with ointment (Mark 14:3–9; Matthew 26:6–13; John 12:1–8). **Luke**'s version is special in placing the incident early in Jesus' ministry rather than just before the passion, and in identifying the woman as a sinner. Previously, Jesus has healed a Gentile's servant (7:1–10) and raised a widow's son from the dead (7:11–17). Now he forgives sins. He is continuing his mission of preaching the Good News to the despised of Israel that he announced in the Nazareth synagogue (4:18).

To help us understand better the contrast between the woman and his host, Simon, Jesus tells a parable about two debtors and asks a fundamental question about love. Luke has several parables that contrast individuals and attitudes. An younger son is compared with an elder son (15:11–32), a tax collector with a Pharisee (18:9–14). Here the person who is forgiven much loves more than the one forgiven little. The woman who has been forgiven many sins celebrates her repentance with an extravagant display of love. Her reward is the salvation that would come to Zacchaeus (19:9), the peace that would be the fruit of Easter (24:36). Jesus' host, Simon the Pharisee, refuses, like the elder brother of the prodigal son, to join in the rejoicing at the return of the lost (15:7). He can only criticize the one he had thought was a prophet. Like the elder son, and the Pharisee in the Temple, he does not recognise his own need for forgiveness and so has no love to show. He denies Jesus the normal courtesies of a host.

We owe to Luke a note about the women companions of Jesus on his way to Jerusalem. These women are of different backgrounds and have different resources. They include Magdalene of the seven demons and Joanna from the royal palace of Herod. They will persevere in Jesus' company until the cross (23:49), witness to the empty tomb (24:10) and pray with the Twelve before pentecost (Acts 1:14). They are model disciples in perseverance, prayer and hospitality.

Sunday 12 C

Zechariah 12:10–11; 13:1
Psalm 62:2–6, 8–9
Galatians 3:26–29
Luke 9:18–24

Who Is Jesus?

The book of **Zechariah** is the prophetic work most quoted in the passion stories of the Gospels. It originated in the dark days after the exile, when God seemed far away. The prophet glimpses better days ahead when the people will once again acknowledge their God. They will repent of their sins and find forgiveness. These words were applied to Christ by John both in the Gospel and in the book of Revelation. It was Christ who was pierced by the soldier's spear (John 19:37; Revelation 1:7) and it was the blood and water that flowed from his side that would be a fountain of forgiveness (John 19:34).

The **Psalm** is traditionally attributed to David during his desert campaigns fleeing from Absalom (2 Samuel 15–16) or from King Saul (1 Samuel 23:14). He knows how God is the remedy for human restlessness, that he will never find a better protector than the God who holds him in his right hand.

For Paul, internal faith in Christ finds external expression in baptism. This is the time for wearing new, clean garments, and in **Galatians** these are a symbol of the Christ whom we put on in baptism. In the eyes of God, all those who wear Christ are equally his children. Human distinctions remain between Jew and Greek (Romans 9:3), between slave and free (1 Corinthians 7:21), between male and female (1 Corinthians 7:10). But God does not recognise such divisions in those who are 'in Christ', because when God looks on them, he sees his Son who is the firstborn among many brothers (Romans 8:29) who share in the promises made long ago to Abraham (3:16).

As Jesus in **Luke** approaches the end of his Galilaean ministry, one question dominates: *who is this Jesus?* Herod asked and found no answer (9:9). According to John, the crowds who had been fed on five loaves and two fish (9:13), saw in him 'the prophet who is to come into the world' (John 6:14). Other popular answers were that he was John the Baptist returned, or Elijah, the fiery prophet who had been taken to heaven in a chariot of fire and had never died (2 Kings 2:11).

Peter tells Jesus that he is 'the Christ of God'. As a Galilean of his time, Peter would not understand this word in its full Christian sense, which has to take into account the cross and resurrection (Romans 1:4). He would be thinking of a new 'anointed one', who would deliver Israel, not from the Philistines as David had done (2 Samuel 5:25), but from the Romans who rule their country. Jesus cannot allow his disciples to speak of him in such dangerous terms. Herod, the king who rules with Rome's permission in Galilee, and Pilate, the Roman governor in Judaea, would see to his swift removal.

Jesus corrects Peter by identifying himself first as the 'Son of Man', who would suffer, be rejected and die. This is part of the divine necessity for Jesus and there is no escaping it (24:26). He next describes himself as one to be followed. Those who accept his invitation have to deny themselves. They are not only to listen to the words of Jesus but to do them (6:47). They have to carry the cross behind Jesus daily, not necessarily the literal cross that Simon carried (23:26), but its equivalent in their conforming their lives to the crucified one. They have to bear the yoke of Jesus (Matthew 11:29) and observe all that he has commanded (Matthew 28:20). They have to do this every day because, for Luke, there would be no early release for the Christian through martyrdom nor any rapid return of Jesus. They have to follow him on the road that leads to Jerusalem (9:51).

Sunday 13 C

1 Kings 19:16, 19–21
Psalm 15:1–2, 5, 7–11
Galatians 5:1, 13–18
Luke 9:51–62

The Journey Begins

The call of Elisha in 1 **Kings** is an unusual type of vocation story. Most prophets in the Old Testament record a direct call by God (Isaiah 6; Jeremiah 1), but Elisha was summoned, on God's instructions, by Elijah, whom he was to succeed. His response to his call is generous. He gives up his twelve yoke of oxen and sanctifies his calling by making a sacred meal of two of them. But he delays in order to fulfil family obligations—a delay that Jesus in the Gospel forbids his own follower.

The **Psalm** is a song of confidence in God by a Levite, a member of the tribe in Israel which possessed no land of its own. God alone is 'my heritage, my cup'. Elisha could make this prayer after his call. Peter quoted this psalm on Pentecost Day. He saw in God's care for the psalmist in his sickness a prophecy of the resurrection of Christ (Acts 2:32).

Now nearing the end of **Galatians**, Paul celebrates the freedom of the Christian from sin and from strict observance of the Mosaic Law, which Christ won through his death. But Paul acknowledges the risk that his converts run of falling back into slavery to sin. This could treat their freedom as licence, as a result of allowing 'self-indulgence' to be their guide in life rather than the love of neighbour which was the fruit of the gospel (Mark 12:31). Such love ensures that the quality of life demanded by the Mosaic Law is achieved. It is a gift of the Holy Spirit (1 Corinthians 13:1–13). They are not to ignore the prompting of the Spirit of God which lives in each of us (4:6). The person who lives by the Spirit cannot live a life of self-interest.

Luke began his account of Jesus' ministry in Galilee with his rejection in Nazareth (4:16–30). He then gave details of Peter's call to discipleship (5:1–10). He repeats this pattern in his description of the beginning of Jesus' journey to Jerusalem, and to Paradise (23:43). This journey pictures a Jesus determined to meet the demands of his destiny (24:26), who gives an example of the perseverance he asks of the disciples (8:15). On this journey, the disciples cease to be mere spectators to what he says and does. In various teachings and encounters, he shows what is required of a disciple and attempts to conform their attitudes to his own.

As he sets out, Jesus is rejected by Samaritans, people with whom Jews did not associate (John 4:9). His disciples, who still think of Jesus in terms of the prophet Elijah (9:19), ask him to punish them with fire from heaven, as Elijah had punished the soldiers of Ahab (2 Kings 1:10). Jesus refuses such a violent response. He will shortly follow up this tolerance of Samaritans with the parable of the good Samaritan who cared for the man wounded by the side of the road (10:30). Later he will praise the Samaritan leper who showed gratitude for his cure (17:16). He gives a personal example of the love for enemies that he preached (6:35–36).

Luke gives us the most attractive of the gospel portraits of Jesus. People rejected by the rest of society streamed to him (15:2). Crowds in general were spellbound by him (19:48). But Jesus makes serious demands on his followers. Their commitment, like his, is to be without compromise. Two people offer themselves as his disciples. The first is invited to share Jesus' own homelessness and forbidden to follow the example of Elisha, Elijah's successor, who first went home to say goodbye. The second is refused permission to bury his father. The spiritually dead can meet such filial obligations, but not those who follow the Saviour who is Christ, the Lord (2:11).

Sunday 14 C

Isaiah 66:10–14
Psalm 65:1–7, 16, 20
Galatians 6:14–18
Luke 10:1–12, 17–20

The Mission of the 72

A key word in the concluding chapter of **Isaiah** is 'rejoice'. The joy here prepares us for the joy of the 72 returning from their mission in the Gospel. The prophet sees God creating a new Jerusalem for 'the man of humble and contrite spirit' (66:2) who does not rely on a religion of ritual alone (Revelation 21:2). The care and comfort that this Jerusalem lavishes on its children mirrors that of God, who is compared to a mother (42:14). Earlier, this prophet compared God to a woman in labour (42:14) and has reminded Zion that just as a woman cannot forget her child, so God cannot forget his own people (49:15).

The **Psalm** reflects the joy of a people conscious of God's care. They recall typical deeds of God on their behalf. He brought them through the sea at the Exodus when they had been delivered from Egyptian oppression (Exodus 14:22), and brought them across the Jordan so that they might enter the Promised Land (Joshua 3:17). Such deeds continue in the mission of the 72 about which we will hear in the Gospel.

Paul concludes **Galatians** with references to Christ, his converts and himself. Christ is his Lord who loved him and gave himself for him. Paul can boast of nothing else (1 Corinthians 3:21); this cross changed his whole way of existence (Philippians 3:8). He now lives in Christ (2:20). As for his converts, through their faith and baptism they are a new creation (2 Corinthians 5:17). God has once again created light from darkness (2 Corinthians 4:6). Paul is different physically, too, since, because of his toils and sufferings on behalf of the gospel (2 Corinthians 11:23–27), his body is marked with scars that prove he belongs to Christ.

Luke is unique in recording a mission of the 72 in addition to a mission of the Twelve (9:1–6) during the lifetime of Jesus. Possibly he is reminding the reader of the 70 elders who assisted Moses (Exodus 24:1). Certainly he is looking forward to pairings such as Paul and Barnabas in Acts who worked for the gospel but did not belong to the original Twelve (Acts 13:2). The harvest is too great to be reaped by such a small group (John 4:35). Legend has it that Luke himself was one of the 72.

The conditions for this mission are demanding. Resources are minimal and the task is urgent. It is dangerous, too. The 72 are like sheep among wolves. They are given no guarantee of success. Sometimes they will be welcomed and sometimes not (Acts 13:50–51). But their message is not their own. Like Jesus, they are to preach the Kingdom of God (4:43). They will learn, 'We all have to experience many hardships ... before we enter the kingdom of God' (Acts 14:22). At the Last Supper Jesus would relax his prohibition on purse and bag for the journey (22:36). From then on, the mission would not be confined to Palestine but directed to the 'ends of the earth', by which was probably understood Rome, the centre of power and empire in those days (Acts 1:8).

Despite all, the mission of the 72 is successful and they return full of joy, just as Paul and Barnabas would after their missionary journey (Acts 13:52). Correctly, they attribute their success not to their own efforts but to the 'name' of Jesus. They report to him. He knows that events on earth have repercussions in heaven (Revelation 12). He reminds them that their task is to oppose not only the powers of this world, but the powers of evil in high places (Ephesians 6:12). Their earthly success has driven Satan's power from heaven and their labours for the gospel have ensured that their own names are written in the heavenly books (Philippians 4:3). They should rejoice because they are citizens of the New Jerusalem of which the prophets spoke (Isaiah 66:10).

Sunday 15 C

Deuteronomy 30:10–14
Psalm 68:14, 17, 30–31, 33–34, 36–37
Colossians 1:15–20
Luke 10:25–37

The Good Samaritan

Moses' third speech in **Deuteronomy** contains an attractive description of the Mosaic Law, which reflects the goodness of God who was its origin. We do not have to send up to heaven or across the seas to find this Law, because it is a word that is very near to us; it is already written in our hearts (Jeremiah 31:33). The Good Samaritan obeyed its demands and chose the way that leads to life (30:15). Paul applied these verses to faith in Christ and the obedience that goes with it (Romans 10:8).

The **Psalm** is a lament, quoted in accounts of the death of Jesus who, like the psalmist, was given vinegar to drink (Psalms 68:21; Matthew 27:34). It fits the situation of the wounded traveller in the parable well. The kindness and compassion of God, which he sought in his prayer, came to him by means of the Good Samaritan, who listened to the plea of the needy.

The letter to the **Colossians** was written to combat various false teachings. Among these was a tendency to treat the exalted Christ as one of several powers that control the universe. We hear today an early Christian hymn that contradicts this. Christ is identified with the Wisdom that was God's agent in creation (Proverbs 8) and is superior to all other powers. By his cross he defeats them all. Like a Roman general enjoying his triumph, he drags these adversaries behind him in his victory procession (Colossians 2:15). Through his earthly career and on the cross to which it led, he became the means of reconciliation and peace between God and humanity. Nor is he idle now, because not only is the Church a body (1 Corinthians 12), but it has a head who is Christ, and he is the source of its unity.

Our readings from **Luke** on these next three Sundays can all be linked to the question of the lawyer: 'Master, what must I do to inherit eternal life?' He is learned enough in the Law to answer his own question: he is to love God and to love his neighbour (Mark 12:30). His problem is, 'Who is my neighbour?' We cannot conceive how Jesus' answer, extolling the qualities of a Samaritan, would have shaken him because of the fierce hostility that existed between Jew and Samaritan (John 4:9). Besides, because the parable of the Good Samaritan is familiar to all who know anything of the Gospels, its impact is easily blunted for all of us.

The story is simple enough. A traveller falls among robbers on a steep, desert road. He is left naked and half dead by the roadside. His need is absolute. Religious people, a priest and Levite, pass by. If they are on their way to Jerusalem to perform religious duties, they have a dilemma: contact with a corpse would disqualify them from their responsibilities (Leviticus 21:1). So they pass by, refusing the absolute need of the sufferer. A third traveller comes. He belongs to those Samaritans who sacrilegiously ruined Jewish Passover celebrations a few years before. Like Jesus when he saw the plight of the bereaved widow (7:13), he is overwhelmed by pity. He spares none of his resources: his oil, his wine, even his donkey. He pays the innkeeper the amount of two days' wages (Matthew 20:10) and promises to return to meet any further debts.

Yes, says the lawyer, this third man proved himself a neighbour. (He could not speak the word 'Samaritan'.) Jesus tells him to do the same. His original question is like those that the crowds addressed to John the Baptist (3:10). John's answers had been decent enough, but were trite compared with the answer given by Christ. Repentance implies a complete change of outlook and behaviour. Peter was looking for this on Pentecost Day when the crowds asked him what they were to do (Acts 2:37).

Sunday 16 C

Genesis 18:1–10
Psalm 14:2–5
Colossians 1:24–28
Luke 10:38–42

Listen to the Word

Abraham unknowingly entertained angels (Hebrews 13:2). **Genesis** tells us how they came, with no appointment or introduction and at the hottest time of the day. Though he does not know that, in welcoming them, he is meeting God, Abraham spares no effort in his hospitality. He is too good a man to expect a reward for his generosity, but God does not let him go without one. His wife, Sarah, will give him a son.

The **Psalm** lists the qualities that are needed for a person to feel at home in the presence of God in the Temple, and is selected, presumably, as a fit description of the guests who came to Abraham. He was to make such qualities his own, and the description also fits Abraham well. This psalm may prepare us for Jesus' parable about the two men who went to the Temple to pray (Luke 18:9–14).

In **Colossians**, Paul reflects on his mission and his message. His mission has brought him suffering and hardships, but elsewhere he has reflected on how when he was weak the power of Christ had its full scope (2 Corinthians 12:9). Difficulties endured in the service of the gospel have not destroyed his confidence. Jesus warned about such difficulties (Mark 13:9) but, thanks to them, Paul experiences the abundance of the consolation that God offers (2 Corinthians 1:5). As for the gospel he preaches, it is not a secret mystery known only to some privileged few (Daniel 2:19), but God's plan of salvation now being revealed publicly to all. It does not consist of abstract propositions, but is making the person and presence of Christ real to the world; in him their hope lies and they can look forward to a share in his glory.

The journey of Jesus continues, and he finds himself in the house of Mary and Martha, known to us from John's Gospel as the sisters of Lazarus whom Jesus raised from the dead (John 11:1). There, too, Martha is the active one, who comes to meet Jesus while Mary stays at home (John 11:20). Luke's story of Martha and Mary, which follows immediately after the story of the Good Samaritan, may be understood as a further part of Jesus' answer to the lawyer's question, 'What must I do to inherit eternal life? (10:25). Here we are offered a story about a woman, balancing, as so often in this Gospel, a story about a man (2:25, 36; 15:4, 8). Many, even those who are not Christians, have imitated the compassion of the Good Samaritan. The disciple of Christ is to add to practical deeds of mercy a zeal for listening to the Word of God such as Mary showed when Jesus visited her and her sister.

Concern and respect for the Word of God runs through Luke's writings. He began by acknowledging his debt to 'ministers of the word' (1:2). The goal of disciples was to be good soil for the Word of God, so that they would 'take it to themselves and yield a harvest through their perseverance' (8:15). The true family of Jesus consisted of those who 'hear the word of God and put it into practice' (8:21). Mary, the mother of Jesus, was one who 'stored up' all the words of Jesus in her heart (2:51). On the Emmaus road, Jesus himself explained the Word of God, 'starting with Moses and going through all the prophets', to such effect that the hearts of his hearers burned within them (24:27, 32). In Acts, 'The word of God continued to spread and to gain followers' (Acts 12:24).

Mary thus shows herself a fine Lucan disciple by sitting at the feet of Jesus and listening with such attention to his words. Yet Martha also serves. She addresses Jesus as her Lord, and Jesus speaks to her directly by name. Our Christianity must combine the Samaritan's practical compassion for the neighbour, Martha's service and Mary's devotion to the Word.

Sunday 17 C

Genesis 18:20–32
Psalm 137:1–3, 6–8
Colossians 2:12–14
Luke 11:1–13

The Lord's Prayer

The wickedness of Sodom and Gomorrah was proverbial. What was God to do about it? What, indeed, is God to do about all human sin and infidelity? The author of **Genesis** wrestles with these questions by introducing a dialogue between Abraham and God, anticipating the later debates we find in the book of Job. In very human language, we see God pondering what to do. We listen to Abraham arguing with God. We come to understand better what is meant by the justice of God. Despite the sin of the many, he is prepared to spare them because of the goodness of the few. Paul knew that even if only a remnant were faithful, then God would not abandon his commitment to the many (Romans 11:5).

The **Psalm** is a song of thanksgiving by one whose prayer has been answered. God is seen as dwelling in a heavenly court (Isaiah 6; Revelation 5). He continues to exercise the qualities of kindness and mercy by which he bound himself to his people through Moses (Exodus 34:6–7) and which he showed to Abraham.

The classic text about baptism in Paul is found in Romans (6:3–5), where he looks forward to our sharing in the resurrection of Christ in the future. In **Colossians**, he goes further, claiming that baptism has already brought us a share in this resurrection. Through it, we have received forgiveness of sins (Acts 2:38). Humanity has run up many debts because of its failure to live up to the demands of the Law; the cross of Christ has brought about their cancellation, because these debts have been nailed to the cross.

The prayer that Jesus taught his disciples is found in two places in the Gospels (Matthew 6:9–13). **Luke**'s version is shorter and its context is significant. It is part of the narrative of Jesus' journey to Jerusalem and follows on the incident of Mary and Martha. It too can be understood as part of the answer to the lawyer's question, 'What must I do to inherit eternal life?' (10:25). The Christian is to have the social conscience of the Samaritan and the eagerness for the Word of God that Mary showed, and must also know how to address God as Father in prayer.

Short though the prayer is, we can compose a commentary on it from the words of the rest of the Gospel. The one who addresses God as 'Father' (Abba) is Jesus himself, both during his public life (10:21) and at his death (23:34, 46). A model for those who pray, 'may your name be held holy', is Mary in her 'Magnificat' (1:46), as well as so many others who thank God for the mercy they experience through Jesus (17:15). Those who pray, 'Your kingdom come', may remember the persistence of the widow begging for justice from the wicked judge (18:1–8). The best prayer for forgiveness of sin comes from the tax collector in the Temple who asks for God's mercy and has no time to bore God with his own achievements like the Pharisee (18:9–14). Jesus himself gives the example for forgiveness of enemies at his execution (23:34) and, by his prayer on the Mount of Olives before his death, gives his disciples instructions on how to avoid temptation (22:39–46).

The story of the person who wants bread from a friend at midnight is a commentary on the words, 'Give us each day our daily bread'. When we pray to God, we pray, not to a sleepy friend, but to a loving Father who is ready to give the Holy Spirit to the children of God who ask him (Romans 8:14–15). Such is the daily bread that God gives us so that we may carry our cross daily (9:23).

Sunday 18 C

Ecclesiastes 1:2; 2:21–23
Psalm 89:3–6, 12–14, 17
Colossians 3:1–5, 9–11
Luke 12:13–21

The Rich Fool

The preacher Qoheleth wrote 300 years before Christ. **Ecclesiastes**, his brief book, is unconventional and untypical of the group of 'Wisdom' books to which it belongs. This is the only Sunday in the year when we hear it. A favourite word, 'vanity', comes at the beginning and end of the book (12:8). The pessimism of our passage prepares us for our meeting with the rich fool in the Gospel. He too had to leave the fruits of his own skill, industry and success to someone else.

The **Psalm** reflects on the shortness of life. The author takes seriously God's words to Adam in Genesis about returning to dust (Genesis 3:19). But, nonetheless, the psalmist continues to praise God and to live his life in God's presence, unlike the fool in the Gospel.

The conclusion of **Colossians**, like other Pauline letters, deals with Christian behaviour. Our way of life as Christians depends on our understanding of the person of Christ, now exalted to heaven, who is the image of the unseen God (1:15–20) and on our human dignity based on our baptismal experience (2:12). Although we are saved in principle, full salvation belongs to the future, even in the case of Paul, who could yet be disqualified from the race (1 Corinthians 9:27); for the present, the vices that threaten the rest of humanity threaten the Christian too. Among these is 'greed', the vice that destroyed the rich fool in the Gospel. Our destiny is to be fully identified with Christ. Because our baptism cancels out distinctions of race, sex and social status in his sight, God is able to see his own Son in us (Galatians 3:28). Our passage begins and ends with the word 'Christ' which is very typical of Paul.

It is in **Luke**'s Gospel that we find the most references to riches and poverty, and today's passage is a good sample. It begins and ends with a reference to inheritance, in both instances leaving open the question of who inherits. Jesus speaks first to an individual who wants him to settle an inheritance problem, but then he addresses the crowds as a whole. Unusually, he answers a question directly and he follows up his answer with a parable. Again unusually, he explains how the parable is to be understood.

Jesus' direct answer is a warning against greed and a security based on material possessions. In this he agrees with the best teachers of the Greek world to which Luke was directing his Gospel, but he carries the argument further because, in this untypical parable, there is only one human character. On a material level, he is very successful because of the abundance of his crops. But whereas this should have been an occasion of thankfulness to God (we remember the grateful leper [17:16]) and an excuse for celebration with his family and employees, his only thought is for himself and the prospect of better and bigger crops. He must build more barns to store them. As for conversation, he only speaks to his own soul. He orders his soul to drink, eat and have a good time. He reminds us of the Pharisee who went to pray in the Temple and prayed about himself (18:11).

But if the rich man has forgotten God, God has not forgotten him. In language reminiscent of the psalmist describing the man who denies God as a fool (Psalm 14:1), God has news for him, both about his soul and his possessions, and the news is not good. He has not made himself rich in the sight of God, and someone else must inherit all his possessions. The first in the list of woes that follows the beatitudes in Luke is addressed to the rich (6:24). Riches for Luke are not evil in themselves; it is the use to which they are put that is important. Lydia in Acts knew how to employ her riches in hospitality (Acts 16:15); Zacchaeus gave half his possessions to the poor (19:8).

Sunday 19 C

Wisdom 18:6–9
Psalm 32:1, 12, 18–20, 22
Hebrews 11:1–2, 8–19
Luke 12:32–48

Life in the Kingdom

The book of **Wisdom**, written shortly before the birth of Jesus, meditates at length on Israel's history. Our passage recalls the night on which the Israelites escaped in haste from Egypt (Exodus 12:33). The Egyptian Pharaoh had decreed that all the male children of the Israelites should be killed, but Moses, who was to lead his people to safety, had escaped (Exodus 1:16). In the final plague suffered by the Egyptians, their firstborn were slaughtered (Exodus 12:12). These verses prepare us for Jesus' appeal to his disciples to show similar urgency in responding to his message as their ancestors had shown when they fled from Egypt.

The **Psalm** celebrates God's concern for his people over many generations. It probably originated late in Israel's history. It portrays a God rich in merciful love (Exodus 34:6) who is the shield, not just of Abraham (Genesis 15:1), but of all who commit themselves to him.

The final part of **Hebrews**, which we read over the next three weeks, also meditates on the history of Israel, bringing forward for admiration and imitation heroic figures whose faith typifies that expected of followers of Christ. Today we hear of Abraham and of the faith he displayed in life. He showed faith in his obedience to God, who instructed him to leave his country and his family (Genesis 12:1). He trusted the promise of God that despite his own age and that of Sarah, he would be the father of many nations (Genesis 15:7). He did not hesitate when he was ordered to sacrifice his son Isaac (Genesis 22). Paul too holds Abraham up as a model believer (Romans 4:17; Galatians 3:6). Abraham continues to be revered by Jew, Muslim and Christian.

In his parable of the rich fool, Jesus warned one of the crowd thronging about him of the dangers of greed and selfishness. This week in **Luke**, Jesus teaches an audience of his disciples about values which will make them feel at home in the Kingdom. They may indeed belong to a tiny flock, a remnant (Romans 11:5; Zephaniah 3:13) but by possessing the gift of the Kingdom, they have everything. The words 'have no fear', once addressed to Abraham (Genesis 15:1), are also addressed to them. Such reassurance is a constant theme of Jesus' teaching to his disciples (Mark 6:50).

The rich fool tried to keep his wealth in earthly barns. The person with the spirit of Jesus is ready to give it away, because our real treasure is stored in heaven (Matthew 6:20). But this does not mean that we no longer belong to this world. True disciples of Jesus are dressed for the journey and ready for action, like the Israelites who escaped from Egypt at the first Passover (Exodus 12:11). They are like the wise virgins in Matthew who awaited the return of the bridegroom (Matthew 25:2). They know that the master whom they await has been among them already as 'one who serves' (22:27), and will himself serve them at the heavenly banquet.

Privileges imply obligations. In the ministry of Jesus, God was visiting his people (1:68). Luke expected the church leaders of his own day to appreciate both the gifts that were theirs and the responsibilities that went with them. They were accountable for the household of God (1 Timothy 3:5). It was as if there were thieves lurking outside, who could break into the house and destroy it at any time (1 Peter 5:9; 1 Thessalonians 5:2); wolves threatened (Acts 20:29). Luke knew from experience that there was both competence and incompetence among Christian leaders. The more responsibility they had been given, the more answerable they were, as Paul told the elders of the Church of Ephesus (Acts 20:28). Jesus demands much of those who would be his disciples (9:62), but he prays for them that their faith may not fail (22:32).

Sunday 20 C

Jeremiah 38:4–6, 8–10
Psalm 39:2–4, 18
Hebrews 12:1–4
Luke 12:49–53

Fire upon the Earth

Jeremiah, the prophet, declined to take the easy way of telling the authorities what they wanted to hear when Jerusalem was besieged by Babylonian armies in 588 BC. He insisted on giving them the bad news, the unwelcome truth that came from God. He knew that his mission was not only 'to build and to plant', but also 'to tear up and to knock down' (Jeremiah 1:10). Like Joseph, the patriarch (Genesis 37:22), he was thrown into a pit to die. Again like Joseph, he was saved by a foreigner (Genesis 37:28).

The **Psalm** is a song of confidence. Like the passage from Jeremiah, it makes reference to delivery from a pit. The psalmist's language recalls Israel's troubles in the Exile. Like Deutero-Isaiah, he speaks a new song to God (Isaiah 42:10). This is a psalm that makes much of personal trust in God.

Paul, in Corinthians, had compared the Christian life to a race in the stadium (1 Corinthians 9:25). He knew that he himself had not yet reached the finishing post (Philippians 3:12). In his last hours, he boasted that he had finished the race (2 Timothy 4:7). **Hebrews** extends this sporting image. We are all competing in the race of faith and a crowd is watching us from the clouds above, composed of the great figures of salvation history, such as Abraham and Moses (Hebrews 11). But there is one who has already run the race of faith and won. This is Jesus and he, too, is watching us. His passion and death were the race he ran. He endured the shame of the cross, and his prize was a seat at God's right hand (Psalm 110:1; Luke 22:69; Philippians 2:8–9). We are to fix our gaze on him, especially when we feel we are in the pit with Jeremiah. 'Because he has himself been through temptation he is able to help others who are tempted' (2:18).

John the Baptist told his followers at the Jordan that Jesus would baptize with fire (3:16). But instead of fire, a dove, a sign of peace, came down from heaven (3:22), and Jesus defined his mission as one of 'good news to the poor' (4:18). Yet today, in **Luke**, Jesus tells his disciples that he has come to bring fire on the earth.

Fire in the scriptures is a symbol of purification. The fire that Jesus came to cast upon the earth was not the physical fire with which Elijah destroyed the soldiers of Ahaziah (2 Kings 1:10–14), and which Jesus had forbidden his disciples to call down from heaven (9:54) but the daily self-denial and discipleship that he taught (9:23). He himself gives the example of how to live such a life through his prayer (3:21) and his perseverance (9:51), through forgiveness (7:48) and social concern (7:13). Jesus describes the coming climax of his life as a baptism. This implies letting go, as when a diver jumps off a high board. When he arrives at the destination of his journey (9:51), he will emerge from the waters of his passion into his resurrection.

Jesus' own mission, a mixture of failure and success, will be mirrored in those of his followers. He has not only come to bring peace (2:14; 10:5; 24:36). The words of Simeon to Mary (2:35) at the finding in the Temple (2:48) foretold division in his own family. Hellenic and Hebrew Christians quarrelled in Jerusalem (Acts 6:1); Paul and Barnabas were condemned by fellow Christians after their mission (Acts 15:2). Paul complained about quarrels splitting the Corinthian Christians (1 Corinthians 1:11). Thus Micah's prophecy of family division found fulfilment among Jesus' first followers (Micah 7:6). Jeremiah's ordeal at the hands of his own people was repeated. As to fire, 'something … that seemed like tongues of fire' rested on his disciples on Pentecost Day (Acts 2:3). This fire that symbolized the Holy Spirit would inspire the disciples as they went out on their mission to the 'ends of the earth' (Acts 1:8).

Sunday 21 C

Isaiah 66:18–21
Psalm 116
Hebrews 12:5–7, 11–13
Luke 13:22–30

Entering the Kingdom

The last section of **Isaiah** begins and ends with a great opening up to the Gentile world. The Temple in Jerusalem will no longer be for Israel alone but 'a house of prayer for all the peoples' (56:7; Mark 11:17), and Gentiles will be among the priests and Levites who serve in it. No longer will their number only include descendants of Zadok of the tribe of Levi (Ezekiel 40:46). These foreigners will come from the west (Tarshish in Spain), the south (Put and Lud in Africa) and the north (Tubal, near Russia). Isaiah's vision anticipates Jesus' words in today's Gospel and the mission of his Church to be his witnesses to the ends of the earth (Acts 1:8).

The **Psalm** is the shortest of them all. All nations are summoned to praise God for his merciful love and fidelity (Exodus 34:6), which he revealed in his covenant with his people. He continues to display his faithfulness to Jacob and loyalty to Abraham (Micah 7:20), despite their lack of faithfulness, loyalty and knowledge of God (Hosea 4:2).

The strict father who is prepared to discipline his son was a familiar figure in Jewish 'Wisdom' tradition (Proverbs 5:12; Sirach 23:2). He knows that application and good order are paths to improvement and achievement. In a pattern, common in **Hebrews**, of exhortation following doctrine, its author uses this image to comfort his hearers in times of stress and discouragement. He appeals to them to use their bodily faculties to their full potential: no more limp hands, trembling knees or injured limbs! All this becomes possible if they can keep before them the picture of 'Jesus, who leads us in our faith and brings it to perfection' (12:2).

In **Luke**, we continue to accompany Jesus the prophet as he travels through the towns and villages to Jerusalem (9:51). At times he addresses his disciples, at times his critics and at times the crowds. Today he speaks to the crowds and, as usual with this audience, his teaching is demanding and urgent. They are to seize the opportunity offered to them, otherwise it may be too late. The question put to him, 'Sir, will there be only a few saved?', receives no direct answer. Only God knows. The questioner's task is to ensure that he will be one of them. Jesus uses various images. To 'try your best' is what an athlete does in a race. Like Paul, he is to fight the good fight and finish the race (2 Timothy 4:7). He is to run with perseverance along the course set before him (Hebrews 12:1). He is to think of the way into the Kingdom as a narrow door.

The picture changes to that of a householder who has locked the door of his house and opens only to those he knows. At first sight, the person with the key seems to be God, but the words, 'We once ate and drank in your company; you taught in our streets', identify him with Christ, who is making his way to Jerusalem. We recall from Matthew the foolish virgins who were locked out of the marriage feast, saying, 'Lord, Lord ... open the door for us' (Matthew 25:11), and Jesus' final words in the Sermon on the Mount to those who boasted of their miracles and exorcisms in his name, 'I have never known you' (Matthew 7:23).

The atmosphere changes again in Jesus' concluding saying. He pictures the great banquet in the Kingdom at the end of time, foreseen by the prophets. 'Yahweh Sabaoth will prepare for all peoples a banquet of rich food' (Isaiah 25:6). Despite the severity of Jesus' sayings about narrow doors and locked doors, the banquet is full. All the patriarchs and prophets are there, together with peoples from the four corners of the earth. The final promise of Isaiah about the nations is fulfilled, but their destination is not the Temple in Jerusalem, but the great banquet in heaven (Isaiah 66:18–21; Revelation 7:9).

Sunday 22 C

Sirach 3:17–20, 28–29
Psalm 67:4–7, 10–11
Hebrews 12:18–19, 22–24
Luke 14:1, 7–14

The Lower Place

Ben-Sira, who wrote the Wisdom of **Sirach**, may have been a teacher in Jerusalem a hundred years before Christ. His message is gentle and pious; he is suspicious of the intellectual speculation encouraged by the Greeks and the other-worldly rhetoric of Jewish apocalyptic writers. He does not approve of questioning the wisdom tradition that he wants to pass on. He would agree with the wisdom writer who preached the fear of the Lord rather than the writing of books and much study (Ecclesiastes 12:12–13). Today's verses encourage humility and warn against pride. They prepare us for the teaching of Jesus in his beatitudes (Luke 6:20–24) and his message to the dinner guests in our gospel reading.

Our **Psalm** ranges over much of the history of salvation; today we hear how God has particularly selected for blessings those to whom the world refuses its favours, such as the orphan, the widow, the lonely, the poor.

As we conclude **Hebrews**, we are introduced to a final contrast between the old and the new covenants. The covenant of Mount Sinai was marked by darkness and storm, thunder and a deafening voice. The whole atmosphere was one of terror and fear. In contrast, the heavenly Jerusalem is characteristic of the new covenant. Millions of angels enjoy a festival. The saints are there and, most importantly, Jesus himself, who pleads on our behalf. The blood he shed has brought us purification. The book of Revelation expands this picture. There, too, is the throne room of God, where the slaughtered Lamb takes his place (Revelation 5:6) and the new Jerusalem, come down from heaven to earth, where God lives among his people (Revelation 21:2–3).

We now pause on Jesus' journey to Jerusalem to find him at table. Greek readers of **Luke** would remember that it was at table that many teachers found opportunity to pass on their instruction and wisdom. But Jesus' companions are described as lawyers and Pharisees; so far such people have proved his critics and opponents (5:30; 7:30), so we expect conflict. Jesus faces it head-on. He takes the initiative.

In verses that we omit, Jesus questions the religious experts present about whether it is lawful to heal on the Sabbath, because a man with dropsy is present. In the silence that ensues he gets no answer, and heals the sick man. Jesus then addresses his fellow guests with a parable. They are to seek out the lowest rather than the highest places when they are invited to a banquet. In the Kingdom that he preaches, the greatest honour belongs to the one who serves rather than the one greedy for status. The former will be exalted (18:14). In a previous chapter we heard about the master who made his slaves sit down at table when they had completed their work (12:37). At the Last Supper, Jesus told his disciples that he was among them as one who served (22:27).

Finally, he has a word for his host. Instead of friends, relations, neighbours, rich people who can repay the invitation, he is to invite the poor, the crippled, the lame and the blind to his banquet, who can only repay at the resurrection. The ministry of Jesus explains this saying. His first public words told how the Spirit had anointed him to preach the good news to the poor (4:18). Then followed healings of the crippled (13:11), the lame and the blind (7:22). Jesus is making the same appeal to his host that he has previously made to his disciples: he is to be 'compassionate as your Father is compassionate' (6:36). Those who heed this gospel are the descendants of the poor, the lame and the blind whom Jesus invited to his banquet, the banquet foretold by prophets such as Isaiah (25:6–8; 55:1).

Sunday 23 C

Wisdom 9:13–18
Psalm 89:3–6, 12–14, 17
Philemon 9–10, 12–17
Luke 14:25–33

The Demands of Discipleship

One of the great prayers in the Old Testament is the prayer of Solomon at Gibeon for an understanding mind so that he could govern God's people (1 Kings 3:9). In a lamentation recalling Greek philosophy, the author of **Wisdom** echoes this prayer, which sees the human soul as weighed down by the body. We need divine wisdom to assist us if we are to find and follow the ways of justice and right. So Paul would write that 'In this present state, it is true, we groan as we wait with longing to put on our heavenly home over the other' (2 Corinthians 5:2).

The **Psalm**, too, is a prayer for 'wisdom of heart'. Life is short, and its end is a return to the dust from which it came (Genesis 3:19). But even such a short life is worthwhile if lived in the consciousness of God's love and praise. The Christian knows that our destiny is to 'stay with the Lord' (1 Thessalonians 4:17).

Verses from his letter to **Philemon** introduce us to Paul and to early Christianity. Paul is totally committed to Jesus Christ: he mentions Christ at the beginning and end of our passage. He wants Philemon to take back his slave Onesimus, who has been assisting Paul. He refers to the slave in family terms: Paul is his father and he wants Philemon to take him back as a brother. The Church and its members are a family (Mark 3:34). Paul, as a caring pastor, is reluctant to give orders: he prefers personal appeals and encourages people to choose right on their own initiative. He does not condemn slavery as such—it was part of the fabric of his world (1 Corinthians 7:21)—but if Philemon consents to accept him back, Onesimus becomes his brother rather than his slave. All, slave or free, are 'one in Christ Jesus' (Galatians 3:28).

His meal with the Pharisees concluded, in **Luke** Jesus now resumes his journey towards Jerusalem, and once more he is surrounded by large crowds. Again his teaching is blunt; he does not want them to miss the opportunity that beckons them now that God is visiting his people in the person and ministry of Jesus (1:68; 7:16).

Not for the first time, Jesus lays down challenging conditions for discipleship. After his first prediction of his passion, he told his followers that they must carry their cross daily (9:23). As he set out on his journey to Jerusalem, he warned three would-be disciples of the fierce demands of discipleship (9:57–62). In this passage, he illustrates the urgency and seriousness of the gospel in three ways.

The disciple must be ready to put family demands in second place. We know how Jesus, as a twelve-year-old, stayed in the Temple to be 'busy with his Father's affairs' rather than returning home with his family (2:41–50). But he did not cancel the commandment of love of parents, as he made clear to the rich young man (18:20). Secondly, the disciple must be open to a life of self-denial. Simon of Cyrene literally carried the cross behind Jesus on his way to Calvary, but he did not carry it alone (23:26). Thirdly, the disciple must be ready to give up all possessions. Jesus himself did this. In Paul's words, 'he was rich, but he became poor for your sake' (2 Corinthians 8:9). So did at least some of the early Christians in Jerusalem (Acts 2:45). The rich young man was invited to sell what he had in order to have treasure in heaven (18:22).

Jesus' hearers knew how careful a farmer was before he built a tower in his vineyard; he made sure he could finish the job. Likewise, a king would not go to war without the resources for victory. Like Solomon in the book of Wisdom, they thought hard before they came to a decision. Enthusiasm alone is insufficient reason to follow Jesus. The cost must be reckoned (5:11; 18:28).

Sunday 24 C

Exodus 32:7–11, 13–14
Psalm 50:3–4, 12–13, 17, 19
1 Timothy 1:12–17
Luke 15:1–32

Parables of the Lost

The God of the Bible is a God who forgives. A dramatic example of this is the story of the worship of the golden calf in **Exodus**. With Moses absent on the mountain-top, Aaron has encouraged the people to worship a calf fashioned out of their golden ear-rings. He told them that this calf, not the God whom Moses venerated, had brought them out of Egypt. Such worship was not uncommon in that culture. King Jeroboam would tell his people that two golden calves he had made had delivered them (1 Kings 12:28). Moses persuades God to forgive his people rather than punish them. The Gospel of today gives us a yet more radical picture of a God who waits and longs to forgive sin.

Tradition associates our penitential **Psalm** with David's sin with Bathsheba (2 Samuel 11). Its rich vocabulary teaches us how destructive sin can be, but the mercy of God is ready to deal with it.

Both Peter, whom Jesus appointed to 'feed his sheep' (John 21:17) and Paul, the instrument that Jesus chose to bring 'my name before pagans and pagan kings' (Acts 9:15) had to live with the memory of great sin. For Peter, it was his three denials in the courtyard of the High Priest when Jesus was on trial (Luke 22:54–62); for Paul, it was his career of persecuting the followers of Jesus before his personal conversion. In **1 Timothy**, a letter from the last days of his life, Paul recalls this sin yet again, in language stronger than ever. He has been a blasphemer, a persecutor, a man of violence, but God has shown mercy to him. We can read about this three times in Acts (9:15; 22:21; 26:17) and in his own writings too (Galatians 1:15; Philippians 3:9).

The severe demands of discipleship spelt out by Jesus to the crowds in **Luke** (14:25–33) fail to discourage all the tax collectors and sinners from listening to him and sharing food at his table. The Pharisees and scribes are shocked at such disregard for the traditional laws of purity, and they tell Jesus so. He replies to them with three parables, each of which has its surprises. A shepherd leaves 99 sheep in the wilderness to find the one that is lost. Which of you, Jesus asks the Pharisees, would do this? They would not keep sheep at all, since they thought it an unclean occupation. There is a woman lighting a lamp and sweeping the house, looking for a lost coin. The celebration for her friends when she finds it may cost her the value of the coin. There is a father who disobeys the injunction to discipline his errant son (Proverbs 29:17); he waits and watches out for the son's return. By giving this son a robe, a ring and sandals, he places him in a higher position after his sin than before it. As for the surly elder brother who refuses to join in the feast, his father pleads with him to return to communion with his family. But he is at first unaware of his brother's return. He does not address his father as 'father' or call his brother 'brother'. He regards his life as one of servitude rather than membership in the family.

Thus Jesus understands God: as the shepherd looking for his sheep, the woman looking for the coin, the father watching for the younger son and pleading with the elder. The Pharisees should have known all this from the prophets. 'I shall look for the lost one', God told Ezekiel (34:16). 'Does a woman forget her baby at the breast, or fail to cherish the son of her womb? Yet even if these forget, I will never forget you', he said through Isaiah (49:15). Through Hosea he described Israel as the child he loved (Hosea 11:1). Luke wanted his readers to know God as Jesus knew him (Romans 8:15). The Pharisees cannot grasp God's extravagant love, and so they cannot share the joy of Jesus at table with the sinners who were coming to repentance. He had come into the world to save sinners (19:10).

Sunday 25 C

Amos 8:4–7
Psalm 112:1–2, 4–8
1 Timothy 2:1–8
Luke 16:1–13

A Crafty Steward

Around 750 BC, Israel enjoyed great material prosperity, at least for one part of the population. Religious shrines flourished, but the poor did not. Their poverty was not the result of laziness, but of economic exploitation by the powerful. **Amos** lists the various shady techniques of swindling and tampering that these people used to enrich themselves even further, while scrupulously observing the Sabbath and other festivals. This biblical passage clearly links economic activity with religious responsibility. It prepares us for the steward in the Gospel.

The **Psalm** is the first of the *hallel* psalms (Mark 14:26). Its language recalls ancient hymns of praise such as the canticle of Moses (Exodus 15:11). It ascribes to God a characteristic which distinguished Israel's God from other deities, namely a concern for the poor (1 Samuel 2:8).

The situation addressed in **1 Timothy** is that of a Church settling down for the long haul in the world. It has to avoid the hostility of state authorities and to pray for them (Romans 13:1); this new religion is not to become a threat to public order. This presumes that a situation does not call for Christians to obey God rather than human authority (Acts 5:29). They are a people ransomed by means of the death and resurrection of Christ (Mark 10:45). The spread of the gospel depends on human agency, such as that of Paul in his role as herald, apostle and teacher (Romans 10:15). And a universal response to divine activity is to be one of reverent prayer, such as Paul himself practised (1 Thessalonians 1:2) and constantly preached (1 Thessalonians 5:17).

One parable from **Luke** last week was about a son who squandered money. This week we hear about a rich man's steward who does the same. Threatened with the loss of his post, the steward tries to remedy the situation by reducing the sums that his master's debtors owe.

The master commends his steward for this conduct. This seems puzzling, since the master appears to be approving of dishonesty, hardly a gospel value. It has been suggested that the money and goods that the steward cancels are due to him, rather than to his master, as the agent responsible for recovering the debt. He is not paid a salary; he makes what he can by charging commission on the sums he lends on his master's behalf. So here he is not claiming the commission due to him. His stratagem costs the master nothing and will be understood and welcomed by the debtors. The master praises him for his prudence in taking action which is not dishonest. The disciples of Jesus are to learn from the astuteness of the steward in meeting a crisis.

Others find the point of the parable not in the steward's behaviour at all, but in the master's. He behaves strangely, like the father in last week's parable, who welcomed, rather than disowned, his wayward son (15:20). This master warns his servant about his misconduct but, surprisingly, does nothing about it. When he hears what his agent is doing to rehabilitate himself, he does not condemn him. It is not impossible that he takes the agent back into service. His unexpected response to inadmissible behaviour recalls that of the prodigal son's father who, instead of disinheriting him, gives him a higher status than ever (15:22). Has Luke included this parable in order to assure the 'stewards' responsible for the Christian community (12:42) that, when they have proved incompetent or even dishonest, their Lord will not rush to condemn them and might even accept them back into office, sadder but wiser? Jesus accepted Peter back, despite the sin of his denials (24:34).

Sunday 26 C

Amos 6:1, 4–7
Psalm 145:6–10
1 Timothy 6:11–16
Luke 16:19–31

Dives and Lazarus

We owe to **Amos**, the herdsman from Tekoa (7:14), one of the most vigorous attacks on the extravagant and the slothful in all scripture. Such people live just for themselves and have no regard for the welfare of their nation. Their curiosity about King David, the greatest of their kings, is limited to his ability to make musical instruments. Their selfishness prepares us for the gospel story.

The **Psalm** is the first of the final set of praise songs in the Psalter. Our verses praise God neither for his powers of creation nor for his mighty deeds in delivering his people, but because of his concern for the weak and defenceless. Such a God is of no interest to the selfish wealthy whom Amos condemns.

We pick out three contrasts in our final extract from **1 Timothy**. The first is between the virtues that Timothy is to make his own and the vices of the false teachers whom the author has just mentioned (1 Timothy 6:3). The second is between the confession that Timothy himself made before many witnesses at his baptism or ordination and the example of Christ Jesus, who witnessed in front of Pontius Pilate before his passion (John 18:28–38). The third contrast is between God, the blessed and only ruler of all, and Caesar, the Roman emperor for whom Christians were certainly to pray (2:1) but whose divine power they could not acknowledge. Jewish tradition praised God with many a doxology (1 Chronicles 29:10); but here we have a doxology that appears to attribute to Christ qualities that traditionally belong to God. In the letter to Titus, Jesus Christ will be called our great God and Saviour (Titus 2:15).

We hear today a third parable from **Luke** that begins, 'There was a rich man' (12:16; 16:1). As in the previous two, the man is unnamed, although tradition has called him Dives. This parable, like last week's, is about the correct use of wealth. Dives behaves like the wealthy folk in Amos; he is probably not even aware of the presence of the second character in the story, Lazarus, who lies starving at his gate. He may think his wealth is a sign of God's favour (Deuteronomy 28:11) and consider the dogs licking Lazarus' wounds a proof of God's anger. Elijah had warned that God, in anger, would send dogs to lick up the blood of king Ahab (1 Kings 21:19).

After his death, Dives learns the truth. He now sees Lazarus clearly, and discovers that he too is a child of Abraham (3:8). Despite his proper burial, he finds himself separated from God. Abraham, the third character in the parable, tells him that he can do nothing to cross the chasm; it is too late. He feels like those sent off to everlasting fire in the story of the sheep and the goats in Matthew (25:46). They have failed to recognise Christ in the hungry and the naked. Their opportunity is past. They, and Dives, have had their reward already (Matthew 6:5).

So far the parable resembles traditional stories known from Egypt about reversal of fortune in the next life, and builds on the teaching of the Magnificat and the Beatitudes (1:52; 6:20). It is the final part that should be emphasized. Dives asks that his brothers be warned lest they incur the same fate. He is given his answer; the warning is contained in prophets such as Amos, whom we heard this week and last. (It also appears in today's psalm.) Dives pleads with Abraham that somebody must go back from the dead. We know that Christ has done this. His life and resurrection have confirmed the teaching of the Prophets and the Psalms, as Jesus told the despairing disciples on the Emmaus road (24:44). Thus Luke warns all those, like Dives, who ignore the Lazarus in their own communities.

Sunday 27 C

Habakkuk 1:2–3; 2:2–4
Psalm 94:1–2, 6–9
2 Timothy 1:6–8, 13–14
Luke 17:5–10

Increase Our Faith

This is the only time that we hear the prophet **Habakkuk** on a Sunday. The final line, that 'the upright man will live by his faithfulness', prepares us for the request that the disciples make of Jesus in our Gospel. The prophet discusses with God one of the oldest religious questions of all: why does God allow the wicked to prosper and ignore the afflictions of his people? Faith answers that God, the one who sees the whole picture, is in ultimate control and will reward virtue in his own time. The proud cannot understand this, but the upright do and live by it. Paul will build his letter to the Romans on this verse (Romans 1:17) and will quote it in Galatians (3:11).

Our **Psalm** was used by pilgrims as they approached the Jerusalem Temple in thanks and joy. A priest speaks in the name of God to warn them against the lack of faith in God that desert hardships had caused their ancestors to display at Meribah (Numbers 20:1–11).

In **2 Timothy**, Paul, in prison awaiting execution, encourages all church leaders in the person of Timothy. What he says is common New Testament teaching. They do not work alone; they were chosen by God (Ephesians 1:4) and act with the power of the Holy Spirit (1 Thessalonians 1:5). They are not to be ashamed of witnessing to Christ (Romans 1:16). They rely on God's power (1 Corinthians 15:10). They are to guard the treasure of faith (2 Corinthians 4:7). Paul is their model; he put into practice the Christian life he defined for the Galatians as 'faith that makes its power felt through love' (Galatians 5:6). Despite his imprisonment, he is confident in the Lord and dares to speak the word with greater boldness and without fear (Philippians 1:14).

Luke offers us the most positive view of Jesus' disciples in the gospel tradition. Only in Luke does one of them ask him to teach them to pray. Jesus answers with the prayer we know as the Lord's Prayer (11:1–4). Now, as they approach Jerusalem, the apostles as a group make a request of Jesus: 'Increase our faith'. Jesus replies with an enigmatic saying about the power of faith to uproot a tree and cast it into the sea. Here he is surely speaking of the sort of faith needed to perform great miracles. We have to believe that nothing is impossible for God (Matthew 19:26).

When Jesus speaks about faith, it is usually the sort necessary for salvation and healing. Thus he commended the faith of the woman cured of bleeding (8:48), the man cured of blindness (18:42), the woman who was a sinner (7:37) and the grateful leper who returned to praise God (17:19). He responded to faith in those who had brought a paralytic to him (5:20) and in the centurion whose servant he was to heal (7:9). Those who show such faith are said to be 'saved'. The disciples, too, are presumed to have faith. When Jesus calmed the storm, he challenged them, 'Where is your faith?' (8:25).

The words of Jesus that follow the apostles' request contrast with his earlier teaching in which he promised watchful servants that their master would make them sit down to eat and would come and serve them (12:37). They would dine at the messianic banquet in heaven (13:29). But such privileges are not theirs by right but by gift. They are among the poor, the crippled, the lame and the blind who have been invited to the banquet (14:21). Their service in the Kingdom is the least response they could make. With Paul, they are to say, 'the grace that he gave me has not been fruitless' (1 Corinthians 15:10). They have no ground for boasting (Romans 3:27). All this reminds us that faith is ultimately a gift of God.

Sunday 28 C

2 Kings 5:14–17
Psalm 97:1–4
2 Timothy 2:8–13
Luke 17:11–19

The Thankful Leper

The first public speech of Jesus in Luke referred to the story of Naaman the leper in **2 Kings** (Luke 4:27). Naaman is the commander of the king of Aram's armies. The prophet Elisha, successor of Elijah, cures him of leprosy. Relevant to today's Gospel is the fact that Naaman, who is a foreigner, not only shows his gratitude to the prophet for being healed but is also converted to the God of Israel. It is for this reason that he takes earth from the land of Israel home with him in order to serve this God with proper worship.

The **Psalm** focuses on the universal rule of Israel's God. It would have been at home on the lips of Naaman, who recognised that God's compassion and concern for social justice were for all the nations, not just Israel (Isaiah 51:4–6).

Paul in **2 Timothy** continues to encourage church leaders in the person of Timothy, his 'brother ... who is God's helper' (1 Thessalonians 3:2). Each idea refers us back to earlier letters of Paul. In mentioning his gospel he reminds us of the beginning of Romans, where its contents are summarised (Romans 1:3–4) and its power described (1:16–17). By speaking of his imprisonment, he puts us in mind of his positive reflections on captivity in Philippians, where he says that his imprisonment has 'actually been a help to the Good News' (1:12). His song of encouragement for martyrs called to confess Christ at the cost of their lives is related to the hymn about the death and exaltation of Christ in Philippians (2:6–11). Like other such summaries of doctrine in these 'pastoral letters', it is a saying that is sure, one that readers would be expected to make their own and to treasure (1 Timothy 1:15; 3:1; 4:9).

Still on the road to Jerusalem, now on the border between Galilee and Samaria, Jesus meets ten lepers. Like the blind man outside Jericho, they cry out to him for mercy (18:38; Mark 10:47). Jesus does not reject their request. Like so many in **Luke**, the lepers encounter his compassion for those whom society rejects; he is continuing the mission, announced in the Nazareth synagogue, of good news to the poor (4:18; 23:43). He cures the lepers or, rather, they go to the priests and discover they are cured (Leviticus 14:2–3). For the second time, Jesus has imitated the works of Elisha in curing lepers (5:12–26).

This cure, like that of Naaman in 2 Kings, has a sequel. One of the lepers sees beyond his healing to the God who, through Jesus, has made it possible. He turns back, gives glory to God and expresses gratitude to Jesus. Like Naaman, he is a foreigner. But he is no ordinary foreigner; he is a Samaritan, one of those who do not associate with Jews (John 4:9).

The narrative concludes with three questions from Jesus. 'Were not all ten made clean?' Nine of them have gone; they do not see beyond their healing. They illustrate Jesus' teaching in the parable of the sower (8:12–14). The word of Jesus has been taken from their hearts, whether by Satan or through their own inability to think beyond the present. 'The other nine, where are they?' Jesus is waiting for them, like the father looking out for his son in another parable (15:20). 'No one has come back to give praise to God, except this foreigner.' The point of Jesus' physical healing was to lead to spiritual healing, to a turning around, a change of direction in repentance (7:47; 24:47). Encountering the mercy of God should move people to praise God (1:46; 11:2). The nationality of this man not only fulfils the programme that Jesus proclaimed in the synagogue at Nazareth (4:27) but also anticipates the successful mission of Philip to the Samaritans (Acts 8:4–25) and indeed of the disciples to the ends of the earth (Acts 1:8).

Sunday 29 C

Exodus 17:8–13
Psalm 120
2 Timothy 3:14–4:2
Luke 18:1–8

The Persistent Widow

Moses was a mediator for his people before God, and prayer was one way he performed this role. He prayed for them after they worshipped the golden calf (Exodus 32:11) and again when they revolted against God by longing for their old life in Egypt (Numbers 14:13–23); he prayed that they might be blessed in the land they were to enter (Deuteronomy 33:1–29). Today in **Exodus** he prays for them in their battle against the fierce Amalekites. His perseverance prepares us for the persevering prayer of the widow in the Gospel.

The **Psalm** reports a dialogue between a temple priest and pilgrims as they prepare for their homeward journey. They recognise God as their creator and their protector. The priest prays that God will save them from dangers from the sun by day and the moon by night, and from all other powers that might harm them (Psalm 91:11).

In the New Testament there are many references to scripture and quotations from it, both explicit and implicit. In those days, this meant the writings of the Old Testament. In **2 Timothy**, we learn of scripture's inspiration by God and its usefulness in meeting various needs of Christian life. Knowledge of scripture is part of the equipment needed for living out the Christian vocation. Elsewhere the word of the prophets is compared to a lamp shining in a dark place, and its origin is attributed to God's Holy Spirit (2 Peter 1:19–21). In Romans, Paul reminds his audience that whatever was written in former days was written for our instruction and as a source of hope (Romans 15:4). St Augustine wrote, 'The New Testament lies hidden in the Old; the Old Testament is enlightened by the New'.

As they approach Jerusalem, Jesus has been urging his disciples to learn from the events of the flood in the time of Noah and about the fate that befell Lot when Sodom was destroyed (17:26–29). He now reinforces his teaching in **Luke** with two parables, the first of which we hear today. In this he tells of a widow who pleads her case before an unjust judge. This widow, instead of being a person who is exploited and without resources, the way widows are usually portrayed in scripture (Job 22:9; Isaiah 1:17), is active, enterprising and persistent. She wins her cause by allowing no peace to the judge who has power to help her. As for the judge, he falls far short of Israel's ideal; he neither fears God nor respects man (2 Chronicles 19:6–7). He only gives way to the widow's entreaties to save himself further battering from her. (The word is taken from boxing: he did not want a black eye!)

Earlier in this Gospel, Jesus gave his disciples a model prayer and followed it up with an instruction about a householder who is woken up at midnight by a friend demanding bread (11:1–8). The point was that we do not address our prayer to a person who is asleep, but to a loving and watchful Father, like the father of the prodigal son (15:20). Here we are reminded that we do not pray to an unjust judge but a father who is merciful and concerned for us, just like Jesus himself who took pity on the widow of Nain when she lost her son (7:13).

But there is a further application, too. Jesus asks his disciples a final question which links the parable with his previous teaching about the last days. Will the Son of Man at his coming find faith on earth? If Luke's readers have taken to heart the examples of faith already met in this gospel story, such as the woman cured of her bleeding (8:48) and the man healed of his blindness (18:42), and have joined the disciples in asking for an increase of faith (17:5), he will certainly find it. After all, Jesus himself, before he went to his death, prayed for Peter that his faith should not fail (22:32).

Sunday 30 C

Sirach 35:12–14, 16–19
Psalm 33:2–3, 17–19
2 Timothy 4:6–8, 16–18
Luke 18:9–14

Two Pray in the Temple

We owe to Ben-Sira an unusual portrait of God as judge. The God presented in **Sirach** is quite unlike the judge in last week's Gospel (Luke 18:2–6). His aim is to set things right, whoever the person who applies to him might be; as Peter told Cornelius, he does not show partiality (Acts 10:34). With him, those whom the world abuses, the orphan and the widow, find just treatment. He executes justice for them (Deuteronomy 10:18). As the psalmist wrote, he is father of orphans and protector of widows (Psalm 68:5). He is a God who listens to the prayer of the tax collector in today's Gospel.

The **Psalm** also celebrates God's concern for the unfortunate. It uses many words to describe them. Whatever their trouble might be, the psalmist is confident that God will eventually redress their wrongs and deliver them from distress.

Paul's last days are described in **2 Timothy**. His words echo others from his major letters. He is a sacrifice being poured out on the altar, as he told the Philippians (2:17). He is a runner reaching the line to claim victory in the stadium, as he described himself to the Corinthians (1 Corinthians 9:25). He has found himself alone at this trial, as Jesus was; but just as Jesus told his disciples at the Last Supper that he was never alone, because the Father was with him (John 16:32), neither is Paul. As he wrote to the Galatians, Christ lives in him (Galatians 2:20). If his life is to end in tribulation, then his words to his Churches in Lystra, Iconium and Antioch are coming true: we must experience many hardships before we enter the kingdom of God (Acts 14:21–22).

Jesus in **Luke** follows up his parable of the persistent widow with another about a Pharisee and a tax collector. The audience is described as those who pride themselves on being virtuous. It concludes with the statement that it was the tax collector who went home 'at rights with God', or justified. We are not to miss the paradoxes in the story. The first shock, sometimes overlooked because of over-familiarity, is that the tax collector, whose profession was regarded as making it impossible for him to live a life faithful to his religion, goes into the Temple to pray at all.

At first hearing, the Pharisee's prayer offers us much to admire. Few could compete with his religious observance and commitment in his fasting and tithing. But the flaw in his prayer is obvious. It is all about himself, and he speaks not one good word about anybody else. His way of prayer could be translated, 'He prayed to himself'. He shows no concern for the widow and the orphan. He does not follow Jesus' instruction, 'when you have done all you have been told to do, say, "We are merely servants"' (17:10). At first sight, the prayer of the tax collector is equally defective. He prays at a distance. If the God of Luke's Gospel resembles the father of the prodigal son, this God might well fail to see him, still less to embrace him (15:20). The psalmist tells us to raise our eyes to heaven when we pray (Psalm 123:1); the tax collector does not. He does not address God as Father, but simply as God (11:2). Yet we can say that he prays one verse of the Lord's prayer in asking for forgiveness of his sins (11:4). This the Pharisee has not done. The tax collector goes home at rights with God. He has made a good beginning, and this the Lord says is sufficient.

The parables of Jesus often tease us. Just as in the parable of the two sons we debate with which of the two the Lord wants us to identify (15:11–32), so in this parable we may recognise characteristics of our own behaviour in both of those who went to pray in the Temple. May we allow the grace of God to do its work for our justification.

Sunday 31 C

Wisdom 11:22–12:2
Psalm 144:1–2, 8–11, 13–14
2 Thessalonians 1:11–2:2
Luke 19:1–10

Zacchaeus the Tax Collector

After meditating on the events of the Exodus, the author of **Wisdom** turns to the relationship of God with creation. Elsewhere in scripture we have learnt of God's love and mercy for all humanity and even the animals: God told Jonah of his concern for the 120,000 who lived in Nineveh, and all the animals too (Jonah 4:11). Here we are told that God loves all that exists, even though for God this amounts to no more than a drop of morning dew. Genesis tells us how God saw that his creation was good (Genesis 1:31). Paul reflected this love when he wrote of all creation groaning in one great act of giving birth (Romans 8:22). The love of God surely embraces Zacchaeus, the tax collector in the Gospel.

The **Psalm**, a summary of many other psalms, offers a last word on the merciful character of God. Traditionally, it has been recited several times a day. It lists the qualities of goodness, kindness and loyalty that Israel recognised in its God (Exodus 34:6), qualities recognised also by the creatures he made (Psalm 104).

Prayer and instruction are included in our extract from **2 Thessalonians**. In the prayer, we ponder the relationship between God, Jesus and ourselves. God is the one who calls us and fulfils our desires. We live in faith; we share in God's glory. God and Jesus are spoken of in almost equal terms. Instruction follows on the prayer. The fruit of such prayer is a sober attitude regarding the Day of the Lord. This was once regarded as a day of darkness, to be dreaded (Amos 5:18). For the Christian it is day of our Lord Jesus when we all gather around him in welcome. Our destiny is to stay with this Lord for ever (1 Thessalonians 4:17).

We know few names of those whom Jesus met on his journey to Jerusalem, but these include the tax collector, Zacchaeus of Jericho. We have met such people before in **Luke**. Tax collectors flocked to John the Baptist for baptism (3:12; 7:29), sat at table with Jesus (5:30; 15:1) and featured in his parables (18:10). Zacchaeus is also wealthy. The rich in this Gospel have generally not fared well. The rich fool put his grain into barns, died and lost everything (12:18). Dives spent his money on clothes and food, did not see Lazarus at his gate and found himself in hell (16:23). Jesus' lament fits well, 'Alas for you who are rich' (6:24).

Like Herod, Zacchaeus is anxious to see Jesus (9:9). He takes action by running and climbing a tree because of his short stature. His behaviour risks ridicule from those who see him, but not from Jesus. Jesus addresses him by name and lets him into the secret of his own mission. 'I must stay at your house today', just as it had been necessary to be 'busy with my Father's affairs' at the beginning of the Gospel (2:49) and, as the Christ, to 'suffer and so enter into his glory' at its end (24:26). Like other tax collectors who listened to Jesus (15:1), Zacchaeus responds positively. He welcomes Jesus into his house. Like the shepherds of Bethlehem (2:11) and the good thief (23:43), he accepts Jesus' 'today' of salvation. Like Martha, he makes Jesus his guest (10:38). What is impossible for men proves possible for God; a rich man is saved (18:27).

Zacchaeus says, 'I am going to give half my property to the poor, and if I have cheated anybody I will pay him back four times the amount'. Had he been doing this all along? He could be an example of the correct use of wealth. The good Samaritan used his oil, wine and beast to help the injured man (10:34). Mark's mother and her servant welcomed Peter into her house (Acts 12:13). Lydia, the wealthy purple-cloth merchant, gave hospitality to Paul (Acts 16:15).

Sunday 32 C

2 Maccabees 7:1–2, 9–14
Psalm 16:1, 5–6, 8,15
2 Thessalonians 2:16–3:5
Luke 20:27–38

Dispute about Resurrection

In 167 BC, privileges allowing the Jewish people to worship their God and to keep his Law were withdrawn by Antiochus Epiphanes, who insisted that they behave like everybody else in a world that was enthusiastically embracing Hellenism, the culture of the Greeks. **2 Maccabees** relates how the old man Eleazar endured a hideous death for refusing to eat pork (6:18–31). Seven brothers and their mother follow his example, confident that God will vindicate them by raising them up to an everlasting renewal of life. This text, from one of the deuterocanonical books, is among the most explicit statements about resurrection in the Old Testament.

The **Psalm** is an appeal for help, such as the seven brothers might have made. The images used to describe God are striking. God hears prayers with his ear, guards his subject like the apple of his eye and protects with the shadow of his wings (Deuteronomy 32:10–11).

Our extract from **2 Thessalonians** pictures the world of early Christianity. This world belongs to Christ the Lord and God the Father; Christ gives an example of fortitude: the Father is the God of love and is a faithful Lord. The gifts on offer include grace, comfort and hope. Paul is a messenger of the word of God, an agent on whom its spread depends. But there are forces ranged against Paul and his converts. There is the evil one; there is the wicked world that this evil one influences. Paul's response is serious prayer; he expects his hearers to imitate him in their prayer. Jesus expected his disciples to do the same (Luke 18:1). It is the enduring message of scripture.

Having arrived in Jerusalem, Jesus teaches in the Temple. He is so popular, **Luke** tells us, that all the people get up early in the morning to listen to him (21:38). Today we hear one example of this teaching; his immediate audience is the Sadducees, the conservative party among the Jews, who did not believe in the resurrection or in angels (Acts 23:8). In dealings with his critics, Jesus often replied with a parable (Luke 15:3–32); here it is his opponents who tell a story. It is the sort of story with which Sadducees would tease Pharisees, the party among the Jews who believed in resurrection.

A woman married and outlived seven brothers successively; whose wife would she be after the resurrection? Jesus does not rebuke his critics for knowing neither the scriptures nor the power of God, as in Matthew (Matthew 22:29). He appeals rather to the doctrine of the 'two ages'. The present age is that of the present, wicked world (Galatians 1:4). The future age is a world without death and so has no need of the new life that comes from marriage. Those who belong to it will be like angels (whose existence the Sadducees denied), 'children of the resurrection'. Jesus quotes God's words to Moses, proclaiming himself a God of the living and not of the dead (Exodus 3:6). He could not be the God of Abraham, Isaac and Jacob if they were no longer alive.

This teaching prepares us for Jesus' own resurrection (24:46). Jesus supports the Pharisees, who accepted the idea of resurrection emerging in the later books of the Old Testament. We heard an example of this in our reading from 2 Maccabees. It is found in Daniel (12:2) and the book of Wisdom (3:4). Some scribes compliment Jesus on his answer (20:38), and some Sadducees may have been among the priests who soon became Christians (Acts 6:7). Resurrection is taken for granted in the New Testament. Paul in Acts defends the 'resurrection of good men and bad alike' before Felix, the Roman governor (Acts 24:15). In 1 Corinthians he devotes a whole chapter to the resurrection (1 Corinthians 15).

Sunday 33 C

Malachi 3:19–20
Psalm 97:5–9
2 Thessalonians 3:7–12
Luke 21:5–19

Warnings about the Future

An over-confident Israel used to anticipate the Day of the Lord as a day of favour and deliverance. Prophets such as Amos (5:18) and Zephaniah (1:14), however, warned that it would be a day of retribution and wrath for a nation hardened in its sin. The experience of exile brought the more realistic view that we find in **Malachi**, a temple prophet 400 years before Christ: this day will be one of sorrow for the evil-doer but a day of healing for the virtuous.

The **Psalm** looks forward to God's appearance on earth. The mountains, rivers and sea he created join humanity in a great symphony of praise. This coming of the Lord will mean a revelation of his justice and compassion (Exodus 34:6). The people to whom God wants to bring salvation, are to reflect God's own compassion in their behaviour (Isaiah 51:5–6).

There were those among the Christians addressed in **2 Thessalonians** who were a scandal to the rest because they were disorderly and idle and refused to work. They may have seen no point in working because of their belief in the imminent return of Christ (1 Thessalonians 1:10). They may have thought that the order given to Adam and Eve to toil in the sweat of their brow (Genesis 3:17–19) had been cancelled by Christ's victory over death. They may have become too dependent on the charity of fellow Christians who looked after the poor in the community (Galatians 2:10). Paul appeals to them to heed his example of self-support and hard work, and to share his horror of burdening anyone by his labours in preaching the gospel (1 Thessalonians 2:1–12). Still less are they to interfere in the work of others.

Our second example of Jesus' teaching in the Temple in **Luke** comes from his 'apocalyptic discourse'. We heard its conclusion on the first Sunday of Advent. Then the topic was the coming of the Son of Man at the end of time. Today it is the events to be expected between the ascension of Jesus and the End. In Luke, Jesus is still inside and not outside the Temple; his audience is not, as in Mark, confined to three apostles (Mark 13:1–3). By the time Luke's Gospel was written, more than a decade had passed since the destruction of the Temple by Roman armies in AD 70.

First, Jesus warns of false prophets, famines, wars and persecutions. Between the time of Jesus and that of Luke writing his Gospel, all of these are known to us from Acts. There were the false prophets Simon in Samaria (Acts 8:9) and Bar-Jesus in Cyprus (Acts 13:7). Agabus foretold a famine that would affect the whole world (Acts 11:28). Christians fled from Jerusalem because of persecution (Acts 8:1). Paul's preaching was greeted with opposition in many cities (Acts 14:19; 16:23) and this is confirmed by him in his letters (2 Corinthians 11:26). The wars and troubles of the year 69, when four Roman emperors struggled for power, would be familiar to Luke's readers. Such upheavals take place in every age.

These were the conditions of life in the age of the early Church. Jesus prepared his disciples for them in his teaching on the way to Jerusalem (9:51–19:28). He promised them the assistance of the Holy Spirit when they were brought up before the courts (12:12); now he promises his own help. Paul's vision of Christ in Corinth is an example (Acts 18:9). Jesus has warned the disciples of the family divisions that his mission of fire upon the earth will cause (12:53); such divisions may end in death. He has himself shown them the way of prayer (18:1; 22:44) and watchfulness (12:36). If they persevere they, like the seed in the good soil, will bear much fruit by their patient endurance (8:15).

Christ the King C

2 Samuel 5:1–3
Psalm 121:1–5
Colossians 1:12–20
Luke 23:35–43

The Penitent Thief

David was the greatest of the kings of Israel, and it was from his line that the messiah was expected to come. Our passage from **2 Samuel** describes David as a shepherd and a king. He is bound to his people by covenant, and he is the one whom the people anointed. These expressions would be applied to Christ as the anointed one. David's kingship anticipates the kingship of Christ, who is named Son of David (Matthew 1:1) in the New Testament. Yet Jesus himself reminds us that, as messiah, he is greater than David, because David addressed the messiah as his Lord (Mark 12:36).

The **Psalm** is a pilgrim song to be sung on arrival in Jerusalem (Deuteronomy 16:16), the city where David moved after his anointing at Hebron (2 Samuel 5:9). For the Christian, the refreshment and security that it offered the pilgrim now come from the heavenly Jerusalem where Christ, as the Lamb, has his throne with God (Revelation 22:1).

Most of Paul's letters begin with a thanksgiving. In **Colossians** this includes quotations from a possible hymn about Christ celebrating baptism. The baptized have been delivered from darkness into light (1 Thessalonians 5:5); they belong to the Kingdom of the beloved Son of God. The authority of this Son, Christ, far exceeds that of any human king. He was the firstborn of creation; all things were made through him and for him. He was the firstborn of those rescued from the power of death, the means of reconciliation when creation was alienated from God through sin. All this was achieved by the blood of the cross. In him we find the fullness of God. This ancient hymn illuminates and is illuminated by another in Philippians (2:1–11).

Luke records five reactions to Jesus as he hung dying on the cross. Three are negative. The religious leaders who had condemned him to death scoff at him, mocking him as a false messiah. The soldiers who crucified him jeer at him because of the inscription above him naming him 'King of the Jews'. One of the criminals crucified with him mocks him. All challenge him to save himself. We know Jesus as one who spent his ministry bringing salvation to others, not himself. The angels at his birth called him 'saviour' (2:11); John the Baptist, quoting Isaiah, proclaimed that through him, 'all mankind shall see the salvation of God' (3:6).

The salvation that Jesus is bringing through his cross is glimpsed in the reaction of the people. They simply watch. After his death, they go home, 'beating their breasts', a sign of repentance (23:48). But one person, the 'good thief', takes the words of the title on the cross seriously. For him, Jesus is king, a king to be addressed by name, 'Jesus, remember me when you come into your kingdom'. He refuses to join in the jeering of his companion and the mockery of the rulers. He acknowledges his own guilt, but adds his voice to those of Pilate and Herod, who witnessed to the innocence of Jesus (23:4, 14, 22).

The Jesus who healed the ear of the priest's servant at his arrest (22:51), who brought consolation to the weeping daughters of Jerusalem as he went to his death (23:28), continues his ministry of good news to the poor (4:18). He promises that on that very day the good thief will be with him in paradise. Paradise was the name given to the garden where Adam and Eve lived before the fall (Genesis 3). It was the place where, according to the Jewish literature of the time, the righteous would spend the afterlife. For the Christian, it means to be with Christ in glory. Paul had once been taken up to Paradise (2 Corinthians 12:4). Like Zacchaeus, the penitent thief recognises his day of salvation (19:9).

INDEX

Since many of these Sunday readings, especially the Gospels, also occur on weekdays, this index is offered in the hope of extending the usefulness of the book to weekdays as well as Sundays.

The Old Testament

(except the Psalms)

The Psalms

The numbering followed in the Missal is that of the Vulgate text, which adopted the numbering of the Greek translation of the Old Testament, called the Septuagint. But most Bibles follow the numbering of the original Hebrew text. These are the differences.

From Psalm 10 to 112, we add one, so that the psalms we read in the Missal are numbered in Bibles 11–113.

Psalm 114 is numbered in Bibles 116:1–9.

Psalm 115 is numbered in Bibles 116:10–19.

Psalms 116–145 are numbered in Bibles 117–146.

Psalm 146 is numbered in Bibles 147:1–11.

Psalm 147 is numbered in Bibles 147:12–20.

The New Testament

Luke

John

Philemon

Hebrews

James

1 Peter

2 Peter

1 John

Revelation